"This work . . . will shift the focus from re-engineering processes to re-inventing industries; from reducing overheads to regenerating strategies; and from what is feasible in the short term to what is possible in the long term." —*The Economist*

"An exciting and valuable book. . . . The ideas are stimulating and original. I predict that this book will be a big success, and that many businessmen will gain competitive advantage from reading it." —**David Sainsbury,** *Financial Times*

"A primer on strategy for the 1990s."
  —**Michael Pellecchia, syndicated columnist**

"One of the best business books of the year."
  —*Soundview Executive Book Summaries*

"This is probably one of the most important management books of the last 20 years, because it's not just about rebuilding and 'blue sky' prospecting, but about focusing on core strengths as a route to future strategies, markets, and profits."
  —*Management Consultancy*

"One of the best business books of the year. . . . A provocative future-oriented book that shows how an organization can seize control of its industry and create future markets. Unlike the recent books promoting downsizing, restructuring, and/or reengineering, this timely volume advances an aggressive framework of 'industry transformation' as the way to be strategic." —*Library Journal*

"A very small number of books have a profound impact on senior management thinking. This book is one." —*Business Executive*

"Required reading for entrepreneurs." —*Entrepreneur*

"Every thoughtful strategic planner and every executive intent on revitalizing a business needs to heed [Hamel and Prahalad's] tocsin." —*Planning Review*

"One of the few books published each year that breaks new ground, instead of simply replowing old furrows. Understanding its contents conveys a certain competitive advantage—which is the best reason for reading business books in the first place."

—**Ted Kinni,** *Quality Digest*

"Pioneering ideas on strategy, leadership competencies and market forces abound in this study." —*Publishers Weekly*

"*Competing for the Future* develops a coherent model for how today's executives can accomplish heroic goals in their company's future. This book will be an invaluable resource for industry leaders who want to stay on top of the market."

—*Colorado Springs Business Journal*

"*Competing for the Future* provides a new and thought-provoking look at strategy formulation for large corporations that participate in global markets. . . . Hamel and Prahalad argue persuasively that traditional approaches to strategic planning are unlikely to prepare a firm for industry leadership in the future."

—*Business Horizons*

"Students of management and practicing managers will benefit from exposure to this dynamic challenge for meeting the future."

—*Choice*

"The book contains more stimulating concepts and fresh ideas than most of the output from academic institutions and will repay the modest effort involved in reading it." —*Director*

"*Competing for the Future* ought to be required reading for all those persons involved in management at any level within an organization." —*Production*

COMPETING FOR THE FUTURE

GARY HAMEL
C.K. PRAHALAD

COMPETING FOR THE FUTURE

HARVARD BUSINESS SCHOOL PRESS
BOSTON, MASSACHUSETTS

Published by the Harvard Business School Press in hardcover, 1994;
in paperback, 1996
Copyright © 1994 by Gary Hamel and C.K. Prahalad
Printed in the United States of America
07 08 09 10   19 18 17

The Library of Congress has catalogued the hardcover edition of this title as
follows:

Hamel, Gary.
    Competing for the future / Gary Hamel, C.K. Prahalad.
        p. cm.
    Includes bibliographical references and index.
    ISBN 0-87584-416-2 (hc)
    1.   Competition. 2. Corporate planning. 3. Competition, International. I.
    Prahalad, C.K. II. Title.
    HD 41.H24 1994   94-18035
    658.4'012 – dc20   CIP

978-0-87584-716-0 (ISBN 13)
ISBN 0-87584-716-1 (pbk)

This book is dedicated to our children . . .
Paul and Jessica
Murali and Deepa
. . . our own stake in the future

Contents

▪ ▪

Preface to the Paperback Edition

Since its publication in autumn 1994, *Competing for the Future,* now translated into more than a dozen languages, has had a profound impact on how companies all over the world think about and prepare for their futures. While the book presents a radically different way of thinking about strategy and competition, the heart of its message, and its appeal, is hope. We believe that every company really does have the opportunity to shape its own destiny; no company is destined to be a laggard. We believe it is possible to move beyond incrementalism to create a broad and enticing new opportunity horizon; a lack of resources needn't limit a company's ambitions nor its accomplishments. We believe a sense of excitement and possibility can replace the fear and resignation that so often accompany downsizing and reengineering. And we believe it is possible to regenerate purpose, meaning, and direction in the absence of a crisis. These beliefs are not the product of simple-minded optimism, but of deep experience. We have seen our concepts and practices put to work in hundreds of companies around the world—we *know* the difference they can make.

We are hopeful, but we are not naive. Substantial challenges face any organization intent on getting to the future first. The first challenge, how to navigate from here to there, arises as both public and private institutions struggle to plot a course through an increasingly *inconstant environment,* where experience is rapidly devalued and familiar landmarks no longer serve as guideposts. Never before has the industrial terrain been changing so quickly or have industry boundaries been so malleable. Never before have competitors, partners, suppliers, and buyers been so indistinguishable. How, then, does one get to the future first, even when there's no map? How does one invent one's own route to the future? This book is for anyone who is more interested in creating the future than in watching it happen.

The second challenge, made altogether more pressing by the first, is how to oppose the forces of *institutional entropy* that, seemingly inevitably, undermine organizational effectiveness and sap institutional vitality. Never before have robust strategies been so quick to atrophy. Never before have precedent and tradition been so dangerous and incumbency worth so little. Enormous managerial energy, and acres of newsprint, have been devoted to turnarounds, rescues, and massive "change" programs, yet isn't the real goal to avoid a crisis-sized transformation problem by creating a capacity for continuous renewal deep within the company? This book is for anyone who views him- or herself as an enemy of entropy.

The third challenge, which must be addressed in concert with the second, is how to stem the tide of *individual estrangement* that threatens to wash over those who have borne the pain of downsizing, delayering, divesting, and refocusing. Never has the level of employee anxiety and disenchantment been higher than it is today in large Western companies. Never before have the costs of top management's shortsightedness been more apparent or poignant. Never before has the firm's loyalty to its members been so in doubt and the individual's loyalty to his or her employer so sorely tested. Rather than calculating the number of people to fire in order to become competitive, companies should be asking How can we create the sense of purpose, possibility, and mutual commitment that will inspire ordinary individuals to feats of collective heroism? This book is for anyone who believes that reenergizing individuals can do more for competitiveness than reengineering processes.

Competing for the Future starts with a fundamental premise: We've reached the limits of incrementalism. Squeezing another penny out of costs, getting a product to market a few weeks earlier, responding to customer inquiries a little bit faster, ratcheting quality up one more notch, capturing another point of market share, tweaking the organizational one additional time—these are the obsessions of managers today. But pursuing incremental advantage while rivals are fundamentally reinventing the industrial landscape is akin to fiddling while Rome burns. This book is not about catching up, it's about getting ahead.

Many companies have already done much of the hard work of catching up on cost, quality, speed, and flexibility. Now they are turning their attention to growth. But there are as many foolhardy ways to grow as there are to downsize. Pouring money into so-called synergistic acquisitions, merging with other behind-the-curve laggards, or getting caught up in a high-tech acquisition "land rush" may temporarily increase the top line but will have virtually no effect on the long-term bottom line.

The choice is not between incrementalist operational improvements on the one hand and ego-driven mega deals on the other. Instead, the goal is to fundamentally reinvent existing competitive space (First Direct's telephone banking service in the United Kingdom) or invent entirely new competitive space (Netscape's Web browsers) in ways that amaze customers and dismay competitors. Sustainable, profitable growth is not the product of a deal, it's the product of foresight. In turn, foresight is not the product of perspicuity, but of unconventional, out-of-the-box thinking.

Ralph Waldo Emerson once wrote, "There are always two parties, the party of the past and the party of the future; the establishment and the movement." A substantial truth lurks in this observation: The future belongs not to those who possess a crystal ball, but to those willing to challenge the biases and prejudices of the "establishment." The future belongs more to the unorthodox than it does to the prognosticators, more to the movement than to the starry-eyed.

We believe that the goal is not to predict *the* future, but to imagine *a* future made possible by changes in technology, life style, work style, regulation, global geopolitics, and the like. And there are as many viable futures as there are imaginative firms that can understand deeply the dynamics at work right now which hold opportunities to become the author of the new. For the future is not what *will* happen; the future is what *is* happening. The present and the future don't abut each other, neatly divided between the five-year plan and the great unknown beyond. Rather they are intertwined. Every company is in the process of becoming—of becoming an anachronism irrelevant to the future, or of becoming the harbinger of the future. The long-term is not something that happens someday; it is what every company is building or forfeiting by its myriad daily decisions. As William Jennings Bryan put it, "Destiny is no matter of chance. It is a matter of choice: It is not a thing to be waited for, it is a thing to be achieved."

But without a point of view about the opportunity for change—for revolution—a company is more likely to forfeit the future than own it. The goal of this book is to help individuals, and the institutions to which they devote their efforts, develop such a point of view and turn it into reality. Only those who can imagine and preemptively create the future will be around to enjoy it.

This book is about strategy—about a company's strategy for shaping its future. In many ways, strategy has been discredited over the past several years. Consulting companies that once focused on strategy are now turning to operational issues. Strategic planning departments are being disbanded. The view that "strategy is the easy part, and implementation is the hard part" goes unchallenged in many quarters. Most strategic planning is strategic in name only, ritualistic and formulaic, seldom deeply creative. No wonder strategy has lost much of its credibility. But make no mistake—strategy is hard work. Creating a compelling view of tomorrow's opportunities and moving preemptively to secure the future are tasks for neither dilettantes nor the merely intellectually curious. Those who want to put the ideas in this book to work in their own companies will find that they have embarked on a task as intellectually and emotionally demanding as any they have undertaken in their professional lives. They will also find the challenge immensely rewarding: Nothing is more liberating than becoming the author of one's own destiny.

We argue that successfully competing for the future requires the capacity to bring about a revolution in one's industry or market space, which in turn requires a revolution in how one creates strategy. Luckily, this revolution needn't start at the top. Anyone can spawn a revolution. Yet front-line employees and middle managers today, inclined to regard themselves as victims, have lost confidence in their ability to shape the future of their organizations. They have forgotten that historically it has been the dispossessed—from Gandhi to Mandela, from the American patriots to the Polish shipbuilders—who have led revolutions. Notwithstanding all the somber incantations that "change must start at the top," one must ask how often the monarchy has led a revolution. In our work and research, we have found the ferment of intellectual revolution more often in the middle of organizations than at the top. Understanding this, any employee, at any level, who cares deeply about the future of his or her company must be willing to become an activist. This is a book for activists.

Competing for the Future provides would-be revolutionaries with the tools and concepts they need to challenge the protectors of the past.

Preface

The book you are holding is the record of a unique partnership spanning seventeen years. In 1977 one of us (Gary) was a doctoral student in international business at the University of Michigan and the other (C.K.) a newly hired associate professor of strategy. We first met when the professor crossed departmental lines to give a seminar to the international business Ph.D. students. What we both remember is that the afternoon quickly turned into an extraordinarily pointed, take-no-prisoners debate between the two of us. Each of us was determined to deliver an unequivocal intellectual *coup de grace*. Others present thought we might never speak to each other again, let alone work together. But the seeds of mutual respect, and, ultimately, friendship, were sown that afternoon. Other, equally contentious debates followed, but we quickly discovered that we had more in common than a passion for academic sparring. We both believed that the ultimate test of business school research is its managerial significance. We were both deeply concerned with the ability of large enterprises to maintain their competitive vitality. And we both felt there was a great deal of managerial and competitive reality that lay beyond the boundaries of existing theory. These shared interests laid the foundation for the ensuing years of joint research, shared consulting assignments, and co-authorship.

The collaboration started in earnest when a consulting relationship C.K. had with a large and respected American firm became the grounds for our first joint research. Though the company declined to release the specifics of the study, the ideas generated became the basis for our first *Harvard Business Review* article, "Do You Really Have a Global Strategy?" As our research and consulting took us to other companies, we were intrigued by how smaller rivals, many from Japan, could apparently prevail against much larger, richer companies. How, we wondered, could competitors with such apparently meager resources manage to successfully challenge corporate giants? What prevented industry leaders from turning aside the challenge of impertinent newcomers? We saw this pattern, of an incumbent's failing to adequately defend itself against smaller, resource-limited challengers, again and again. How could we square what we were observing with the prevailing theory about the market power of incumbents and the advantages of market share? What theory could explain how Canon managed to make such a huge dent in Xerox's market share? How could Honda manage to outgun, in so many ways, the behemoths of Detroit? And what about Sony versus RCA?

The marked differences we observed in resource effectiveness could not be explained by incremental differences in operational efficiency, nor by institutional factors such as the cost of labor or capital. No static comparison of cost structures could account for the seeming ability of some companies to constantly invent new ways of accomplishing more with less. What, we asked ourselves, could account for such disparities in resource effectiveness?

It was clear that the challengers were driven by something more than short-term financial goals. As we looked back across their investments, alliances, international expansion strategies, and new product announcements, we observed a consistency to their actions that presupposed a point of view about the future. As we interviewed managers in these companies, they often referred to amazingly ambitious goals—goals that stretched far beyond the temporal bounds of typical strategic "plans." Where did such aspirations come from? How did they get by the "reality test" that truncates ambition in so many companies? And how could such seemingly incredible goals be made tangible and real to employees at all levels?

Many times the challengers had succeeded in creating entirely new forms of competitive advantage and in dramatically rewriting the rules of engagement. Flexibility advantages were built atop speed advantages, which were built atop supplier-management advantages, which were built atop quality advantages. What interested us was not the particulars of any single advantage; those could be easily accounted for by traditional notions of competitive advantage. Instead, we were intrigued by the process of advantage creation. What drove some companies, and not others, to continuously search for new advantages? What was the dynamic at work?

We saw companies making commitments to particular skill areas—optical media, financial engineering, miniaturization—far in advance of the emergence of specific end-product markets. Senior executives seemed to see competition as a race to build competencies, not simply to gain immediate market share. What was the basis, we asked ourselves, for such commitments? How could one write a business case for a market that might not emerge for a decade or more? What was the logic behind the emotional and intellectual commitment so much in evidence? How did executives select which capabilities to build for the future?

We had to conclude that some management teams were simply more "foresightful" than others. Some were capable of imagining products, services, and entire industries that did not yet exist and then giving them birth. These managers seemed to spend less time worrying about how to position the firm in existing "competitive space" and more time creating fundamentally new competitive space. Other companies, the laggards, were more interested in protecting the past than in creating the future. They took the industry structure as a given, seldom challenging the prevailing conventions. But where did the foresight come from? How was it possible to imagine markets that hadn't yet come into being?

Existing theories of strategy and organization, while providing a solid base for discovery, do not fully answer these questions. While they help us understand the structure of an extant industry, they provide little insight into what it takes to fundamentally reshape an industry to one's own benefit. While they illuminate the attributes of a transformational leader, they say little about what it takes for a leadership team to develop a prescient, well-grounded point of view about the future, much less to make it happen. While they provide a scorecard for keeping track of relative competitive advantage, they fail to capture the dynamic of competence-building.

The gap, then, between theory and observation provoked this book. We wrote it at a time when companies were disbanding corporate strategy departments, when consulting firms were engaged more often to improve operating efficiency than to plot strategy, and when many companies were rushing to downsize rather than to create the markets and industries of tomorrow. It is, perhaps, not too overstated to say that strategy has been in crisis. Our goal in this book is to enlarge the concept of strategy so that it more fully encompasses the emerging competitive reality—a reality in which the goal is to transform industries, not just organizations; a reality in which being incrementally better is not enough; a reality in which any company that cannot imagine the future won't be around to enjoy it. In closing the gap between theory and reality, we hope to return to strategy a little of its lost luster.

While this book is about strategy, about "how to think," it draws heavily on the experience of companies around the world that have managed to overcome resource disadvantages and build positions of global leadership. It devotes even more attention to companies that have managed to escape the curse of success and have rebuilt industry leadership a second and third time. Nevertheless, the companies held as exemplars in this book don't necessarily pass a comprehensive test of "excellence." There is no single company that fully embodies the approach to strategy, competition, and organization we are advocating, though some come closer than others. We believe there is plenty of upside potential for every company willing to commit to the action agenda laid out in these pages.

So *Competing for the Future* is not for dilettantes; it is not for the merely intellectually curious. It is a handbook for those who are not content to follow, for those who believe that the best way to win is to rewrite the rules, for those who are unafraid to challenge orthodoxy, for those who are more inclined to build than cut, for those more concerned with making a difference than making a career, and for those who are absolutely committed to staking out the future first.

Acknowledgments

We have had the opportunity to interact with tens of thousands of managers over the last decade and a half, and this book is, in large part, the product of that interaction. Through a series of research programs, through executive education (on behalf of the London Business School and the University of Michigan, and in dozens of companies), and through consulting assignments in many of the world's leading companies, we've learned much about what it takes to successfully compete for the future. We owe an enormous debt to the managers from whom we learned and to the companies that gave us an opportunity to test our ideas.

In particular, we would like to thank Rob Wilmott and Peter Bonfield, the past and present chief executives of ICL plc. Our research and executive development partnership with ICL, formed in the mid-1980s, provided much of the early impetus for our thinking on global competition, strategic alliances, and "strategic intent." A similar relationship with Motorola, under the sponsorship of then Chairman Bob Galvin and CEO George Fisher, provided us an opportunity to form and test our ideas around the notion of core competence. Executives at EDS made a significant contribution to the development of our thinking on "strategic architecture" and the process of strategy "regeneration." We would like to thank especially Les Alberthal, chairman of EDS, as well as Nick Barretta and Greig Trosper. Other companies that provided fertile ground for action research included AT&T, Cargill, Trinova, Ford, Rockwell, Philips, Colgate-Palmolive, and Eastman Chemical. We would also like to acknowledge the contribution of the Gatsby Charitable Foundation in providing financial support for our research.

We have benefited greatly from a wide variety of research that has preceded this book. Our intellectual debt to strategy pioneers Ken Andrews, Igor Ansoff, Alfred Chandler, and to many others is substantial. Our work resonates with their concern for the setting of corporate direction and the accumulation of distinctive competencies. We are also indebted to Michael Porter, who so successfully integrated corporate strategy and industrial economics. He reminded his colleagues that corporate strategy can be neither created nor pursued in a competitive vacuum. Any strategy that is not grounded in a deep understanding of the dynamics of competitive rivalry will fail. Hence our emphasis in this book on *competition* for the future. Professor Henry Mintzberg has made a similarly valuable contribution to our learning. We are entirely sympathetic to his view of strategy outcomes as always evolutionary and often unpredictable. Professor Mintzberg's view of strategy as an organic process and Professor Porter's somewhat more analytical and deterministic view of strategy are often seen as antithetical to each other. Yet we believe that both scholars have illuminated important truths about the nature of strategy. Strategy is both a process of understanding and shaping competitive "forces" and a process of open-ended discovery and purposeful incrementalism.

Like the pioneers, we believe that top management must develop a point of view about desired competitive outcomes. Like Professor Porter, we believe that that point of view must be fully cognizant of the aspirations and strategies of rivals seeking to occupy the same competitive space. Like Henry Mintzberg, we believe that much cannot be known about the future, and that planning can never be a wholly acceptable substitute for discovery and learning.

Our book is just one thread in a tapestry of new perspectives on strategy and competition. Through seminars, reading, and personal conversations we have benefited enormously from the fresh ideas brought to the strategy marketplace by Richard Pascale, Peter Senge, James Brian Quinn, Hiroyuki Itami, Kenichi Ohmae, Ikujiro Nonaka, Richard Rumelt, David Teece, Robert Burgleman, Ingemar Dierickx, Karel Cool, Jay Barney, Yves Doz, and several others. Rather than providing a footnote at every point where their ideas coincide with ours, we simply wish to direct the reader's attention to the substantial body of sound, innovative thinking that is contained in the work of these "new age" strategy scholars. Though these researchers have, for the most part, worked in parallel, rather than in serial, and have often used different words to describe similar phenomena, their perspectives on the challenges facing managers are broadly similar to our own. Like us, they emphasize "invisible assets," "learning," "innovation," "capabilities," "knowledge," "vision," and "leadership." Like us, they are working hard to ensure that the strategic tools and perspectives available to managers are up to the task of crafting strategy for the twenty-first century. We have drawn inspiration from these scholars and assurance that perhaps we are on the right track after all. For readers interested in the work of the strategy pioneers that formed the point of departure for this book, or in the more recent work of scholars whose work complements that of our own, we provide a bibliography at the end of this volume.

There is another individual whose wisdom has benefited our work enormously, one who is both a pioneer and a latter-day guru—Professor Peter Drucker. Professor Drucker has never lost sight of the fact that, for a theory or concept to be useful, it must ultimately be translated into the language and context of managers and managerial action. He has also been an unfailing beacon, lighting the way toward the management issues of tomorrow. Whatever small amount of managerial relevance and thoughtful foresight we achieve in this book owes much to Professor Drucker's shining example.

Our editor at the Harvard Business School, Carol Franco, deserves much credit for this book. It was her encouragement, as well as her penchant for deadlines, that ensured the project was completed before the turn of the millennium. Karen Moss, Gary Hamel's able assistant at the London Business School, did a heroic job of keeping the world at bay, thus creating time for writing. Thanks are also due Mark Bleackley, a Ph.D. candidate at the London Business School who provided substantial research support. Dr. Jim Scholes, a consulting colleague and friend for more than ten years, helped substantially with the preparation of Chapter 5. His contribution is gratefully acknowledged.

Most of all we must thank our wives, who exercised a degree of forbearance far beyond that which we had any right to expect. The demands of producing this book often pushed family responsibilities into second place. The unfailing enthusiasm and support of ElDona and Gayatri made us feel less guilty than we should have. To them goes our biggest and most heartfelt "Thanks!"

Getting Off the Treadmill

. . . .

Look around your company. Look at the high-profile initiatives that have been launched recently. Look at the issues
that are preoccupying senior management. Look at the criteria and benchmarks by which progress is being measured.
Look at the track record of new business creation. Look into
the faces of your colleagues and consider their dreams and fears.
Look toward the future and ponder your company's ability to
shape that future and regenerate success again and again in the
years and decades to come.

Now ask yourself: Does senior management have a clear and
broadly shared understanding of how the industry may be different
ten years in the future? Are its "headlights" shining farther out
than those of competitors? Is its point of view about the future
clearly reflected in the company's short-term priorities? Is its point
of view about the future competitively unique?

Ask yourself: How influential is my company in setting the new
rules of competition within its industry? Is it regularly defining
new ways of doing business, building new capabilities, and setting
new standards of customer satisfaction? Is it more a rule-maker
than a rule-taker within its industry? Is it more intent on challenging
the industry status quo than protecting it?

Ask yourself: Is senior management fully alert to the dangers
posed by new, unconventional rivals? Are potential threats to the
current business model widely understood? Do senior executives
possess a keen sense of urgency about the need to reinvent the
current business model? Is the task of regenerating core strategies

receiving as much top management attention as the task of reengineering core processes?

Ask yourself: Is my company pursuing growth and new business development with as much passion as it is pursuing operational efficiency and downsizing? Do we have as clear a point of view about where the next $10 million, $100 million, or $1 billion of revenue growth will come from as we do about where the next $10 million, $100 million, or $1 billion of cost savings will come from?

Ask yourself: What percentage of our improvement efforts (quality improvement, cycle-time reduction, and improved customer service) focuses on creating advantages new to the industry, and what percentage focuses on merely catching up to our competitors? Are competitors as eager to benchmark us as we are to benchmark them?

Ask yourself: What is driving our improvement and transformation agenda—our own view of future opportunities or the actions of our competitors? Is our transformation agenda mostly offensive or defensive?

Ask yourself: Am I more of a maintenance engineer keeping today's business humming along, or an architect imagining tomorrow's businesses? Do I devote more energy to prolonging the past than I do to creating the future? How often do I lift my gaze out of the rut and consider what's out there on the horizon?

And finally: What is the balance between hope and anxiety in my company; between confidence in our ability to find and exploit opportunities for growth and new business development and concern about our ability to maintain competitiveness in our traditional businesses; between a sense of opportunity and a sense of vulnerability, both corporate and personal?

These are not rhetorical questions. Get a pencil. Rate your company.

How does senior management's point of view about the future stack up against that of competitors?

Conventional
and Reactive
●　　●　　●　　●　　●
Distinctive
and Far-sighted

**Which issue is absorbing more of
senior management's attention?**

Reengineering   •   •   •   (•)   •   Regenerating
Core Processes   Core Strategies

**Within the industry, do competitors view
our company as more of a rule-taker or a rule-maker?**

Mostly a   •   •   (•)   •   •   Mostly a
Rule-taker   Rule-maker

**What are we better at, improving operational efficiency
or creating fundamentally new businesses?**

Operational   (•)   •   •   •   •   New Business
Efficiency   Development

**What percentage of our advantage-building efforts
focus on catching up with competitors versus
building advantages new to the industry?**

Mostly   Mostly
Catching Up   (•)   •   •   •   •   New to the
to Others   Industry

**To what extent has our transformation agenda
been set by competitors' actions versus
being set by our own unique vision of the future?**

Largely   Largely
Driven by   •   (•)   •   •   •   Driven by
Competitors   Our Vision

**To what extent am I, as a senior manager,
a maintenance engineer working on the present
or an architect designing the future?**

Mostly an   •   •   •   (•)   •   Mostly an
Engineer   Architect

**Among employees, what is the balance
between anxiety and hope?**

Mostly   •   •   •   (•)   •   Mostly
Anxiety   Hope

If your marks fell somewhere in the middle, or off to the left, your company may be devoting too much energy to preserving the past and not enough to creating the future.

We often ask senior managers three related questions: First, what percentage of your time is spent on external, rather than internal, issues—understanding, for example, the implications of a particular new technology versus debating corporate overhead allocations? Second, of this time spent looking outward, how much of it is spent considering how the world could be different in five or ten years, as opposed to worrying about winning the next big contract or how to respond to a competitor's pricing move? Third, of the time devoted to looking outward *and* forward, how much of it is spent in consultation with colleagues, where the objective is to build a deeply shared, well-tested view of the future, as opposed to a personal and idiosyncratic view?

The answers we get typically conform to what we call the "40/30/20 rule." In our experience, about 40% of senior executive time is spent looking outward, and of this time, about 30% is spent peering three, four, five, or more years into the future. And of the time spent looking forward, no more than 20% is spent attempting to build a collective view of the future (the other 80% is spent looking at the future of the manager's particular business). Thus, on average, senior management is devoting less than 3% (40% $\times$ 30% $\times$ 20% = 2.4%) of its energy to building a *corporate* perspective on the future. In some companies the figure is less than 1%. As a benchmark, our experience suggests that to develop a prescient and distinctive point of view about the future, a senior management team must be willing to spend about 20 to 50% of its time, over a period of several months. It must then be willing to continually revisit that point of view, elaborating and adjusting it as the future unfolds.

It takes substantial and sustained intellectual energy to develop high-quality, robust answers to questions such as what new core competencies will we need to build, what new product concepts should we pioneer, what new alliances will we need to form, what nascent development programs should we protect, and what long-term regulatory initiatives should we pursue. We believe such questions have received far too little attention in many companies.

They have received too little attention not because senior managers are lazy; most are working harder than ever. Stress, burnout, and perpetual jet lag are less occasional occupational hazards than a way of life for most executives today. It is not even the sheer, bloody, time-consuming difficulty of answering these questions that scares top teams off. These questions go unanswered because to address them senior managers must first admit, to themselves and to their employees, that they are less than fully in control of their company's future. They must admit that what they know today—the knowledge and experience that justify their position in the corporate pecking order—may be irrelevant or wrong-headed for the future. These questions go unanswered because they are, in a sense, a direct challenge to the assumption that top management really is in control, really does have better headlights than anyone else in the corporation, and already has a clear and compelling view of corporate direction. So the urgent drives out the important; the future goes largely unexplored; and the capacity to act, rather than the capacity to think and imagine, becomes the sole measure of leadership.

If it's not the future, just what is occupying senior management's attention? In two words—restructuring and reengineering. Whereas downsizing and core process redesign are legitimate and important tasks, they have more to do with shoring up today's businesses than creating tomorrow's industries. Neither is a substitute for imagining and creating the future. Neither will ensure continued success if a company fails to regenerate its core strategies. Any company that succeeds at restructuring and reengineering, but fails to create the markets of the future, will find itself on a treadmill, trying to keep one step ahead of the steadily declining margins and profits of yesterday's businesses.

BEYOND RESTRUCTURING

The painful upheavals in so many companies in recent years reflect the failure of one-time industry leaders to keep up with the accelerating pace of industry change. For decades the changes that confronted Sears, General Motors, IBM, Westinghouse, Volkswagen, and other incumbents were, if not exactly glacial in speed, at least more or less linear extrapolations of the past. Sears could count on the fact that successive generations of rural Americans would find its catalog the most convenient way to outfit their homes and themselves; GM could be sure that as incomes rose, young consumers, like their parents before them, would trade up from Chevys to Oldsmobiles and from Buicks to Cadillacs; IBM could expect revenues to rise forever upward as big companies added more "mips" to their central data-processing departments and as proprietary operating systems protected IBM's accounts from competitor encroachment. The watchword for top management in these companies was "steady as she goes." Companies were run by managers, not leaders; by maintenance engineers, not by architects.

Yet few companies that began the 1980s as industry leaders ended the decade with their leadership intact and undiminished. IBM, Philips, Dayton-Hudson, TWA, Texas Instruments, Xerox, Boeing, Daimler-Benz, Salomon Brothers, Citicorp, Bank of America, Sears, Digital Equipment Corp. (DEC), Westinghouse, DuPont, Pan Am, and many others saw their success eroded or destroyed by the tides of technological, demographic, and regulatory change and order-of-magnitude productivity and quality gains made by nontraditional competitors. Buffeted by these forces, few firms seemed to be in control of their own destiny. The foundations of past success were shaken and fractured when, in all too many cases, the industrial terrain changed shape faster than top management could refashion its basic beliefs and assumptions about which markets to serve, which technologies to master, which customers to serve, and how to get the best out of employees.

These and many other companies found themselves confronted with sizable "organizational transformation" problems. Of course, any company that is more of a bystander than a driver on the road to the future will find its structure, values, and skills becoming progressively less attuned to an ever-changing industry reality. Such a discrepancy between the pace of change in the industry environment and the pace of change in the internal environment spawns the daunting task of organizational transformation. The organizational transformation agenda typically includes downsizing, overhead reduction, employee empowerment, process redesign, and portfolio rationalization. As important as these initiatives are, their accomplishment cannot restore a company to industry leadership, nor ensure that it intercepts the future.

When a competitiveness problem (stagnant growth, declining margins, and falling market share) finally becomes inescapable, most executives pick up the knife and begin the brutal work of restructuring. The goal is to carve away layers of corporate fat, jettison underperforming businesses, and raise asset productivity. Executives who don't have the stomach for emergency room surgery, like John Akers at IBM or Robert Stempel at GM, soon find themselves out of a job.

Masquerading under names like refocusing, delayering, decluttering, and right-sizing (one is tempted to ask why the "right" size is always smaller), restructuring always has the same result: fewer employees. In 1993, large U.S. firms announced nearly 600,000 layoffs—25% more than had been announced in a similar period in 1992 and nearly 10% above the levels of 1991, which was technically the bottom of the recession in the United States. While European companies had long tried to put off their own day of reckoning, bloated payrolls and out-of-control employment costs had, by the early 1990s, made downsizing as inevitable in Europe as it was in the United States. Some European companies such as Volkswagen, eager to preserve industrial peace, sought to maintain employment levels by reducing the number of hours worked by each employee. The depressing assumption seemed to be that because there was no hope of raising output, the only solution was to share fewer jobs among more people.

Despite the excuses about global competition and the job-destroying impact of productivity-enhancing technology, the fact was that most of the employment contraction in large U.S. companies was caused not by distant foreign competitors intent on "stealing U.S. jobs," but by U.S. senior managers who had fallen asleep at the switch. For the most part, the companies that have been most aggressive in reducing headcount won't make it on to anyone's "most admired" list (see Table 1-1). These companies tend to be a rogue's gallery of undermanaged or wrongly managed companies.

Although some responsibility for Europe's pitiful record of job creation could be laid at the feet of politicians and their overgenerous social spending (between 1965 and 1989 European industry

TABLE 1-1 SOME COMPANIES REDUCING HEADCOUNT IN 1993

Reduced Headcount Between 5 and 10%		Reduced Headcount 10% or More	
BASF	8	J.E. Seagram	17
Data General	8	Owens-Illinois	16
Westinghouse	7	Monsanto	11
Borden	6	Union Carbide	13
Dresser	5	IBM	13
Bethlehem Steel	7	Digital	17
General Motors	5	Amdahl	30
Honeywell	6	Kodak	17

Source: "The Fortune 500," *Fortune*, 18 April 1994, pp. 257–280.
Note: This also includes headcount reductions through divestment.

created approximately 10 million new jobs while U.S. industry created close to 50 million new jobs), much of the problem was, again, management-made. The guilty included self-protective executives in Europe's sclerotic telecommunications companies determined to prevent European companies from enjoying the fruits of the information revolution, timid managers in European car companies who preferred protectionism at home to the challenge of learning to compete head on with U.S. and Japanese automakers outside of Europe, and subsidy-hungry managers in many of Europe's high-technology companies who, having accepted billions of ecus from Europe's long-suffering taxpayers, nevertheless failed to create world-beating new businesses.

With no or slow growth, these companies soon found it impossible to support their burgeoning employment rosters, traditional R&D budgets, and significant investment programs. The problems of low growth were often compounded by inattentiveness to ballooning overheads (IBM's problem), diversification into unrelated businesses (such as Xerox's foray into financial services), and the paralysis imposed by unfailingly conservative corporate staff. It is not surprising that shareholders are giving moribund companies new marching orders: Make this company "lean and mean"; "make the assets sweat"; "get back to basics." Return on capital employed, shareholder value, and revenue per employee became the primary arbiters of top management performance. Although perhaps inescapable and in many cases commendable, the resulting restructuring has destroyed lives, homes, and communities—to what end? For efficiency and productivity. Although arguing with these objectives is impossible, their single-minded—and sometimes simple-minded—pursuit has often done as much harm as good. Let us explain.

Imagine a chief executive who, fully aware that if he or she doesn't make effective use of corporate resources someone else will be given the chance, launches a tough program to improve return on investment. Now, ROI (or RONA, or ROCE, and so forth) has two components: a numerator—net income—and a denominator—investment, net assets, or capital employed. (In a service industry, a more appropriate denominator may be headcount.) Managers throughout our not-so-hypothetical firm also know that raising net income is likely to be a harder slog than cutting assets and headcount. To grow the numerator, top management must have a point of view about where the new opportunities lie, must be able to anticipate changing customer needs, must have invested preemptively in building new competencies, and so on. So under intense pressure for a quick ROI improvement, executives reach for the lever that will bring the quickest, surest improvement in ROI—the denominator. To cut the denominator, top management doesn't need much more than a red pencil. Thus the obsession with denominators.

In fact, the United States and Britain have produced an entire generation of denominator managers. They can downsize, declutter, delayer, and divest better than any managers in the world. Even before the current wave of downsizing, U.S. and British companies had, on average, the highest asset productivity ratios of any companies in the world. Denominator management is an accountant's shortcut to asset productivity.

Don't misunderstand. We have nothing against efficiency and productivity. We believe, and will argue strongly, that a company must not only get to the future first, it must get there for less. Yet there is more than one route to productivity improvement. Just as any firm that cuts the denominator and holds up revenue will reap productivity gains, so too will any company that succeeds in growing its revenue stream atop a slower growing or constant capital and employment base. Although the first approach may sometimes be necessary, we believe that the second approach is usually more desirable.

In a world where competitors are capable of achieving 5, 10, or 15% real growth in revenues, aggressive denominator reduction, under a flat revenue stream, is simply a way to sell market share profitably. Marketing strategists term this a "harvest strategy" and consider it a no-brainer. Take a national example. Between 1969 and 1991, Britain's manufacturing output (the numerator) went up by a scant 10% in real terms. Yet over this same period, the number of people employed in British manufacturing (the denominator) declined by 37%. The result was that during the early and mid 1980s—the Thatcher years—U.K. manufacturing productivity increased faster than any other major industrialized country except Japan. Though Britain's financial press and Conservative ministers trumpeted this "success," it was, of course, bittersweet. While new legislation limited the power of trade unions, and the relaxation of statutory impediments to workforce reduction allowed management to excise inefficient and outmoded work practices, there was not a corresponding increase in the ability of British firms to create new markets at home and abroad. In fact, with scarcely any net gain in real manufacturing output over the period, British companies were, in effect, surrendering global market share. One half expected to arrive at Heathrow one morning, pick up the *Financial Times,* and find that Britain had finally matched Japanese manufacturing productivity—and that the last remaining person at work in U.K. manufacturing was the most productive son-of-a-gun on the planet.

The social costs of restructuring are high. And although an individual firm may be able to avoid some of these costs, society cannot. In Britain, the service sector could not absorb all the displaced workers and underwent its own vicious downsizing in the recession beginning in 1989. Of course, much of the cutting in British companies and around the world was necessary, even if first-line workers often bore more than their fair share of the pain. Unproductive layers of management had to be excised, dumb acquisitions unwound, and inflexible work practices abandoned. Yet few companies seemed to ask themselves: How will we know when we're done restructuring? Where is the dividing line between cutting fat and cutting muscle?

One of the inevitable results of downsizing is plummeting employee morale. Employees have a hard time squaring all the talk about the importance of human capital with seemingly indiscriminate cutting. They are too often confronted with a lose-lose proposition: "If you don't become more efficient, you'll lose your job. By the way, if you do become more efficient, you'll lose your job." What employees hear is that they're the firm's most valuable assets; what they know is that they're the most expendable assets.

Many middle managers and first-line employees must feel like the laborers who built the pharaohs' tombs. Every pharaoh hoped to build for himself a tomb of such intricate and deceitful design that no marauder would ever be able to enter it and purloin the pharaoh's wealth. Think of the laborers as middle managers in the midst of corporate restructuring. All the workers knew that when the tomb was finished they would be put to death—this was how the pharaoh destroyed any memory of how to find the wealth. Imagine what would happen when the pharaoh showed up on a work site and inquired of a supervisor, "How's it going, are you about done yet?" "Not yet boss, it'll be a few more years, I'm afraid." No wonder tombs were seldom finished within the pharaoh's lifetime! And no wonder so few first-level and mid-level employees bring their full emotional and intellectual energies to the task of restructuring.

Restructuring seldom results in fundamental improvement in the business. At best it buys time. One study of 16 large U.S. companies with at least three years of restructuring experience found that although restructuring usually did improve a firm's share price, the improvement was almost always temporary. Three years into restructuring, the share prices of the companies surveyed were, on average, lagging even farther behind index growth rates than they had been when the restructuring began. The study concluded that a savvy investor should look at a restructuring announcement as a signal to sell rather than buy.[1] Downsizing belatedly attempts to correct the mistakes of the past; it is not about creating the markets of the future. The simple point is that getting smaller is not enough. Downsizing, the equivalent of corporate anorexia, can make a company thinner; it doesn't necessarily make it healthier.

Any company that is better at denominator management than numerator management—any company that doesn't have a track record of ambitious, profitable, organic growth—shouldn't expect Wall Street to cut it much slack. What Wall Street says to such companies is, "Go ahead, squeeze the lemon, get the inefficiencies out, but give us the juice (i.e., the dividends). We'll take that juice and give it to companies that are better at making lemonade." The financial community knows that a management team that is good at denominator reduction may not be good at numerator growth. Look at how IBM's share price tanked when the company finally cut its dividend. Investors obviously didn't believe that IBM was likely to redeploy the cash saved in a way that would ultimately produce more shareholder wealth.

Though many factors influence dividend payout ratios (the proportion of earnings paid out to shareholders), and although ratios among companies in the developed world may be slowly converging after having diverged since the mid-1970s, it is not totally by accident that the world's best denominator managers—U.S. and British managers—pay back more of their firm's earnings to shareholders than do Japanese and German managers. Again and again Wall Street has shown itself quite content to watch a firm profitably restructure itself out of business, when top management seems incapable of profitably creating the future.

BEYOND REENGINEERING

Recognizing that restructuring is ultimately a dead end, smart companies have moved on to reengineer their processes. Reengineering aims to root out needless work and get every process in the company pointed in the direction of customer satisfaction, reduced cycle time, and total quality.[2] Once again, the stopwatches are out: How do we do things faster and with less waste? The difference between this twenty-first century Taylorism and the original is that now companies are asking employees, rather than the "experts," to redesign processes and work flows. Interestingly, though the ostensible goal of reengineering is to focus each and every process on customer satisfaction, it is almost always the promise of reduced costs, rather than heightened customer satisfaction, that convinces a top team to sign up for a major reengineering project. In fact, many companies have taken reengineering charges against earnings in the same way they took restructuring charges in earlier years.[3] Few companies seem to have asked themselves what is the opportunity cost of the hundreds of millions—or even billions—of dollars that have been written off for reengineering and restructuring. What if all that cash and all that "redundant" brain power had been applied to creating tomorrow's markets? Far from being a tribute to senior management's steely resolve or far-sightedness, a large restructuring and reengineering charge is simply the penalty that a company must pay for not having anticipated the future.

There is a difference, though, between restructuring and reengineering. Reengineering offers at least the hope, if not always the reality, of getting better as well as getting smaller. Any company that is more successful at restructuring than reengineering will find itself getting smaller faster than it is getting better. Several of the largest U.S. companies have recently found themselves in this unenviable position. Although restructuring is never more than a necessary thing, reengineering can be a good thing. Yet there is a dilemma. Let us explain. *The Machine That Changed the World,* an exhaustive and insightful study of the changing economics of car design and production, was published in 1990.[4] "Lean manufacturing," the authors' term for the extraordinarily efficient manufacturing system pioneered by Toyota, is a central theme of the book. Yet as one reads the book, one is compelled to ask: When did Toyota begin its pursuit of lean manufacturing? Answer: more than 40 years ago. And another question comes: Why did it take U.S. automakers 40 years to decode the principles of lean manufacturing? Answer: because those principles challenged every assumption and bias of U.S. auto executives.

Detroit is today catching up on quality and cost with its Japanese competitors. (Of course, Detroit was helped by a yen that appreciated by 20% against the dollar between 1991 and 1993 and a new U.S. president who, at the beginning of his term, threatened Japanese car producers with a massive antidumping suit. Not surprisingly, Japanese automakers raised their prices and surrendered market share.) Supplier networks have been reconstituted, product development processes redesigned, and manufacturing process reengineered. Yet the cheerful headlines heralding Detroit's comeback miss the deeper story. Sure, Detroit is catching up on cost and quality, but what was lost in terms of employment and global market share? The answer: hundreds of thousands of jobs, about 25 percentage points of market share in the United States, and any near-term hope of U.S. automakers' beating Japanese rivals in the booming markets of Asia.

The point is that in many companies, process reengineering and advantage-building efforts are more about catching up than getting out in front.[5] A few years ago one of us sat in on a leading strategy consulting firm's exposition of its methodology for helping clients do things faster. "Competing on time" was, in the opinion of the presenters, the next big competitive advantage. Although no one argued with this premise or the proposed methodology, the consultants were reminded that in the 1970s they had identified global scale and experience effects as key advantages to be pursued and, indeed, many automakers, chemical companies, semiconductor producers, and others had been persuaded to make preemptive investments in large-scale plants, each hoping to secure the required minimum share of world capacity. The result, in several industries, was severe overcapacity and vicious price cutting. Later, in the 1980s, they had urged their clients to pursue quality, which was certainly a laudable goal. Now they were recommending speed as the tonic for uncompetitiveness. In each case, it was pointed out, the consultants had come up with the right answer, but in each case the answer had come about ten years too late. They were helping their clients catch up rather than take the lead.

So while U.S. car companies could celebrate the fact that they were pulling even with their Japanese rivals on cost and quality,

Japanese producers were setting new competitive hurdles—breathtaking engine performance, razor-edge handling, luxury, new design aesthetics, and product development aimed at lifestyle niches. It remained to be seen whether Detroit would be the pacesetter in the next round of competition—to produce vehicles as exciting as they were fuel efficient and reliable—or whether they would once again rest on their overused laurels.

In a recent survey, nearly 80% of U.S. managers polled believed that quality would be a fundamental source of competitive advantage in the year 2000. Yet, barely half of Japanese managers predicted quality to be a source of advantage in the year 2000, though 82% believed it was currently an important advantage. Rated first as a source of competitive advantage in the year 2000 by Japanese managers was a capacity to create fundamentally new products and businesses.[6] Does this mean that Japanese managers are going to turn their backs on quality? Of course not. It merely indicates that by the year 2000 quality will no longer be a competitive differentiator; it will simply be the price of market entry. These Japanese managers realize that tomorrow's competitive advantages must necessarily be different from today's.

We come across far too many companies where top management's advantage-building agenda is still dominated by quality, time-to-market, and customer responsiveness. Although no one questions that such advantages are prerequisites for survival, to be still working on the advantages of the 1980s in the 1990s is hardly a testimony to management foresight. Though managers often try to make a virtue out of imitation, dressing it up in the fashionable colors of "adaptiveness," what they are adapting to all too often are the preemptive strategies of more imaginative competitors.

REGENERATING STRATEGY

Again, let us be clear. Catching up is necessary, but it's not going to turn an also-ran into a leader. Divisions of IBM, GM, and DEC have all won the Baldrige for quality—an award for better, not different. Becoming smaller and better are not enough. Think again about the laggards of the late 1980s and early 1990s: Sears, TWA, Westinghouse, Sanyo, Upjohn. Could Sears retake the high ground by getting even better at "bait-and-switch," convincing even more customers that they really wanted a $600 washing machine when they had come in for a $300 model? Would it have helped Sears to become an even more efficient and customer-focused catalog retailer (instead of killing off its encyclopedic catalog)? What if IBM created a lightning-fast mainframe development process, and won even more loyalty with central data-processing managers? What if American and United perfected the art of running a hub-and-spokes airline system—would this help them woo well-heeled international business passengers away from British Airways and Singapore? Our point is simple: It is not enough for a company to get smaller and better and faster, as important as these tasks may be; a company must also be capable of fundamentally reconceiving itself, of regenerating its core strategies, and of reinventing its industry. In short, a company must also be capable of getting different (see Figure 1-1).

Just as some companies have gotten smaller faster than they've gotten better, others have gotten better without becoming much

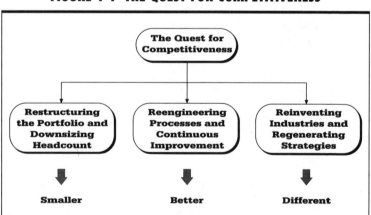

FIGURE 1-1 THE QUEST FOR COMPETITIVENESS

different. Consider Xerox. During the 1970s and 1980s Xerox surrendered a substantial amount of market share to Japanese competitors such as Canon and Sharp. Recognizing that it was on a slippery slide to oblivion, Xerox benchmarked its competitors and fundamentally reengineered its processes. By the early 1990s Xerox had become a textbook example of how to reduce costs, improve quality, and satisfy customers. But in all the talk of the new "American Samurai," two issues were overlooked. First, although Xerox succeeded in halting the erosion of its market share, it failed to recapture much share from its Japanese competitors. Canon still produces more copiers than any company in the world. Second, despite a pioneering role in laser printing, networking, icon-based computing, and the laptop computer, Xerox has failed to create any substantial new businesses outside its copier core. Although Xerox may have invented the office as we know it, it profited very little from its inventiveness. In fact, Xerox has probably left more money on the table, in the form of underexploited innovation, than any company in history. Why all this underexploited innovation? Because to create new businesses, Xerox would have had to regenerate its core strategy and reinvent its very concept of self: its channels, manufacturing processes, customers, criteria for promoting managers, metrics for measuring success, and so on. A company surrenders today's businesses when it gets smaller faster than it gets better. A company surrenders tomorrow's businesses when it gets better without getting different.

It is entirely possible for a company to downsize and reengineer without ever confronting the need to regenerate its core strategy, without ever being forced to rethink the boundaries of its industry, without ever having to imagine what customers might want in ten years' time, and without ever having to fundamentally redefine its "served market." Yet without such a fundamental reassessment, a company will be overtaken on the road to the future. Defending today's leadership is no substitute for creating tomorrow's leadership.

We meet many managers who describe their companies as "market leaders." (With enough creativity in delimiting market boundaries, almost any company can claim to be a market leader.) But market leadership today certainly doesn't equal market leadership tomorrow. Think about two sets of questions:

Today	5 to 10 Years in the Future
Which customers are you serving *today?*	Which customers will you be serving *in the future?*
Through what channels do you reach customers *today?*	Through what channels will you reach customers *in the future?*
Who are your competitors *today?*	Who will be your competitors *in the future?*
What is the basis for your competitive advantage *today?*	What will be the basis for your competitive advantage *in the future?*
Where do your margins come from *today?*	Where will your margins come from *in the future?*
What skills or capabilities make you unique *today?*	What skills or capabilities will make you unique *in the future?*
In what end product markets do you participate *today?*	In what end product markets will you participate *in the future?*

If senior executives don't have reasonably detailed answers to the "future" set of questions, and if the answers they do have are not substantially different from the "today" answers, there is little chance their companies will remain market leaders. Whatever market a company might dominate today, it is likely to change substantially over the next ten years. There's no such thing as "sustaining" leadership; it must be reinvented again and again.

The competitiveness problem faced by so many companies today is not a problem of "foreign" competition, but a problem of "nontraditional" competition. It's not the United States versus Japan versus Europe (Japan and Europe face even more daunting competitive problems than does the United States). The real competitive problem is laggards versus challengers, incumbents versus innovators, the inertial and imitative versus the imaginative. Challengers typically invent more efficient solutions to customer problems (for example, movies on demand over broad-band cable versus movies available from the local video rental outlet, or discount warehouse shopping versus traditional department store shopping). The new solutions emerge not because the challengers are incrementally more efficient than the incumbents, but because they are substantially more unorthodox. They discover the new solutions because they are willing to look far beyond the old.

At best, laggards follow the path of least resistance. Only when customers demanded it did Ford Motor Co. make "Quality Job 1." Only after Southwest Airlines became the most profitable airline in America did United and American challenge their long-held assumptions about how to compete. At worst, laggards follow the path of greatest familiarity. Challengers, on the other hand, follow the path of greatest opportunity, wherever it leads. A company doesn't need to be an upstart to be a challenger. Whereas CNN, Microsoft, and The Body Shop have often exhibited all the rebellious tendencies of adolescents, elders like Merck, British Airways, and Hewlett-Packard have also challenged the orthodoxies of industry incumbents.

FROM ORGANIZATIONAL TRANSFORMATION TO INDUSTRY TRANSFORMATION

The organizational transformation challenge faced by so many companies today is, in many cases, the direct result of their failure to reinvent their industries and regenerate their core strategies a decade or more ago. Laggards have crisis-proportion organizational transformation problems (reskilling employees, selling off businesses wholesale, slash-and-burn restructuring) because they surrendered leadership in the task of industry transformation. Take IBM. Although many observed that IBM had, in the early 1990s, the wrong kind of organization, skills, systems, and behaviors for a radically transformed information technology industry, such observations missed the deeper point. The real issue was not that IBM had the wrong kind of organization, skills, or people but that it woke up far too late to reconfigure its organization, skills, and people in time to intercept the trends that were dramatically reshaping its industry. For much of the 1980s, IBM had been driving toward the future while looking out the rear-view mirror. Despite spending close to $6 billion a year on R&D and hiring the best and brightest worldwide, IBM missed, as a corporation, almost every important clue as to how its industry was changing (though many lone individuals within the company saw the changes coming).

To take a counterexample, the organization and skills of AT&T and Hewlett-Packard 20 years ago were just as inappropriate to today's industry context as were IBM's. Yet, on average, HP and AT&T moved more quickly to adapt to the changing industry environment than did IBM. It was HP's deep insights into opportunities like engineering workstations, reduced instruction set (RISC) architecture, and the market for small printers and other peripherals that propelled the company's transition from an instruments company to a ground-breaking information technology company.

Ironically, the dimensions of the organizational transformation task faced by most companies were established by newcomers who changed the rules of the game rather than by the foresight of the incumbents themselves. Having failed to reinvent their industries 10 or 20 years earlier, and still having no unique point of view about where *they* want to drive the industry, incumbents have no choice but to transform themselves into pale imitations of industry interlopers. In short, for most companies, the organizational transformation agenda is reactive rather than proactive.

Successfully managing the task of organizational transformation can make a firm lean and fleet-footed; it cannot turn a firm into an industry pioneer. And although being a fast follower is better than being a slow follower, neither is a recipe for extraordinary growth and profitability. To be a leader, a company must take charge of the process of industry transformation.

All this prompts us to ask just how much of the reengineering problem companies are actually working on today. Although process reengineering dominates the top management agenda in many companies, we've argued that to create the future, a company must also be capable of "reengineering" its industry. The logic is simple: To extend leadership a company must eventually reinvent leadership, to reinvent leadership it must ultimately reinvent its industry, and to reinvent its industry it must ultimately regenerate its strategy. For us, top management's primary task is reinventing industries and regenerating strategy, not reengineering processes.

To create the future a company must (1) change in some fundamental way the rules of engagement in a long-standing industry (as Charles Schwab did in the brokerage and mutual fund businesses), (2) redraw the boundaries between industries (as Time Warner, Electronic Arts, and other companies are attempting to do in the field of "edutainment"), and/or (3) create entirely new industries (as Apple did in personal computers). A capacity to invent new industries and reinvent old ones is a prerequisite for getting to the future first and a precondition for staying out in front.

Table 1-2 provides examples of newcomers who have changed industry rules, of incumbents who have successfully regenerated their core strategies to accommodate the relentless pace of change in their industries, and of incumbents who have managed to both regenerate their strategies and reinvent their industry. Gaining an understanding of how to accomplish this last, most difficult task, is central to the mission of this book.

TABLE 1-2 COMPANIES REINVENTING INDUSTRY, REGENERATING STRATEGY, OR BOTH

	Reinvented Their Industry	Regenerated Their Strategy
■ CNN	X	
■ Wal-Mart	X	
■ ISS	X	
■ Service Corp. Int'l	X	
■ AT&T		X
■ Compaq		X
■ J.P. Morgan		X
■ Bankers Trust		X
■ Merck	X	X
■ Bell Atlantic	X	X
■ British Airways	X	X
■ Hewlett-Packard	X	X

Too many managers charged with the task of managing organizational transformation forget to ask, "Transform to what?" The point is that the organizational transformation agenda must be driven by a point of view about the industry transformation agenda: How do we want this industry to be shaped in five or ten years? What must we do to ensure that the industry evolves in a way that is maximally advantageous for us? What skills and capabilities must we begin building now if we are to occupy the industry high ground in the future? And how should we organize for opportunities that may not fit neatly within the boundaries of current business units and divisions? A point of view about the desired trajectory for industry transformation enables a company to create a proactive agenda for organizational transformation.

It was its point of view about the potential direction of the industry that encouraged Apple Computer, in 1992, to establish a division responsible for personal-interactive electronics, though this move didn't spare Apple from the need to take painful action to shore up its existing personal computer business. Merck's insights into the changing environment in the pharmaceutical industry led to the company's surprising decision to purchase Medco, a large mail-order pharmaceutical distribution company. Likewise, British Airways' understanding of the future of the airline business provided the impetus for a series of equity investments and joint ventures with airlines in the United States, continental Europe, and Asia, all aimed at making BA the world's first truly global airline.

Our premise is that a company can control its own destiny only if it understands how to control the destiny of its industry. Organizational transformation is a secondary challenge. The primary challenge is to become the author of industry transformation.

In July 1993, shortly after taking over the reins at Chrysler, CEO Bob Eaton brought together dozens of senior executives to discuss the company's second-quarter earnings. After praising his executives for producing Chrysler's best results since 1984, he quoted several commentators who had praised Chrysler's turnaround. Having gotten the assembled managers to the verge of smugness, Eaton revealed that the accolades had been written in 1956, 1965,

1976, and 1983. At least once a decade Chrysler had undergone a miraculous resurrection. "I've got a better idea," the CEO went on. "Let's stop getting sick. . . . My personal ambition is to be the first chairman never to lead a Chrysler comeback."[7] Staying off the critical list is a laudable objective, but one few companies manage.

No company can escape the need to reskill its people, reshape its product portfolio, redesign its processes, and redirect its resources. Organizational transformation is an imperative for every enterprise. The real issue is whether transformation happens belatedly—in a crisis atmosphere—or with foresight—in a calm and considered atmosphere; whether the transformation agenda is set by more prescient competitors or derives from one's own point of view about the future; whether transformation is spasmodic and brutal or continuous and peaceful. Palace coups and bloodletting make great press copy, but the real objective is a bloodless revolution. There is often a high price to be paid for brutal and belated transformation: The most talented people anticipate the carnage and flee for safety (the first rats off the ship are the best swimmers), civilian casualties are high (it is not always those most responsible for the conflict that suffer the most grievously), architectural treasures are looted (when healthy businesses are forced to slash headcount and investment to compensate for lousy strategic decisions), and populations are left demoralized (personal survival becomes the all-consuming task). The goal is a transformation process that is revolutionary in result, but evolutionary in execution.

Only when restructuring and reengineering fail to halt corporate decline do most companies consider the need to regenerate their strategy and reinvent their industry. Most companies work from left to right in terms of the agenda portrayed in Figure 1-1. When performance declines the first assumption is that the company has gotten fat, so investment and headcount are attacked. If this fails to bring about a lasting improvement in performance, as is usually the case, senior managers may conclude that the company has also gotten lazy, and that core processes are rife with needless bureaucracy and "make-work." A reengineering program is adopted with the objective of shaping up sloppy processes. But as we have argued, restructuring and reengineering may ultimately be too little, too late if a company's industry is changing in a profound way and if the company has fallen far behind that change curve. Too often, profound thinking about the future and how to shape it occurs only when present success has been substantially eroded. To get ahead of the industry change curve, to have the chance of conducting a bloodless revolution, top management must recognize that the company may be blind as well as fat and lazy. It must attack the strategy regeneration and industry reinvention agenda in concert with, or better yet, in anticipation of, the restructuring and reengineering agenda.

TOWARD A NEW VIEW OF STRATEGY

Our starting premises are simple: Competition for the future is competition to create and dominate emerging opportunities—to stake out new competitive space. Creating the future is more challenging than playing catch up, in that you have to create your own road map. The goal is not simply to benchmark a competitor's products and processes and imitate its methods, but to develop an independent point of view about tomorrow's opportunities and how to exploit them. Pathbreaking is a lot more rewarding than benchmarking. One doesn't get to the future first by letting someone else blaze the trail.

So what is it that compels some companies rather than others to take up the difficult challenge of inventing the future? What allows some companies to create the future despite enormous resource handicaps, while others spend billions and come up short? Why do some companies seem to possess over-the-horizon radar while others seem to be walking backward into the future? In short, what does it take to get to the future first? At a broad level, it requires four things: (1) an understanding of how competition for the future is different; (2) a process for finding and gaining insight into tomorrow's opportunities; (3) an ability to energize the company top-to-bottom for what may be a long and arduous journey toward the future; and (4) the capacity to outrun competitors and get to the future first, without taking undue risks.

Implicit here is a view of strategy quite different from what prevails in many companies. It is a view of strategy that recognizes that a firm must *unlearn* much of its past before it can find the future. It is a view of strategy that recognizes it is not enough to optimally position a company within existing markets; the challenge is to pierce the fog of uncertainty and develop great *foresight* into the whereabouts of tomorrow's markets. It is a view of strategy that recognizes the need for more than an incrementalist, annual planning rain dance; what is needed is a *strategic architecture* that provides a blueprint for building the competencies needed to dominate future markets.

It is a view of strategy that is less concerned with ensuring a tight fit between goals and resources and is more concerned with creating *stretch goals* that challenge employees to accomplish the seemingly impossible. It is a view of strategy as more than the allocation of scarce resources across competing projects; strategy is the quest to overcome resource constraints through a creative and unending pursuit of better *resource leverage.*

It is a view of strategy that recognizes that companies not only compete within the boundaries of existing industries, they compete to *shape the structure* of future industries. It is a view of strategy that recognizes that competition for *core competence* leadership precedes competition for product leadership, and that conceives of the corporation as a portfolio of competencies as well as a portfolio of businesses. It is a view of strategy that recognizes that competition often takes place within and between *coalitions* of companies, and not only between individual businesses.

It is a view of strategy that recognizes that product failures are often inevitable, but nevertheless provide the opportunity to learn more about just where the mother lode of future demand may lie. It is a view of strategy that recognizes that to capitalize on foresight and core competence leadership, a company must ultimately preempt competitors in critical global markets; that the issue is not so much time to market, but time to *global preemption.*

These are the themes, then, in *Competing for the Future:*

THE NEW STRATEGY PARADIGM

Not Only	But Also

The Competitive Challenge

Not Only	But Also
Reengineering processes	Regenerating strategies
Organizational transformation	Industry transformation
Competing for market share	Competing for opportunity share

Finding the Future

Not Only	But Also
Strategy as learning	Strategy as forgetting
Strategy as positioning	Strategy as foresight
Strategic plans	Strategic architecture

Mobilizing for the Future

Not Only	But Also
Strategy as fit	Strategy as stretch
Strategy as resource allocation	Strategy as resource accumulation and leverage

Getting to the Future First

Not Only	But Also
Competing within an existing industry structure	Competing to shape future industry structure
Competing for product leadership	Competing for core competence leadership
Competing as a single entity	Competing as a coalition
Maximizing the ratio of new product "hits"	Maximizing the rate of new market learning
Minimizing time-to-market	Minimizing time to global preemption

Although the voices calling for a new organizational paradigm (leaner, flatter, virtual, modular, etc.) have been numerous and vocal, there has been no concomitant clamor for a new strategy paradigm. We believe, though, that the way many companies "strategize" is just as out of date, and just as toxic, as the way they organize. However lean and fit an organization, it still needs a brain. But the brain we have in mind is not the brain of the CEO or strategic planner. Instead it is an amalgamation of the collective intelligence and imagination of managers and employees throughout the company who must possess an enlarged view of what it means to be "strategic." This book is as much about how to build and apply that new view of strategy as it is about how to get to the future first.

The goal of this book then can be simply stated: to help managers imagine the future and, having imagined it, create it. We want to help them get off the restructuring treadmill and get beyond the reengineering programs that simply rev up today's performance. We want to help them capture the riches that the future holds in store for those who get there first.

Perhaps this sounds paradoxical: It might make sense to help *a* company get to the future first, but how can one help *companies* get there first? Surely for every leader there must be a follower. Not necessarily. There is not one future but hundreds. There is no law that says most companies must be followers. Getting to the future first is not just about outrunning competitors bent on reaching the same prize. It is also about having one's own view of what the prize is. There can be as many prizes as runners; imagination is the only limiting factor. Renoir, Picasso, Calder, Serat, and Chagall were all enormously successful artists, but each had an original and distinctive style. In no way did the success of one preordain the failure of another. Yet each artist spawned a host of imitators. In business, as in art, what distinguishes leaders from laggards, and greatness from mediocrity, is the ability to uniquely imagine what could be.

2

How Competition for the Future Is Different

· ·

We are standing on the verge, and for some it will be the precipice, of a revolution as profound as that which gave birth to modern industry. It will be the environmental revolution, the genetic revolution, the materials revolution, the digital revolution, and, most of all, the information revolution. Entirely new industries, now in their gestation phase, will soon be born. Such prenatal industries include microrobotics—miniature robots built from atomic particles that could, among other things, unclog sclerotic arteries; machine translation—telephone switches and other devices that will provide real-time translation between people conversing in different languages; digital highways into the home that will offer instant access to the world's store of knowledge and entertainment; urban underground automated distribution systems that will reduce traffic congestion; "virtual" meeting rooms that will save people the wear and tear of air travel; biomimetic materials that will duplicate the wondrous properties of materials found in the living world; satellite-based personal communicators that will allow one to "phone home" from anywhere on the planet; machines capable of emotion, inference, and learning that will interact with human beings in entirely new ways; and bioremediation—custom-designed organisms that will help clean up the earth's environment.

Existing industries—education, health care, transportation, banking, publishing, telecommunications, pharmaceuticals, retailing, and others—will be profoundly transformed. Cars with on-board navigation and collision avoidance systems, electronic books and personally tailored multimedia educational curricula, surgeries performed in isolated locales by a remote controlled robot, and disease prevention via gene replacement therapy are just some of the opportunities that are emerging to reshape existing products, services, and industries.

Many of these mega-opportunities represent billions of dollars in potential future revenues. One company has estimated the potential market for information services in the home, via interactive TV, to be worth at least $120 billion per year in 1992 dollars—home video ($11 billion), home catalog shopping ($51 billion), video games ($4 billion), broadcast advertising ($27 billion), other information services ($9 billion), and more.[1] Many of these mega-opportunities have the potential to fundamentally transform the way we live and work, in much the same way that the telephone, car, and airplane transformed twentieth-century lifestyles.

Each of these opportunities is also inherently global. No single nation or region is likely to control all the technologies and skills required to turn these opportunities into reality. Markets will emerge at different speeds around the world, and any firm hoping to establish a leadership role will have to collaborate with and learn from leading-edge customers, technology providers, and suppliers, wherever they're located. Global distribution reach will be necessary to capture the rewards of leadership and fully amortize associated investments.

The future is now. The short term and the long term don't abut one another with a clear line of demarcation five years from now. The short term and long term are tightly intertwined. Although many of tomorrow's mega-opportunities are still in their infancy, companies around the world are, at this moment, competing for the privilege of parenting them. Alliances are being formed, competencies are being assembled, and experiments are being conducted in nascent markets—all in hopes of capturing a share of the world's future opportunities. In this race to the future there are drivers, passengers, and road kill. (*Road kill,* an American turn of phrase, is what becomes of little creatures who cross the highway in the path of an oncoming vehicle.) Passengers will get to the future, but their fate will not be in their own hands. Their profits from the future will be modest at best. Those who drive industry revolution—companies that have a clear, premeditated view of where they want to take their industry and are capable of orchestrating resources inside and outside the company to get there first—will be handsomely rewarded.

Thus, the question of which companies and countries create the future is far from academic. The stakes are high. The wealth of a firm, and of each nation in which it operates, largely depends on its role in creating tomorrow's markets and its ability to capture a disproportionate share of associated revenues and profits.

Perhaps you have visited the Henry Ford Museum at Greenfield Village in Dearborn, Michigan. Although the home of Ford Motor Co.'s world headquarters, Dearborn's additional claim to fame is Greenfield Village and the museum where you can see the industrial history of the United States. The exhibits are a testimony to pioneers who created new industries and revolutionized old ones: Deere, Eastman, Firestone, Bell, Edison, Watson, the Wright brothers, and, of course, Ford. It was the foresight of these pioneers that created the industries that created the unprecedented prosperity that created the American lifestyle. Any visitor strolling through the museum who has enjoyed the material comforts of a middle-class American lifestyle can't help but recognize the enormous debt he or she owes to these industrial pioneers. Similarly, any German citizen owes much to the pioneers who built that country's innovative, globe-spanning chemical companies, world-class machine tool industry, and automakers that set the benchmarks for excellence for nearly a century. The success of Japanese firms in redefining standards of innovation and performance in the electronics and automobile industries propelled Japan from an industrial also-ran into a world economic superpower and paid for all those Waikiki holidays and Louis Vuitton handbags.

Failure to anticipate and participate in the opportunities of the future impoverishes both firms and nations. Witness Europe's concern over its abysmal performance in creating high-wage jobs in new information technology-related businesses, or Japan's worry over the inability of its financial institutions to capture the high ground of innovation and new business creation, or America's anxiety that Japanese companies may steal a march in the commercialization of superconductivity. Even protectionist-minded politicians realize that a nation that can do little more than protect the industries of the past will lose its economic standing to countries that help create the industries of the future.

The future is not an extrapolation of the past. New industrial structures will supersede old industrial structures. Opportunities that at first blush seem evolutionary will prove to be revolutionary. Today's new niche markets will turn out to be tomorrow's mass markets. Today's leading edge science will become tomorrow's household appliance. At one time IBM described the personal computer as an "entry system"—the expectation was that anyone buying a PC would move up to more powerful computers, and that PCs could happily coexist with mainframes. Ten years later, desktop workstations and local client-server computers were displacing mainframes from more and more applications. Although today's wireless telephones—both cellular and cordless—may seem no more than an adjunct to traditional tethered telephones, in ten years all wired phones will likely seem anachronistic. Twenty years ago few observers expected mutual funds to significantly erode the "share of savings" captured by banks and savings and loans. But savers became investors and by 1992, mutual funds in the United States represented 96% of the money that private investors put into the stock market. Mutual funds accounted for 11.4% of total financial assets in the United States, up from only 2.0% in 1975, whereas the share taken by commercial banks and savings and loans fell from 56.2% in 1975 to 37.3% in 1992.[2] Again, there is no way to create the future, no way to profit from the future, if one cannot imagine it.

To compete successfully for the future, senior managers must first understand just how competition for the future is different from competition for the present. The differences are profound. They challenge the traditional perspectives on strategy and competition. We will see that competing for the future requires not only a redefinition of strategy, but also a redefinition of top management's role in creating strategy.

COMPETITION FOR TODAY VERSUS COMPETITION FOR TOMORROW

Pick up a strategy textbook or marketing handbook and the focus will almost certainly be on competition within extant markets. The tools of segmentation analysis, industry structure analysis, and value chain analysis are eminently useful in the context of a clearly defined market, but what help are they when the market doesn't yet exist? Within an existing market most of the rules of competition have already been established: what price-performance trade-offs customers are willing to make, which channels have proved most efficient, the ways in which products or services can be differentiated, and what is the optimal degree of vertical integration. Yet in emerging opportunity arenas like genetically engineered drugs, multimedia publishing, and interactive television, the rules are waiting to be written. (In existing industries, the rules are waiting to be rewritten.) This vastly complicates the business of making strategic choices. So how is the context for strategy-making different when the focus is on tomorrow rather than today, and when there is little or no clarity about industry structure and customer preferences?

Market Share versus Opportunity Share

Strategy researchers and practitioners have focused much attention on the problem of getting and keeping market share. For most companies, market share is the primary criterion for measuring the strength of a business's strategic position. But what is the meaning of market share in markets that barely exist? How can one maximize market share in an industry where the product or service concept is still underdefined, where customer segments have yet to solidify, and customer preferences are still poorly understood?

Competition for the future is competition for *opportunity share* rather than market share. It is competition to maximize the share of future opportunities a company could potentially access within a broad *opportunity arena*, be that home information systems, genetically engineered drugs, financial services, advanced materials, or something else.

The question that must be answered by every company is, given our current skills, or *competencies* as we will call them, what share of future opportunities are we likely to capture? This question leads to others: Which new competencies would we have to build, and how would our definition of our "served market" have to change, for us to capture a larger share of future opportunities? Whether for a country or a company, the issue is much the same: how to attract and strengthen the skills that form the competencies (e.g., opto-electronics, biomimetics, genetics, systems integration, financial engineering) that provide a gateway to future opportunities.

To gain a disproportionate share of future profits it is necessary to possess a disproportionate share of the requisite competencies. Because such competencies represent the patient and persistent accumulation of intellectual capital rather than a God-given endowment, governments can legitimately play a role in strengthening such competencies (through educational policy, tax incentives, recruitment of inward investment, government-sanctioned private-sector joint ventures, etc.).[3] Singapore, for example, has employed just such means to enhance the range and quality of nationally resident competencies. But to know which competencies to build, policy-makers and corporate strategists must be prescient about the broad shape of tomorrow's opportunities. Top management must be just as obsessed with maximizing opportunity share as with maximizing market share. As we will see, this means a commitment to build competence leadership in new areas, long before the precise form and structure of future markets comes completely into view.

Business Units versus Corporate Competencies

Competition for the future is not product versus product or business versus business, but company versus company—what we term "interfirm competition." This is true for several reasons. First, because future opportunities are unlikely to fit neatly within existing SBU boundaries, competing for the future must be a corporate responsibility, and not just the responsibility of individual business unit heads. (This responsibility may be exercised by a group of corporate officers or, preferably, a cohort of SBU heads working horizontally across the organization.) Second, the competencies needed to access the new opportunity arena may well be spread across a number of business units, and it is up to the corporation to bring these competencies together at the appropriate point within the organization. Third, the investment and timeframe required to build the new competencies necessary to access tomorrow's markets may well tax the resources and patience of a single business unit.

It is important that top managers view the firm as a portfolio of competencies, for they must ask, "Given our particular portfolio of competencies, what opportunities are we uniquely positioned to exploit?" The answer points to opportunity arenas that other firms, with different competence endowments, may find difficult to access. For example, it would be hard to imagine any other firm than Eastman Kodak creating a product like Photo-CD, which required an in-depth understanding of both chemical film and electronic imaging competencies. Canon may understand electronic imaging and Fuji may understand film, but only Kodak had a deep understanding of both.

So the question for top managers is, "How do we orchestrate *all* the resources of the firm to create the future?" This was the question George Fisher faced when he left Motorola to become Kodak's new chief executive. At IBM, Lou Gerstner put together a top team to look for transcendent opportunities. Given IBM's still impressive set of competencies, the question was, "What can we do that other companies might find difficult to do?" Companies like Matsushita and Hewlett-Packard, long champions of bottom-up innovation and business unit autonomy, have recently been searching for opportunities that blend the skills of multiple business units. Even Sony, which has traditionally granted near total autonomy to individual product development teams, has realized that more and more of its products must function as part of complex systems. It has therefore moved to restructure its audio, video, and computer groups for better coordination of new product development.[4]

Creating the future often requires that a company build new core competencies, competencies that typically transcend a single business unit—both in terms of the investment required and the range of potential applications. Within Sharp, for example, it is not up to each business unit to decide how much to invest in perfecting flat screen displays. Sharp competes as a corporation against Toshiba, Casio, and Sony to build world leadership in this area.

The sheer size, scope, and complexity of future opportunities may also require a corporate rather than an individual unit perspective. Mega-opportunities don't yield easily to "skunk works" or undirected entrepreneurship. A lone employee with a bit of free time and access to a small slush fund may create Post-it Notes but is unlikely to bring the interpreting telephone from conception to reality or make much progress on creating a new computing architecture. Consistent, focused competence-building requires something more than "thriving on chaos."

Stand-Alone versus Integrated Systems

Most textbooks on the management of innovation and new product development assume that the company controls most of the resources needed for the commercialization of that innovation. Such an assumption is increasingly likely to be wrong. Many of the most exciting new opportunities require the integration of complex systems rather than innovation around a stand-alone product. Not only does no single business unit have all the necessary capabilities, neither does a single company or country. Few companies can create the future single-handedly; most need a helping hand. Motorola, IBM, and Apple banded together to create a new semiconductor-based computer architecture. Hoping to take advantage of the potential convergence between the videogame industry and the telecommunications industry, AT&T has formed partnerships with, or taken small equity stakes in, a number of computer game makers. Even Boeing has often found it necessary to reach out to foreign partners for the development of its next-generation aircraft.

The need to bring together and harmonize widely disparate technologies, to manage a drawn-out standards-setting process, to conclude alliances with the suppliers of complementary products, to co-opt potential rivals, and to access the widest possible array of distribution channels, means that competition is as much a battle between competing and often overlapping coalitions as it is a battle between individual firms. Competition for the future is both inter-corporate and intercoalition. As we will see, an understanding of how to put such a coalition together and keep it pointed toward a common future is central to the task of competing for the future.

Speed versus Perseverance

Yet another way in which competition for the future is different from competition for the present is the timeframe. Today speed is of the essence.[5] Product life cycles are getting shorter, development times are getting tighter, and customers expect almost instantaneous service. Yet the relevant timeframe for exploring and conquering a new opportunity arena may be ten years, twenty years, or even longer. AT&T first built a prototype of a videophone in its labs in 1939, first demonstrated a videophone to the public at the New York World's Fair in 1964, and finally introduced a model for home use in 1992, 53 years after its first prototype. And even now, video telephony has yet to become a mass market product. Marc Porat, president and CEO of General Magic, a company that is developing the software for tomorrow's personal communication devices, believes it may take a decade or more to turn his company's vision of intelligent, ubiquitous, mobile personal communications into a reality.[6] Leadership in fundamentally new industries is seldom built in anything less than 10 or 15 years, suggesting that perseverance may be just as important as speed in the battle for the future.

Obviously, no company is likely to persevere for 20 years unless it has a deep, visceral commitment to the particular opportunity. JVC, a subsidiary of Matsushita and the world leader in VCRs, began developing videotape competencies in the late 1950s and early 1960s, yet it wasn't until the late 1970s, nearly 20 years later, that JVC hit the jackpot with its VHS-standard machines. What keeps a company going for this length of time? Just what did JVC see in the VCR, or AT&T in the video telephone, or Apple Computer in the Lisa and then the Macintosh, that compelled them to pick themselves up time and time again when they stumbled on the inevitable hurdles, and keep pressing on toward the finish line? What they saw was the potential to deliver new and profound customer benefits. For JVC, it was the desire to "take control [of program scheduling] away from the broadcasters and give it back to the viewers." An engineer would term this "timeshift," but a technical description of the opportunity dramatically underplays its potential impact on lifestyles. Such commitment was also evident at Apple (making computers user friendly), at Ford in its early years (putting a car in every garage), at Boeing (bringing air travel to the masses), at CNN (providing the news around the clock), and at Wal-Mart (offering friendly service and rock-bottom prices to rural Americans).

Organizational commitment and perseverance are driven by the desire to make a difference in people's lives—the bigger the difference, the deeper the commitment. This suggests another difference between competition for the future and competition for the present, namely, the prospect of making an impact, rather than the certitude of immediate financial returns. In contrast, strategic moves within the confines of existing markets are likely to be predicated on traditional financial analysis. But this is not possible in the early stages of competition for the future. No one in the early 1960s could have produced a meaningful set of pro-formas around the VCR opportunity. By the early 1970s, when one might have legitimately made a stab at developing a business case, it was too late for anyone who had not been working on videotape competencies since the early 1960s to catch up without help from one of the pioneers.

This is not to say that commitment to a new opportunity arena is based solely on gut feeling, or that companies at work to create the future are not hoping for substantial financial rewards. A commitment substantial enough to beget the perseverance required to create the future must be based on something more than a hunch.

There are ways of judging the potential impact of a market-creating innovation that may still be many years in the future. Questions to consider might include: How many people will be affected by this innovation? How valuable will they find this innovation? What is the potential scope for the application of this innovation? In the case of the VCR, there were a host of specific indicators one might have considered: How many people had televisions? How fast was the penetration of televisions in the home growing? How many hours did the average person watch television? How often were they away when some potentially interesting program was being broadcast? How often were they forced to choose between two appealing shows broadcast simultaneously? Were there programs they would like to watch more than once? Would they find it more convenient to watch movies at home than at the cinema? Would movie studios and other software providers be willing to release movies not shown on TV as prerecorded software? Might video-cameras be attractive to consumers? and so on.

There should be no mushy-headed wishfulness involved in competing for the future. The absence of a business case does not mean that one commits to a whopping great investment in some hair-brained scheme. As we will see, the investment commitments in the early stages of competition for the future may be quite modest; small as they may be, however, the emotional and intellectual commitment to the future needs to be near absolute. Steve Jobs and Steve Wozniak had virtually no money, but their commitment to creating a computer for every "man, woman, and child" was unshakable.

One of President Reagan's favorite stories provides an illustration. Waking up to her tenth birthday, a young farm girl rises before the sun and runs out to the barn, hoping her parents have bought her a pony. She flings open the barn door, but in the dim light can see no pony, just mounds of horse manure. Being an optimist she declares, "With all this manure around, there must be a pony in here somewhere." Similarly, companies that create the future say to themselves, "With all this potential customer benefit, there must be a way to make some money in here somewhere." A company that cannot commit emotionally and intellectually to creating the future, even in the absence of a financially indisputable business case, will almost certainly end up as a follower.

Think of the people who left Europe in the nineteenth century or Asia in the twentieth century to start a new life in the United States. At the outset of their journeys, few immigrants could have foretold exactly when and how they would achieve economic success in the new world, yet they set out for the "land of opportunity" nevertheless. More than that, many of them willingly accepted great hardship during the journey itself. The important point is that the commitment to be a pioneer precedes an exact calculation of financial gain. A company that waits around for the numbers to "add up" will be left flat-footed in the race to the future. Without a clear-eyed view of the ultimate prize, a company is all too likely to abandon the race when unexpected hazards are encountered en route. Nevertheless, as we will emphasize again and again, a company must ultimately find a profitable route to the future.

Structured versus Unstructured Arenas

We now come to what are the two most important ways in which competition for the future is different from competition for the present: (1) It often takes place in "unstructured" arenas where the rules of competition have yet to be written, and (2) it is more like a triathlon than a 100-meter sprint. We will see that these differences demand a very different way of thinking about strategy and the role of senior management.

Some industries are more "structured" than others, in that the rules of competition are more clear-cut, product concepts better defined, industry boundaries more stable, technology change more predictable, and customer needs more precisely measurable. Unpredictable and turbulent change can come to any industry today (think of how long the three big U.S. television networks dominated their cozy little industry), and new opportunity arenas like genetic engineering are almost universally unstructured. More and more industries, by their very nature, seem to be perpetually underdefined, or even undefinable.

Take the "digital industry." It is not one industry, but a collection of industries that are simultaneously converging and disintegrating.[7] It is an industry that has been around since the invention of the transistor, but is now, more than ever, underdefined. Figure 2-1 depicts the digital industry, circa 1990. While some firms like AT&T spanned several industry groupings, the industry could be broadly partitioned into seven more or less distinct components: (1) computer system suppliers (from Compaq to IBM, and Apple to Hewlett-Packard), (2) information technology service companies (EDS, Cap Gemini, Andersen Consulting), (3) companies whose primary interest was in operating systems and application software for computers (Microsoft and Lotus, most notably, but also Novell, Computer Associates, Oracle, and a myriad of smaller companies focused on specific "vertical" markets), (4) the owners and operators of the digital networks that transmit data and voice (including AT&T, McCaw, MCI, cable television companies, television and radio broadcasters, and regional telephone operating companies), (5) the providers of information content (Time Warner, Berteles-mann, MCA, Bloomberg Financial Markets, Polygram, Columbia Pictures, Dow-Jones, Reed International, and McGraw-Hill to name a few), (6) the manufacturers of professional electronics gear (Xerox, Canon, Kodak, and Motorola; defense electronics companies like Rockwell; and factory automation equipment manufacturers), and (7) the familiar consumer electronics producers (Sony, Philips, Matsushita, and Samsung among others). In the early 1990s, industry observers, corporate strategists, trade journals, and consultants mapped the digital industry more or less along these lines.

The problem, for any company intent on getting to the future first, is that this is a map of the past and not of the future. For companies looking forward, it had become clear by the early 1990s that the labels used to distinguish among the different components of the digital industry were fast losing their descriptive power. It seemed unlikely that the future digital industry would be usefully partitioned into software versus hardware, computing versus communications, professional versus consumer, content versus conduit, services versus products, and horizontal markets versus vertical markets. Was the Macintosh a hardware or software innovation?

FIGURE 2-1 THE EVOLVING DIGITAL SPACE

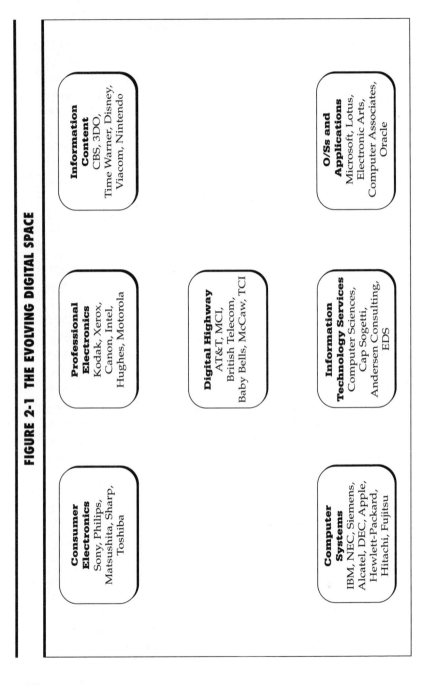

Information Content
CBS, 3DO,
Time Warner, Disney,
Viacom, Nintendo

Professional Electronics
Kodak, Xerox,
Canon, Intel,
Hughes, Motorola

Digital Highway
AT&T, MCI,
British Telecom,
Baby Bells, McCaw, TCI

Consumer Electronics
Sony, Philips,
Matsushita, Sharp,
Toshiba

O/Ss and Applications
Microsoft, Lotus,
Electronic Arts,
Computer Associates,
Oracle

Information Technology Services
Computer Sciences,
Cap Sogetti,
Andersen Consulting,
EDS

Computer Systems
IBM, NEC, Siemens,
Alcatel, DEC, Apple,
Hewlett-Packard,
Hitachi, Fujitsu

How could one call Sharp's Personal Organizer a hardware product when software accounted for the biggest part of its development budget? What about all those hardware companies—Sony, Matsushita, and Toshiba—buying their way into the entertainment software industry? Did it make sense to distinguish between computing and communications when more and more personal computers were using the local telephone network to hook up to Prodigy or CompuServe, or when corporate customers demanded integrated networking of data, voice, and video? What was the distinction between professional versus consumer electronics when Motorola, because of the success of its cellular phones, was compelled to admit that it had become, de facto, a consumer electronics company? And when Time Warner wired homes in Orlando for two-way, interactive video and information services, just where was the dividing line between content and conduit? Pummeled by regulatory changes, advances in digital technology, changes in lifestyles, the raw ambition of companies intent on getting to the future first, and companies paranoid at the prospect of being left behind, the digital industry seemed to be in a state of permanent turmoil.

The digital industry may be more complex and variegated than most, but it is certainly not unique in the challenges it poses to the traditional tools and methods of strategy analysis. Deregulation, globalization, fundamental breakthroughs in science, and the strategic importance of information technology are blurring boundaries in a wide variety of industries. The boundaries between ethical and over-the-counter drugs have been blurring, as have been the boundaries between pharmaceuticals and cosmetics. Industry borders have been blurring between commercial banking, investment banking, and brokerages; between computer hardware and software vendors; and between publishers, broadcasters, telecommunication companies, and film studios. Adding to this stew is a trend toward disintermediation—whether that be Wal-Mart dealing directly with manufacturers or corporate borrowers bypassing banks—and a trend toward corporate confederacies and away from pervasive vertical and horizontal integration, like Toyota and its suppliers. The result, in all these cases, is an industry "structure" that is exceedingly complex and almost indeterminate.

In an environment of turbulent and seemingly unpredictable change, being "adaptive" is not good enough. A rudderless ship in gale force winds will simply go round in circles. Neither is it enough to adopt a "wait-and-see" attitude. A company that pulls in its sails and waits for the calmer seas will find itself becalmed in an industry backwater. However tumultuous the industry, executives still have to make strategic choices. On the other hand, how can a company, possessing only a map of the past, make an intelligent decision about which technologies to pursue, which core competencies to build, which product or service concepts to back, which alliances to form, and what kind of people to hire?

Strategy, as taught in many business schools and practiced in most companies, seems to be more concerned with how to position products and businesses within the existing industry structure than how to create tomorrow's industries. Of what use are the traditional tools of industry and competitor analysis to executives caught up in the melee to create the world's digital future, or to managers trying to understand the opportunities presented by the collapsing boundaries of the financial services industry or the genetics revolution? Of what use are the principles of competitive interaction, drilled into the heads of countless MBA students as they worked their way through the comparatively simple cases of Coca-Cola versus Pepsi, the chain saw industry, DuPont in titanium dioxide, and Procter & Gamble versus Kimberly-Clark in the disposable diaper business? At least in these cases one could easily determine where the industry began and ended. It's not that difficult to determine who is making soft drinks, for example, and who is not. But where does the digital industry begin and end? Or the genetics industry? Or the entertainment industry? Or the retail financial services industry? On any given day, for example, AT&T might find Motorola to be a supplier, a buyer, a competitor, *and* a partner. In well-established industries it is easy to identify product and customer segments. With no preexisting "value chain," how can one anticipate where and how money can be made in the industry, decide which activities to "control," and know how vertically or horizontally integrated to be?

Traditional industry structure analysis, of the kind that is the subject of strategy textbooks, is of little help to executives competing in unstructured industries. On the other hand, simply doing away with existing industry boundaries, as we have done in Figure 2-2, provides no more help to companies trying to make sense of such a tumultuous industry.

Strategic planning typically takes, as its point of departure, the extant industry structure. Traditional planning seeks to position the firm optimally within the existing structure by identifying which segments, channels, price points, product differentiators, selling propositions, and value chain configurations will yield the highest profits. Although a view of strategy as a positioning problem is certainly legitimate, it is insufficient if the goal is to occupy the high ground in tomorrow's industries. If strategy is seen only as a positioning game, it will be difficult for a company to avoid becoming trapped in an endless game of catch-up with farsighted competitors.

FIGURE 2-2 THE DIGITAL INDUSTRY SPACE WITHOUT BOUNDARIES

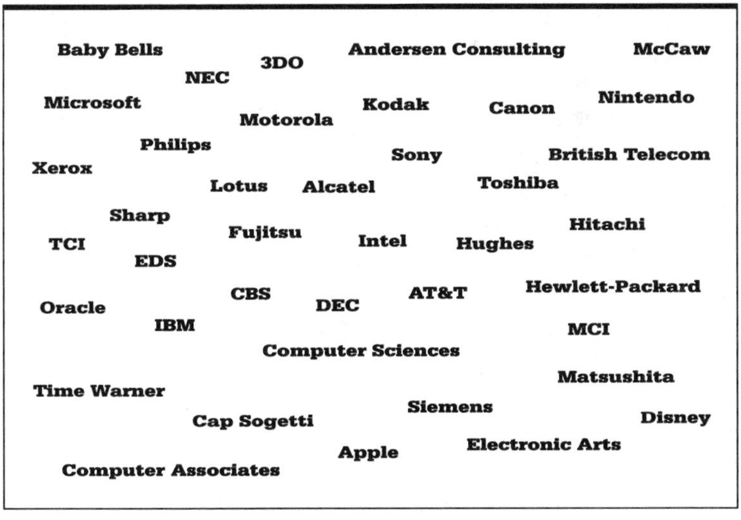

Baby Bells   3DO   Andersen Consulting   McCaw
NEC
Microsoft   Kodak   Canon   Nintendo
Motorola
Philips   Sony   British Telecom
Xerox
Lotus   Alcatel   Toshiba
Sharp   Hitachi
TCI   Fujitsu   Intel   Hughes
EDS
Oracle   CBS   DEC   AT&T   Hewlett-Packard
IBM   MCI
Computer Sciences
Matsushita
Time Warner
Cap Sogetti   Siemens   Disney
Apple   Electronic Arts
Computer Associates

Usually, the current industry structure and the rules of competitive engagement therein have been defined by the industry leader. Although it may be possible to find a profitable niche within the present industry terrain—as Japanese mainframe computer makers did for a while, mimicking IBM—there is typically little growth and prosperity to be found in the shadow of the industry leader. Companies that see strategy as primarily a positioning exercise are industry rule-takers rather than rule-breakers and rule-makers; they are unlikely to be the defining entity in their industry, now or ever.

In short, strategy is as much about competing *for* tomorrow's industry structure as it is about competing *within* today's industry structure. Competition within today's industry structure raises issues such as: What new features should be added to a product? How can we get better channel coverage? Should we price for maximum market share or maximum profits? Competition for tomorrow's industry structure raises deeper questions such as: Whose product concepts will ultimately win out? Which standards will be adopted? How will coalitions form and what will determine each member's share of the power? And, most critically, how do we increase our ability to influence the emerging shape of a nascent industry?

What is up for grabs in an unstructured industry is the future structure of the industry. Sooner or later, to one degree or another, and however briefly, new structures will emerge. Conceiving of strategy as a quest to proactively configure nascent industries, or fundamentally reconfigure existing industries to one's own advantage, is a very different perspective than a view of strategy as positioning individual businesses and products within today's competitive environment. If the goal is competing for the future, we need a view of strategy that addresses more than the problem of maximizing profits in today's markets.

Single-Stage versus Multistage Competition

While much attention has been lavished by managers and business consultants on the product development process and the competition between rival products or services in the marketplace, this really represents only the last 100 meters of a much longer race. Product development is a 100-yard dash, while industry development and transformation is a triathlon, where contestants cycle for 100 miles, swim a mile or two, and then run a marathon. Each event represents a distinct challenge to the triathelete.

Competition for the future of the digital industry is still in its early stages, but by reviewing one particular race, the race to develop the VCR, we can observe the distinct stages of competition for the future. We use the VCR as an example both because enough time has passed so that objective judgments can be made about who won and why, and because the VCR was the first major innovation in consumer electronics that was commercialized first in mass markets by Japanese, rather than U.S. or European companies. And although companies like Motorola and Apple today are attempting to resurrect a consumer electronics industry led by U.S. firms, it was the VCR that established the unequivocal dominance of Japanese companies in consumer electronics. The VCR also added billions of largely uncontested profits to the coffers of its Japanese pioneers. Like many other industry development marathons, the race to commercialize the VCR spanned decades, rather than years. The first videotape recorder was produced by a California company, Ampex, in 1959, but it wasn't until the late 1970s that Matsushita introduced its VHS standard and broke the tape at the finish line.

The first hurdle for any would-be pioneer was to commit to the videotape opportunity arena. Three companies saw clearly the potential for videotape—Philips, Sony, and Matsushita (JVC)—and each worked diligently for close to two decades to produce a VCR for home use. At JVC, what was initially the commitment of a small team to the videotape opportunity soon became a corporatewide commitment. Neither RCA, the color television pioneer, nor Ampex, the inventor of videotape, ever demonstrated the same unflinching commitment to the VCR, although both companies made aborted attempts to produce a home machine.

The second hurdle was to acquire the competencies that would be necessary to shape and profit from the future. The challenge of creating a compact videocassette that would pack two, four, or six hours of color recording onto a tape that was a fraction of the length and width of tapes used to produce a half hour of black and white recording time on reel-to-reel video recorders was a daunting one—what engineers call a "nontrivial technical problem." For more than 15 years Philips, Sony, and Matsushita raced to perfect their videotape competencies. Learning how to manufacture the extremely precise, revolving video-recording heads presented a major competence-building challenge to all comers. An executive at JVC believed that making a VCR was at least ten times more complex than making a television set.

The third hurdle was to discover what configuration of price, features, size, and software was necessary to unlock the mass market. After all, consumers had never seen a VCR before. They could hardly be relied on to provide manufacturers with precise product development specs. How much record time did consumers want? Would they pay as much as $2,500 for a machine? Was slow motion an important feature? The only way to answer those questions was to go into the market again and again, each time improving the product, and coming that little bit closer to the demands of the consumer.

Matsushita launched several VCR models into the market before the company struck gold with VHS. Sony's U-matic VCR, which ultimately became a standards-setter in the professional VCR market, was originally introduced as a "consumer video." But the machine's size and price made it unattractive to home users. The more rapid the pace of market experimentation, the quicker the learning about what customers really want in a product. While Japanese competitors were experimenting in the marketplace, RCA was experimenting only in the lab. RCA didn't launch its consumer videoplayer until 1980. Therefore, it was not surprising that RCA's product, which lacked a record capability, missed the mark badly with consumers.

A fourth hurdle was to establish one's own technical approach to video recording as the industry standard. The battle here was among Sony's Beta, JVC's VHS, and Philips's V2000, each incompatible with the other. It was clear that whoever won the standards battle would reap great benefits in terms of software availability, licensing income, and economies of scale in component production.

The losers would find themselves, millions of R&D dollars later, in a technological cul-de-sac that they could escape only by switching to a competitor's standard. Sony took an early lead, and had 85% of the U.S. VCR market by the end of 1976. But when JVC introduced a machine with a two-hour record time, compared to Sony's one-hour, Sony's lead began to evaporate. The coup de grace came when JVC succeeded in co-opting a number of key partners into its battle with Sony. Telefunken in Germany, Thomson in France, Thorn in Great Britain, and RCA and GE in the United States were all early VHS licensees, initially sourcing components and finished VCRs from JVC and Matsushita.

The wide selection of VHS brands and models, relative to Beta, soon convinced software suppliers to put their money behind VHS, and within two years the market battle between Beta and VHS was over. Philips's V2000, launched in Europe some 18 months after VHS, was dead on arrival despite the fact that Philips had more or less kept pace with its Japanese competitors over the 15-year competence acquisition phase. But in the 18-month gap between the launch of VHS and the launch of V2000, Matsushita managed to sell several million VCRs around the world, making it almost impossible for Philips to catch up with Matsushita's blistering pace of cost reduction and feature improvement. Thus, although the VCR marathon was a full 26 miles, the winner didn't emerge until the last mad scramble for the finish line. But in a marathon, winning by a nose is often as good as winning by a mile. Indeed, attempting to far outdistance a competitor too early in the race may well lead a company into spending too much too soon or running out of resources before the future arrives—the fate that befell Ampex (even though Ampex and Sony were roughly the same size in 1959 when Ampex invented videotape recorders). Although JVC won only by a yard or two, no one who wasn't in the race at the beginning was anywhere near the finish line when it ended.

The final challenge was to keep up in the battle for market share (as opposed to the battle for standards share). The weapons were fast-paced feature enhancement and cost reduction. Sony and Philips ultimately converted to the VHS camp, but Matsushita's early volume advantage gave it an edge in the race to steadily improve price and performance. In 1993, more than 15 years after the launch of VHS and more than 30 years after Matsushita began its pursuit of the videotape opportunity, Matsushita retained its title as the world leader in VCRs.

Whether the race to shift the pharmaceutical industry toward gene-engineered drugs, to allow customers to bank and shop via their PCs or televisions, or to produce cars with noncombustion engines, the race to the future occurs in three distinct, overlapping stages: competition for *industry foresight* and *intellectual leadership*, competition to *foreshorten migration paths*, and competition for *market position and market share*. We will introduce these themes briefly now, and then return to them in later chapters.

Competition for Industry Foresight and Intellectual Leadership This is competition to gain a deeper understanding than competitors of the trends and discontinuities—technological, demographic, regulatory, or lifestyle—that could be used to transform industry boundaries and create new competitive space. This is competition to be prescient about the size and shape of tomorrow's opportunities. This is competition to conceive fundamentally new types of customer benefits, or to conceive radically new ways of delivering existing customer benefits. In short, it is competition to imagine the future.

Competition to Foreshorten Migration Paths In between the battle for intellectual leadership and the battle for market share is typically a battle to influence the direction of industry development (the battle to control and foreshorten migration paths). Many years may elapse between the conception of a radically transformed industry future and the emergence of a real and substantial market. Dreams don't come true overnight, and the path between today's reality and tomorrow's opportunities is often long and tortuous.

In the second stage of competition there is a race to accumulate necessary competencies (and overcome technical hurdles), to test and prove out alternate product and service concepts (by progressively discovering what customers really want), to attract coalition partners who have critical complementary resources, to construct whatever product or service delivery infrastructure may be required, and to get agreement around standards, if necessary. If competition in the first stage is competition to *imagine* a new opportunity arena, competition in the second stage is competition to actively *shape* the emergence of that future industry structure to one's own advantage.

Competition for Market Position and Market Share Finally, one gets to the last stage of competition. By this stage, competition between alternate technological approaches, rival product or service concepts, and competing channel strategies has largely been settled. Competition shifts to a battle for market share and market position within fairly well-defined parameters of value, cost, price, and service. Innovation is focused on product line extensions, efficiency improvement, and what are usually marginal gains in product or service differentiation. (Figure 2-3 shows the three stages of competition for the future.)

Competition for the future can be likened to pregnancy. Like competition for the future, pregnancy has three stages—conception, gestation, and labor and delivery. These three stages correspond to competition for foresight and intellectual leadership, competition to foreshorten migration paths, and competition for market position and share. It is the third phase of competition that is the focus of attention in most strategy textbooks and strategic planning exercises. Typically, the assumption is that the product or service concept is well established, the dimensions of competition are well-defined, and the boundaries of the industry have stabilized. But focusing on the last stage of market-based competition, without a deep understanding of premarket competition, is like trying to make sense of the process of childbirth without any insight into conception and gestation.

The question for managers to ask themselves at this point is which stage receives the bulk of our time and attention: conception, gestation, or labor and delivery? Our experience suggests that most managers spend a disproportionate amount of time in the delivery room, waiting for the miracle of birth. But as we all know, the

FIGURE 2-3 THREE PHASES OF COMPETITION FOR THE FUTURE

Intellectual Leadership	Management of Migration Paths	Competition for Market Share
Gaining industry foresight by probing deeply into industry drivers.	Preemptively building core competencies, exploring alternate product concepts, and reconfiguring the customer interface.	Building a worldwide supplier network.
Developing a creative point of view about the potential evolution of: • Functionality • Core competencies • Customer interface	Assembling and managing the necessary coalition of industry participants.	Crafting an appropriate market positioning strategy. Preempting competitors in critical markets. Maximizing efficiency and productivity.
Summarizing this point of view in a "strategic architecture."	Forcing competitors onto longer and more expensive migration paths.	Managing competitive interaction.

miracle of birth is most unlikely, unless there's been some activity nine months previously. Again, we believe that managers are spending too much time managing the present, and not enough creating the future. But to create the future, a company must first be able to forget some of its past. Learning to forget is the subject of Chapter 3.

3

Learning to Forget

●●●

Like dinosaurs threatened by cataclysmic climatic changes, companies often find it impossible to cope with a radically altered environment. The oft-used analogy of dinosaurs is, thankfully, not entirely apropos to companies. Dinosaurs died off because the species was unable to adapt fast enough to changing conditions. Evolution is a slow process, relying as it does on small, unplanned genetic mutations—some of which incrementally improve the species' chances of survival, and most of which don't. Fortunately for corporate dinosaurs, a company's "genetic coding" can be altered in various ways. In fact, any company that fails to reengineer its genetic coding periodically will be as much at the mercy of environmental upheaval as tyrannosaurus rex.

Just what do we mean by "corporate genetics"? Every manager carries around in his or her head a set of biases, assumptions, and presuppositions about the structure of the relevant "industry," about how one makes money in that industry, about who the competition is and isn't, about who the customers are and aren't, about what customers want or don't want, about which technologies are viable and which aren't, and so on. This genetic coding also encompasses beliefs, values, and norms about how best to motivate people; the right balance of internal cooperation and competition; the relative ranking of shareholder, customer, and employee interests; and what behaviors to encourage and discourage. These beliefs are, at least in part, the product of a particular industry environment. When that environment changes rapidly and radically, those beliefs may become a threat to survival.

MANAGERIAL FRAMES

Acquired through business schools and other educational experiences and from consultants and management gurus, absorbed from peers and the business press, and formed out of career experiences, a manager's genetic coding establishes the range and likelihood of responses in particular situations. In this sense they bound or "frame" a firm's perspective on what it means to be "strategic," the available repertoire of competitive stratagems, the interests that senior management serves, the choice of tools for policy deployment, ideal organization types, and so on. *Managerial frames*, the corporate equivalent of genetic coding, limit management's perception to a particular slice of reality. Managers live inside their frames and, to a very great extent, don't know what lies outside. At one time, thinking of savers as investors was a fairly novel idea for most bankers. For computer makers a decade ago, the idea that videogames might be a leading-edge application for computer graphics technology would have been well outside the frame. All of us are prisoners, to one degree or another, of our experience.

Although each individual in a company may see the world somewhat differently, managerial frames within an organization are typically more alike than different. The tighter the criteria on what kind of people get hired, the more similar their educational background, the more comprehensive the employee induction process, the more widespread and inescapable corporate training programs, the more formal the mentoring of juniors by seniors, the longer the tenure of executives with the firm and within the industry, the fewer outsiders hired near the top, and the more successful the company has been in the past, the more uniform will be managerial frames across the company. Almost by definition, in any large organization there is a dominant managerial frame that defines the corporate canon.

Over time, this dominant managerial frame becomes as pervasive and influential as, well, genetic coding. Managerial frames become part of the organizational fabric as they are enacted through the firm's administrative structure and processes. The definition of business unit boundaries (what business are we in?), capital budgeting systems (the analytical tools used and the relative weight given to evaluative criteria), reward systems (the particular behaviors that are encouraged, tolerated, and discouraged), the strategic planning process (the kinds of information requested and the time horizon considered), the training and socialization process (the skills taught, the myths celebrated, and the values imparted), the accounting and information systems (what data are collected, how they are organized, who uses them, and for what purposes), competitive intelligence gathering (which firms get tracked and what is benchmarked), and other administrative systems all reinforce certain perspectives and biases and discount or exclude others. They are the timbers that comprise the managerial frame.

The deeply encoded lessons of the past that are passed from one generation of managers to another pose two dangers for any organization. First, individuals may, over time, forget why they believe what they believe. Second, managers may come to believe that what they don't know isn't worth knowing. A failure to appreciate the contingent nature of corporate beliefs afflicts many companies. Yesterday's "good ideas" become today's "policy guidelines" and tomorrow's "mandates." Industry conventions and "accepted best practices" assume a life of their own. Dogmas go unquestioned, and seldom do managers ask how we got this particular view of organization, strategy, competition, or our industry. Under what environmental conditions did they emerge? On what are our beliefs contingent? The result is a wholly inappropriate reverence for precedent. Let us illustrate.

A friend of ours once described an experiment with monkeys. Four monkeys were put into a room. In the center of the room was a tall pole with a bunch of bananas suspended from the top. One particularly hungry monkey eagerly scampered up the pole, intent on retrieving a banana. Just as he reached out to grasp the banana, he was hit with a torrent of cold water from an overhead shower. With a squeal, the monkey abandoned its quest and retreated down the pole. Each monkey attempted, in turn, to secure the banana. Each received an equally chilly shower, and each scampered down without the prize. After repeated drenchings, the monkeys finally gave up on the bananas.

With the primates thus conditioned, one of the original four was removed from the experiment and a new monkey added. No sooner had this new, innocent monkey started up the pole than his (or her) companions reached up and yanked the surprised creature back down the pole. The monkey got the message—don't climb that pole. After a few such aborted attempts, but without ever having received a cold shower, the new monkey stopped trying to get the bananas. One by one, each of the original monkeys was replaced. Each new monkey learned the same lesson: Don't climb the pole. None of the new monkeys ever made it to the top of the pole; none even got so far as a cold shower. Not one understood precisely why pole climbing was discouraged, but they all respected the well-established precedent. Even after the shower was removed, no monkey ventured up the pole. We're not suggesting that managers are monkeys! We are suggesting that precedents, enacted into policy manuals, corporate processes, and training programs often outlive the particular industry context that created them.

The second, and perhaps greater hazard, is that individuals don't know what they don't know and, worse yet, don't know that they don't know. This is the great challenge for every organization: How do we come to know what we don't know? How can we identify, and then transcend, the boundaries to our own knowledge? The well-worn aphorism—what you don't know *can* hurt you—is entirely apropos. What Xerox didn't know about Canon's perspective on the copier business, what Sears didn't know about the outlook of discount merchandisers and niche retailers, and what Detroit failed to comprehend about the goals of Japanese car makers undermined the success of those tradition-bound companies. Not that what was important to know was, in any sense, unknowable, only that it lay beyond the boundaries of the existing managerial frame.

The Need for Genetic Diversity
We know from the biological sciences that the long-term health of any population of organisms is dependent on a minimum level of genetic variety. The same is true for the population of organisms we call a company. Recently, one of us addressed the top 20 officers of one of the largest U.S. companies. Four questions were put to

the executives: First, "How many of you have spent your entire professional life in this industry?" All the hands went up. Second, "How many of you have worked only for this company during your career?" All the hands went up. Third, "How many of you got to the top of this company through the sales and marketing function?" All but two hands went up. And finally, "How many of you have never worked for more than five years consecutively outside the United States?" Once again, almost all the hands went up. Our point was that unless the company did something to dramatically increase genetic variety, it would find it very difficult to compete with new, nontraditional competitors.

At different times, one has been able to observe a startling lack of genetic variety across whole industries: the U.S. airline industry in the late 1980s and early 1990s, the U.S. car industry in the 1970s, the European chemical industry in the 1980s, the U.S. banking industry in the 1970s, and business schools from the 1960s through the 1980s. Take one example of genetic sameness: the major U.S. airlines. By the early 1990s American, United, Delta, and Northwest all had a strikingly similar set of conventions: hub-and-spokes route structure, minimalist in-cabin service, mileage-based loyalty programs, and ownership of reservation systems. Consider the airlines' uniformly low service standards. Scan the newspapers and business magazines of the early 1990s. How often did a U.S. air carrier crow about the quality of service it offered travelers on domestic routes? Typically, the only advertised claims were about the size of the carrier's network and the fact that its planes generally arrived on time. This is equivalent to an auto company bragging that its cars really do have four wheels and can be relied on to get you from point A to point B. Only on international routes, where airlines like British Airways and Singapore Airlines set unfailingly high standards, were U.S. carriers forced to emphasize service, and even then they typically lagged far behind their international rivals in terms of customer satisfaction rankings.

The result has been a downward spiral of customer expectations, where ever poorer service begets ever lower expectations and ever more price sensitivity. In this environment, the only way an airline can keep fliers loyal is to bribe them with free miles (the airline's equivalent of auto rebates). The nadir of this downward spiral was an article in an inflight magazine, where the airline's chief executive patiently explained that because passengers weren't willing to pay for it, the company was removing the piece of lettuce that had heretofore adorned a fruit cup. In stark contrast, British Airways and Singapore, consistently among the world's most profitable airlines, constantly search for areas in which they can add new levels of customer service that yield more in terms of loyalty and price realization than they cost to create. They too offer free mileage programs, but more as a bonus and less as a bribe. Virgin Atlantic, another rule-breaker, worked hard to combine innovative and friendly service with keen pricing. By early 1994, Virgin was flying more passengers across the Atlantic every month than either American Airlines or United Airlines. In fact, the most financially successful airlines in the early 1990s were those that departed furthest from the conventions of the U.S. majors.

A lack of genetic variety was understandable, and almost forgivable, as long as competition took place within a "closed system." It wasn't Ford, after all, that challenged GM's most fundamental management beliefs. It wasn't Unisys that shook IBM to its core. It wasn't Montgomery Ward that surprised Sears. Whole industries become vulnerable to new rules when all the incumbents accept, more or less, the same industry conventions. An industry full of clones is an opportunity for any company that isn't locked into the dominant managerial frame. To assess the opportunity to exploit a lack of genetic variety in an industry, one might ask

- Is the industry reasonably concentrated, with fairly stable market-share positions among the incumbents? (That is, are the incumbents spending most of their time watching each other, and are they counting on "gentlemanly" competition to keep their margins up?)

- Alternately, is the industry highly fragmented? (That is, has no one yet discovered opportunities to capture economies of scale?)

- When you ask managers across the industry what's the secret to making money in this industry, do you get more or less the same answer? (That is, is everyone following the same profit recipe?)

- Have most of the top management teams spent their entire careers in the industry? (That is, has in-breeding reduced genetic variety?)

- Is the industry's take-up rate for new technology slower than most? (That is, are there opportunities to use technology to change the rules of the game?)

- Have the leaders tended to rely on high barriers to entry, rather than product and process innovation, to protect their profitability? (That is, have the leaders been able to rest on their laurels?)

- Has the basic concept of the product or service remained unchanged for a significant period of time? (That is, is there an orthodoxy about what customers want and how to serve them?)

- Do regulatory issues preoccupy top managers across the industry? (That is, do managers blame industry problems on regulators rather than search for creative solutions?)

Land is a mystery to fish, and by the time a fish discovers land, it is usually too late—the poor creature's on a hook. In the same way, a company's genetic coding limits its perception of novel opportunities and nontraditional competitors. The perceptual barriers that result from a lack of genetic diversity are often the highest and most impenetrable in those managers who possess the most political clout. (This is a nice way of saying the bottleneck is usually at the top of the bottle.) Senior executives are prone to believe that their organizational status confirms that they know more about the industry, customer needs, competitors, and how to compete than the people they manage. But what they know more about is, all too often, the past. The rules of competitive success in yesterday's world were etched into their minds as they climbed the corporate ladder. Unless these perceptual barriers, these bulwarks against the unconventional, are breached, a company will be incapable of inventing its future.

Every manager must face a cold hard fact: Intellectual capital steadily depreciates. What you, dear reader, know about your industry is worth less right now than it was when you began reading this book. Customer needs have changed, technological progress has been made, and competitors have advanced their plans while you've been perusing these pages. (No, don't stop reading! Just make sure you spend even more time thinking about how your industry is changing.) Here's our definition of a laggard: A laggard is a company where senior management has failed to write off its depreciating intellectual capital fast enough, and has underinvested in creating new intellectual capital. A laggard is a company where senior managers believe they know more about how the industry works than they actually do, and where what they do know is out of date.

Success reduces genetic variety. To the extent that success confirms the firm's strategy ("if we're so rich, we must be doing the right thing"), managers may come to believe that doing more of the same is the surest way to prolong success, and that any competitor that is not doing it "our way" can't be very smart. And if the competitor is relatively resource poor, well, that's even more reason to dismiss the up-and-comer. For just this reason GM was for too long more concerned with Ford than it was with Toyota, the news division at CBS paid more attention to NBC and ABC than to CNN, Xerox worried more about the encroachment of Eastman Kodak and IBM in the copier business than about Canon, and IBM fretted too much about the dangers of the "JCMs" (Japanese computer manufacturers) and not enough about Sun, Hewlett-Packard, EDS, and Microsoft.

Enlarging the Managerial Frame

As the competitive environment becomes more complex and variegated, the need for greater genetic variety—a broader range of managerial beliefs and a greater repertoire of managerial actions—grows apace. Any firm that hopes to survive must create within itself a reasonable proportion of the genetic variety to be found in the industry at large. In nature, genetic variety comes from unexpected mutations. The corporate corollary is skunk works, intrapreneurship, spinoffs, and other forms of bottom-up innovation. Like biological mutations, such instances of spontaneous, incremental innovation typically fail to make a big or immediate impact on the fortunes of the company. And like mutations in nature, most lead nowhere; most are evolutionary dead ends. This is not to argue against unplanned corporate mutations. But one is inevitably left with the question of what to do with the majority of employees and managers who are ill-adapted to the future. What is needed is genetic reengineering on a broad scale, not random mutations on a small scale.

Another way to introduce more genetic variety into a population is to bring in new members who cross-breed with the old. The corporate equivalent to cross-breeding is hiring managers from outside. Often this takes the form of bringing in a new CEO or raiding a competitor for a key divisional vice president. In a convention-ridden industry, musical chairs among the incumbents may not contribute much to genetic variety. On the other hand, an outsider can. When British Airways wanted to change its marketing approach it hired an executive from Mars, the world's leading candy company. When Philips wanted to fundamentally rethink its approach to research and development, it hired Hewlett-Packard's R&D director.

There is, however, a limit to just how fast and how deeply an unconventional senior executive can alter the genetic coding of a large, hide-bound company. The hope in hiring an outsider is that he or she will cross-breed with enough people to substantially alter the genetic pool. But cross-breeding is a slow way to change the genetic coding of a large organization. Even in the best of circumstances, a new CEO can directly influence the perceptions, beliefs, biases, and assumptions of only a limited number of people. "Management by walking about," satellite link-ups, and "town hall" meetings can all help enlarge the newcomer's range of influence but, in a large organization, the newcomer's influence will still be less than all-pervasive. At best, the outsider's appointment sends a strong signal that a change in genetic makeup is long overdue. Ultimately, genetic variety must be part of the woof and warp of the firm, not locked up in the basement like a crazy aunt (skunk works) or bolted on to the top like Frankenstein's head (a new appointment from outside).

So what can a company do to change its genetic coding? First, it should be careful not to overtighten the bolts that hold the managerial frame together. In practice, this may mean leaving a bit of play in administrative procedures (must every business use the same, mandated, strategic planning format?); it may mean being a bit more reluctant to use the lessons of the past to train employees for the future (little is gained by training an army to use the pike or longbow on the eve of the invention of the musket); or it may mean a greater willingness to hire and promote individuals who aren't "just like us" (it is all too easy for top management to perpetuate a serious genetic flaw by yielding to the temptation to hire and promote in its own image).

More generally, preserving some degree of genetic variety in a company requires corporate leaders to be very careful about just what and how much of their beliefs and perspectives get institutionalized in the firm's administrative systems. There is often a thin line between the admirable desire to institutionalize learning and best practice and the need to prevent managerial frames from becoming rigid and inflexible. In this sense, the problem with bureaucracy is not only that it amounts to unnecessary overhead, but that it enforces, through the administrative rituals that it controls, a single, dominant managerial frame. The more powerful the bureaucrats, the less the genetic variety. This was certainly the case at IBM. IBM's motto may have been "Think!" but it needed a rider: "For goodness sake, don't all think alike."

A commitment to maximizing the share of voice of employees who are genetically "different" is also critical to ensuring the survival of genetic variety in a company. Top management must learn to seek out and reward unorthodoxy. The chairman of one of the world's most successful pharmaceutical companies has a simple approach. Knowing that any project that reaches the board has already passed dozens of reviews and has been presold and more or less preapproved, the chairman regularly tracks down projects that were rejected long before they reached the board. His logic is simple:

> I know that whatever we get to see at the board level is going to be pretty consistent with our existing model of the business. I'm looking for the projects that are a bit off the wall, that could change our model of the business.[1]

It is important to distinguish between genetic diversity and cultural diversity. Many laggards are international companies. Many possess enormous cultural diversity in their ranks. Many celebrate such diversity as a source of strength and innovation. Yet much of the potential for creativity offered by cultural diversity is often surrendered to an allegiance to very undiverse views about the industry and how to compete in it. On one occasion one of us addressed a large group of young consultants in one of the world's biggest consulting companies; more than 70 countries were represented in the auditorium. Yet each consultant had gone through the same rigid training process, and each had emerged with a managerial frame of roughly the same dimensions. There is a fine line between socialization and brainwashing. Companies that worship cultural diversity yet enforce, by design or default, an orthodox set of industry perspectives and management precepts, are as competitively vulnerable as those that are myopically ethnocentric.

Enlarging managerial frames depends, more than anything else, on curiosity and humility. It is these traits that make a senior manager willing to tolerate first-level employees who think the boss is a neanderthal, and to exercise the patience required to span the hierarchical divides that form a barrier to "upward learning." It is humility that motivates a senior management team to delve inside competitors' heads to test the limits of its own managerial frames. It is interesting to note that whereas Japanese managers have a reputation for conforming closely to cultural norms for deportment, dress, deference, and diligence, they have worked assiduously to learn from management cultures other than their own. Take a simple example. The Japanese seem to suffer no embarrassment from the fact that their premier prize for quality bears the name of a foreigner, Dr. Deming. On the other hand, it is almost inconceivable that the president of the United States would hand out an Ishikawa prize for quality, and thereby honor the debt that Western industry owes Japan's home-grown quality guru.

Many companies, principally U.S. it must be said, have paid heavily for the pride of authorship. Quality? Yes, Americans invented that. Value engineering, that's ours, too. We just didn't implement too well. These sentiments are heard in executive suites from Manhattan to Long Beach. Although there's more than a little truth here, the implication is that there's not much to learn that we didn't already know. A Japanese manager in one of our studies put it succinctly. "American managers are better teachers than students." A few companies, Motorola and Ford among them, readily admit to learning from Japan. But Japan has no more a monopoly on management wisdom than the United States. If the boundaries that demarcate success and failure are not national boundaries, neither should they be the delineators of better or worse managerial frames. If Japanese managers should ever come to regard themselves as having more to teach the rest of the world than to learn from it, their competitors will be able to break out the champagne. Japan's successful companies must not forget the lessons of their own recent past: Only by humbly considering the merits of other managerial frames can one enlarge and enrich one's own.

UNLEARNING THE PAST

Preserving a degree of genetic variety is sometimes enough to stave off extinction. But what if the environment is already changing rapidly? What if the company is already full of out-of-date "clones?" In such cases there is a need for "gene replacement therapy." Genes that are defective, in the new industry context, must be supplanted by healthy ones. In business terms, removing defective genes is best described as "unlearning."

Although much in vogue, creating a "learning organization" is only half the solution. Just as important is creating an "unlearning" organization. Why do children learn new skills much faster than adults? Partly because they have less to unlearn. Why do music teachers and sports coaches put so much emphasis on the early development of the "right habits?" Because they know that learning is easier than unlearning. (Just ask any self-taught golfer with a seriously out-of-kilter swing!) To create the future, a company must unlearn at least some of its past. We're all familiar with the "learning curve," but what about the "forgetting curve"—the rate at which a company can unlearn those habits that hinder future success?

The more successful a company has been, the flatter its forgetting curve. One very successful company with which we're acquainted recently celebrated its twenty-fifth anniversary. For the occasion it commissioned a number of artists to produce 25 paintings depicting the elements (strategies, markets, skills, and practices) that had contributed to the firm's enviable track record. The paintings were displayed in the company's headquarters tower. One of us suggested—only half in jest—that every year top management put in storage at least one painting in acknowledgment of the fact that the particular theme of the painting had more to do with the firm's past than its future. The point we were really making was that a company must work as hard to forget as it does to learn.

There's an important message here for successful industry challengers. Before new challengers get too arrogant, before Bill Gates says too many more disparaging things about IBM, or Ted Turner pokes any more fun at the traditional broadcast networks, or Intel celebrates the misfortune of its Japanese competitors, they should take a moment to reflect. The challengers' continued success is no more ensured than that of the incumbents they have displaced. While the challengers may revel in their success, many seem oblivious to the fact that the incumbents they have unseated were once challengers themselves. Microsoft and EDS are held up as models of the new "computerless computer company." Ted Turner of CNN fame; Anita Roddick, founder of The Body Shop; Andy Groves, outspoken CEO of Intel; Sir Colin Marshall, the urbane chairman of British Airways; and T.J. Rodgers, opinionated boss of Cypress

Semiconductor, have all been proclaimed business visionaries. Yet they stare out from the covers of the same business magazines that earlier toasted John Akers (IBM), Ken Olsen (DEC), Robert Stempel (General Motors), and David Kearns (Xerox). With surprising speed, yesterday's heresies become today's dogmas.

Flush with success, challengers often forget the most basic rules of corporate vitality: To be a challenger once, it is enough to challenge the orthodoxies of the incumbents; to be a challenger twice, a firm must be capable of challenging its *own* orthodoxies. However much a challenger is feted on Wall Street, benchmarked by competitors, or reverently studied by MBA students, one thing is inescapable: To reinvent its industry a second time, a challenger must regenerate its core strategies. It must reconceive its definition of the marketplace, redraw the boundaries of the firm, redefine its value propositions, and rethink its most fundamental assumptions about how to compete. Ron Summer, former president of Sony America and now working for Sony in Europe, makes the point eloquently: "Where a company is going is more important than where it is coming from. As industry boundaries get erased, corporate birth certificates won't count for much."[2]

To get to the future, a company must be willing to jettison, at least in part, its past. Someone once remarked that "God created the world in six days, but He didn't have an installed base." But what prevents most companies from creating the future is not an installed base of obsolete capital equipment (the case in the U.S. auto industry), not an installed base of end products that must be maintained and updated (the excuse some IBMers used for devoting such a large proportion of the firm's R&D resources to the mainframe business), and not an inefficient installed base of distribution infrastructure (a bedevilment for banks with large, underutilized branch networks). What prevents companies from creating the future is an installed base of thinking—the unquestioned conventions, the myopic view of opportunities and threats, and the unchallenged precedents that comprise the existing managerial frame.

Creating the future doesn't require a company to abandon all of its past. Indeed, a critical question for every firm is: What part of our past can we use as a "pivot" to get to the future, and what part of our past represents excess baggage? Selectively forgetting the past is difficult to do for two reasons—one emotional, one economic. Senior managers typically have a lot of emotional equity invested in the past. Think of all those senior managers at DEC who cut their teeth selling VAX computers to corporate clients; all those top engineers at Xerox who spent a lifetime designing bigger, more complex copiers; all those at CBS who revered the memory of Edward R. Murrow and Walter Cronkite and hoped to sustain forever the glory days of network broadcast news; all those bankers who lived by the rule of 3-6-3 (borrow money at 3%, lend it at 6%, and hit the golf course by 3:00 P.M.). Managers are understandably discomforted when faced with the fact that the intellectual capital accumulated over a professional lifetime may be of little value in a radically changing industry environment. For those who built the past, the temptation to preserve it can be overwhelming.

THE NEED TO REBUILD

A firm's stake in the past is economic as well as emotional. For a successful firm, the definition of served market, the value proposition put forward to customers, the margin and value-added structure, the particular configuration of assets and skills that yields those margins, and supporting administrative systems together constitute an integral and well-tuned profit "engine" (see Figure 3-1). While the profit engine may perform wondrously in one industry environment, any change to that environment typically threatens the engine's efficiency. Optimizing the performance of the engine for one set of conditions (e.g., nitro fuel drag racing) may render it almost useless in another set of conditions (e.g., the 24 hours of Le Mans). Regulatory changes in the U.S. financial services industry, and the emergence of "nonbanks" as strong competitors for savings, reduced the efficiency of the profit engine of many traditional banks. In retailing, Sears' old-fashioned gasoline engine was ultimately out-classed by Wal-Mart's jet turbine engine. But Sears finally recognized the need to rebuild its profit engine from

FIGURE 3-1 DECOMPOSING THE ECONOMIC ENGINE

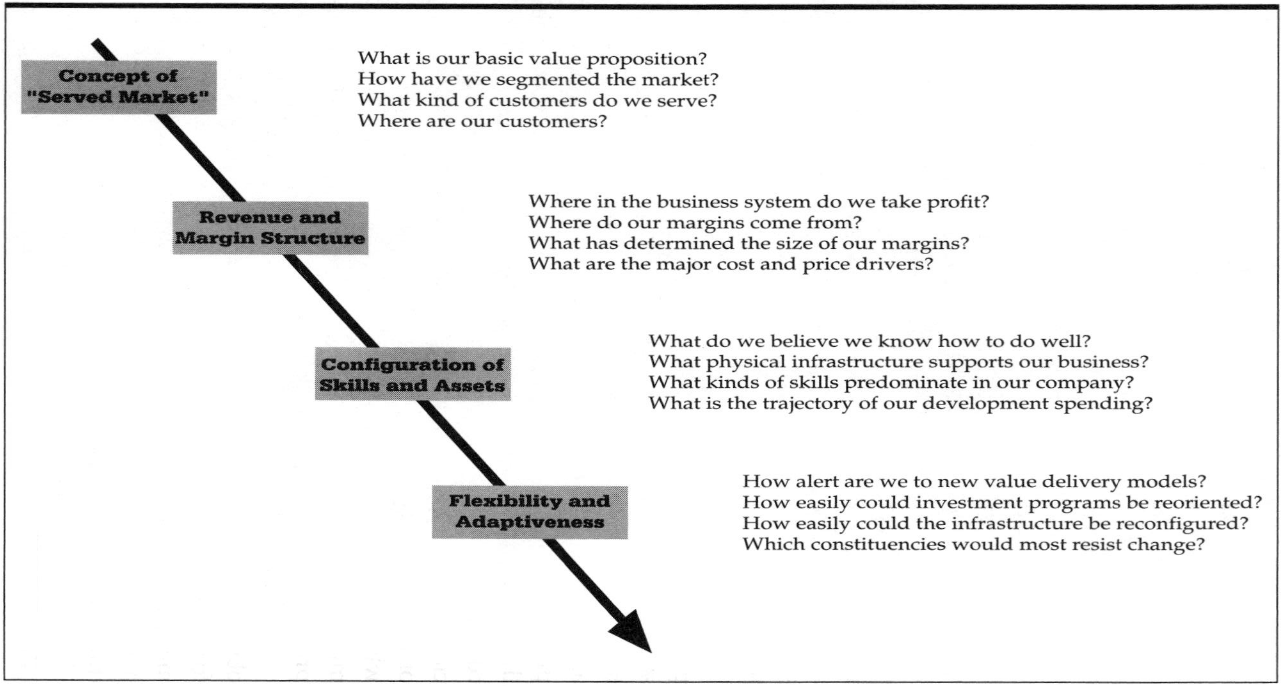

Concept of "Served Market"

What is our basic value proposition?
How have we segmented the market?
What kind of customers do we serve?
Where are our customers?

Revenue and Margin Structure

Where in the business system do we take profit?
Where do our margins come from?
What has determined the size of our margins?
What are the major cost and price drivers?

Configuration of Skills and Assets

What do we believe we know how to do well?
What physical infrastructure supports our business?
What kinds of skills predominate in our company?
What is the trajectory of our development spending?

Flexibility and Adaptiveness

How alert are we to new value delivery models?
How easily could investment programs be reoriented?
How easily could the infrastructure be reconfigured?
Which constituencies would most resist change?

the ground up and abandoned catalog sales and a policy of selling only under its own brand name, and shifted from a merchandising policy that emphasized hard goods to one that emphasizes soft goods.

The threat to a firm's profit engine may come from improvements made by a competitor to a particular component of that engine: redefining the boundaries of the served market (as Canon did for copiers); coming up with a new value proposition (as money market mutual funds in the United States did in the 1980s when they started looking at individuals as investors rather than as merely savers); discovering how to take margins out of a different part of the business system (capturing a price premium for built-in quality rather than relying on service revenues); or reconfiguring assets and skills to produce the same value more economically (as Service Corp. International did when it bought up independent funeral homes and consolidated "backroom" operations like embalming and hearse transport to reap economies of scale[3]). The profit engine is different from a value chain: It encompasses deep-seated beliefs about what business we're in, what we're delivering to customers, how money is made in this business, what assets and skills are critical, and who our competitors are. Think of the profit engine as something quite real and managerial frames as the owner's manual for a specific engine. The point is that every company must be alert to anything that could undermine the efficiency of its engine as a profit generator. It must constantly inquire of itself whether its definition of "served market" is too narrow, whether its margin structure can be sustained, and whether there might be another, much more efficient way to deliver a particular product or service (see Figure 3-2).

Over time, new, more efficient profit engines make older engines obsolete. Video dial tone is fast becoming a more efficient engine for delivering movies into the home than a video rental outlet. For many people, the purchase of computer software by phone, with next day delivery, represents a more efficient engine than traipsing down to the local computer store. Biz Mart, Office Max, and their ilk created a fundamentally more efficient engine for delivering office supplies to small and medium-sized businesses. Charles

FIGURE 3-2 FINDING THE LIMITS OF THE CURRENT ECONOMIC ENGINE

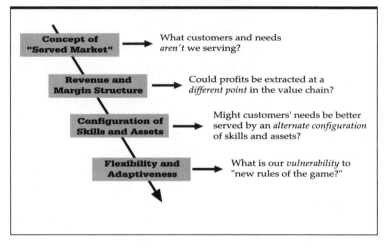

Schwab invented a more efficient engine for delivering brokerage services than that of Merrill Lynch. Supercharging a piston engine (pursuing restructuring and reengineering) is not enough if a competitor has invented a jet turbine engine. Every company must sooner or later build a new economic engine for itself.

Like a grizzled old mechanic who bemoans the complexity of modern automobiles, incumbents typically have an understandable incentive to preserve the existing economic engine. At the extreme, they may be reluctant to admit to, much less proactively harness, the forces of industry transformation. In 1991, a senior executive from CBS told a congressional committee that digital television "defies the laws of physics."[4] Considering the possibility of hundreds, rather than tens of television channels, the president of CBS has said, "I know of no evidence that viewers are crying out for more television."[5] Of course, digital television does defy many of the laws of physics if one attempts to deliver it via terrestrial broadcasting, but it is a snap to deliver over broad-band cable. Likewise, few are crying out for more television of the sort produced by the U.S. networks (who really wants another gore-and-guts police reality show?). On the other hand, there is every chance the people will, in the future, see television as something more than a passive entertainment device. It will offer the chance for interactive shopping, teleconferencing, and game playing. The only question is, what share of television's future is CBS likely to get?

It is hard to imagine any circumstance in which a firm wouldn't benefit more from proactively managing industry evolution, even when the industry is evolving in a way that undermines the efficiency of the firm's current profit engine, than from letting someone else control the pace and direction of industry transition. One should not be surprised to find Xerox managers more than willing to admit today that they should never have let Japanese companies take the initiative in small copiers, even though success in this industry segment somewhat undermined Xerox's margin structure. Similarly, Sears managers must wish they had moved earlier to understand and exploit the potential for discount brand-name retailing; broadcasters at CBS, NBC, and ABC must kick themselves for letting CNN steal a march in the global news business; and Detroit auto executives must bemoan that they so willingly ceded the "unattractive" small-car segment to Japanese rivals in the 1970s. Even the august Daimler-Benz, with its announced plan to slash costs and produce an "entry-level" Mercedes (probably to be made outside Germany), seems to have come to the realization that in global competition the only defense is a vigorous offense. The best way to ensure that one is not at risk from more imaginative competitors is to be the first to conceive of alternate value-delivery mechanisms, the first to cannibalize one's own products and services, and the first to get to the future, even when that future undermines past successes. As Andy Groves at Intel puts it, "You have to be your own toughest competitor."

Perhaps the most-used excuse for sitting tight is that, to create the future, it is necessary to kill the base business or to gut it for cash, technical resources, or managerial skills. Although the argument is often overstated, a company may face a genuine conundrum when the industry is evolving in a 180-degree direction. To some extent, this was the problem for mainframe-dependent IBM and for the major U.S. television broadcast networks. The only way out for a firm in such a predicament is to recognize the "threat" early enough so that the transition from one profit engine to another can be orderly and well managed.

A few years back the *Financial Times* ran a cartoon that showed an IBM executive standing guard in front of a massive door to a castle that had been overrun by an invading horde. The door was labeled "Open Systems," but rather than go through the door, the marauders had gone around the guard and battered down the walls. Said the IBMer with all due solemnity, "Let the unlocking of this door mark the beginning of an era of openness." The message was clear: The trend toward open systems was a *fait accompli*, and the rest of the world wasn't waiting for IBM to make up its mind about the wisdom of supporting open rather than proprietary operating systems. Having failed to embrace open systems, IBM was unable to exert much influence in the development of those trends and ill-positioned to exploit them.

The wasted years that come from a lack of sensitivity to industry trends, and the propensity to deny uncomfortable truths, so often imperil a firm's base business that, by the time the need to change is inescapable, the cash, people, and intellectual energy needed to regenerate a firm's core strategies have been largely dissipated. Thus, the question for today's challengers: Can they reinvent themselves and their industries *in time* and thus avoid the pain and bloodshed inflicted on so many industry incumbents by less hidebound newcomers?

Few companies are capable of regenerating the deep-down sense of what they are, what industry they're in, who their customers are, and what those customers want in time. There are exceptions. Motorola regenerated itself when it decided to get into semiconductors, again when it made the commitment to cellular telephony, and yet again when it conceived of itself as a consumer electronics company (as well as a professional electronics company). J. P. Morgan regenerated itself when it transformed itself from a commercial bank to an investment bank. The Gap regenerated itself when it went from a pile-them-high, sell-them-cheap retailer of jeans to a retailer of trendy, value-priced fashion basics.

To escape the gravitational pull of the past, managers must be convinced that future success is less than inevitable. No company will walk away from some of its past unless it feels that repeating the past won't guarantee future success. To create an incentive to prepare for tomorrow today, senior managers must first be convinced of the impermanence of present success. The urgency thus engendered is critical to providing an incentive to enlarge traditional managerial frames and begin the painful work of genetic reengineering. Of course the trick is to create this urgency while a company is still at the peak of its success.

How does one create a sense of urgency in advance of an incipient crisis, before the environment becomes unrelentingly hostile? How does one get enough people to recognize the need to learn before it's too late? When the pace of genetic evolution falls behind the pace of environmental change, a species, like the dinosaurs, can get wiped out. The corporate equivalent is wholesale layoffs and massive restructuring. Only with anticipatory unlearning can one hope for a bloodless revolution.

Clearly there will be no incentive to selectively forget the past unless managers and employees believe that repeating the past won't sustain success in the future. While every thoughtful person will concede this point at a conceptual level, unlearning won't begin unless every thoughtful person understands it at a visceral and emotional level. Managers and employees have to be brought face to face with the inevitability of corporate decline; weak signals that portend coming disaster must be amplified; everyone must understand at what point, and under what conditions, the present economic engine runs out of steam.

By considering industry trends and potential discontinuities, whether technological, demographic, regulatory, or social, it is possible to fast forward corporate history and glean a preview of what might bring the current profit engine to a grinding halt. This is a desperately important exercise for every company. If a top management team cannot clearly articulate the five or six fundamental industry trends that most threaten its firm's continued success, it is not in control of the firm's destiny. Any company that wants to avoid a genuine profit crisis must create a quasi-crisis years in advance.

Take an example. The revenues of one of the world's most successful service companies grew from $1 billion to $5 billion in the 1980s. Top management was justifiably proud of this performance. With no fundamental change in strategic direction, it projected revenues would race ahead to $20 billion by the turn of the century. Yet when one looked more closely, future success looked anything but ensured. At $1 billion the company had 10,000 employees, at $5 billion the payroll was 55,000. Was the company's goal, we inquired of top management, to be one of the biggest employers in the world? Because if it reached the $20 billion target, with no change in the efficiency of its economic engine, that is exactly where it would end up (given that most other companies were reducing headcount). The point was taken: The company had been pursuing "valueless growth" in that the value-added per employee had actually been declining in inflation-adjusted terms.

There was yet another danger signal. The oft-stated goal of the firm was to be the "premier" service provider in its industry. Yet in reviewing the list of large corporate clients that had signed on in recent years, management realized that its customers were more likely to be the laggards than the leaders in their respective industries. How could the company become the premier service provider in its industry if its clients were anything but premier in their own industries, we asked. These simple insights, shared among hundreds of senior managers, were enough to convince top brass that a major effort was needed to overhaul the company's profit engine and explore new roads to the future.

Boeing has worked hard to ensure that every employee understands that there is no way to intercept the future by repeating the past. Boeing's fast-forward look at the future in the late 1980s convinced the company that airlines would be under intense profit pressure through the turn of the century, and that demand for Boeing's new jets would fall precipitously. While Boeing had expected the world's airlines to retire about 300 aircraft from service every year in the early 1990s, the number turned out to be closer to 100 aircraft per year. Despite the higher operating costs of older aircraft, many airlines found it cheaper to keep old, fully depreciated planes in service than to fork out tens of millions of dollars for more modern jetliners. The only solution was to change the calculus for airlines by dramatically reducing the time and cost of producing new jetliners. But management wondered, how can we get employees to understand why such heroic goals were necessary? How can we tap into the emotional and intellectual energy that is necessary to regenerate success? In the end, Boeing commissioned a video in which an ersatz news reporter in the not-too-distant future recorded the demise of the once-great company. As glum workers handed in their badges and filed out of Boeing's cavernous plants, a newsman announced the sad end of an era in aviation history. Substantially sobered, the once lethargic leader committed itself to completely automating the design of new aircraft, reducing the build time of new aircraft by as much as 50%, and making even bigger cuts in inventory levels, all with the goal of reducing the cost of producing an airliner by 25%. Even Boeing's toughest competitor, Airbus, was willing to concede that if Boeing met its targets, it would transform the industry.[6]

In the early 1980s Motorola launched a similar effort to intercept the future. Fully cognizant of the inroads Japanese competitors had made in consumer electronics (Motorola had already sold its television business to a Japanese rival), the company began to worry that its professional electronics businesses might one day be equally vulnerable to Japanese competition. This was already a fact in semiconductors, and Asian competitors were nipping at Motorola's heels in businesses like two-way mobile radios, cellular telephones, and pagers. Further, the dividing line between professional and consumer electronics was becoming more blurred, and Japanese companies were beginning to bring their legendary mass-manufacturing and mass-marketing skills to bear in businesses like cellular phones. At one memorable board meeting, a senior vice president even had the temerity to assert that the company's quality "stank." Motorola's initial response was to create an awareness-building program, "Rise to the Challenge," which made thousands of employees aware of the early warning signs of potential doom. Again, the apprehension created, coupled with a big helping of can-do attitude, propelled the company to heroic operational improvements and a fundamental reassessment of corporate direction. In anticipating the convergence of consumer and professional electronics and preparing in time, Motorola succeeded in turning back the tide of Japanese competition—a feat accomplished by few other electronics companies. As the 1990s dawned, Motorola remained a world leader in each of its core businesses. As these examples illustrate, unlearning begins when employees are confronted with the potential disconnect between the success recipes of the past and the competitive challenges of the future. An organization must be discomforted before it will unlearn.

Any company that drives forward while looking out the rearview mirror will, sooner or later, run into a brick wall. The goal of making that brick wall apparent to employees is not to create a sense of anxiety. Anxiety is immobilizing. The goal is to produce a sense of urgency. Anxiety is the product of a sense of helplessness, when everyone realizes that what the company is doing is too little, too late, and that there's no way to avoid a spectacular crash. Urgency comes when everyone knows there is a brick wall out there, but that the wall is far enough away so there is still time to turn the wheel and avoid the crash. Top management's responsibility is to make sure that wall always appears just a little bit closer than it really is.

What a senior vice president at Microsoft said about his own firm may be said of any successful company: "[We] have a vested interest in the structure of the industry as it exists today."[7] Yet any company whose stake in the past or the present is bigger than its stake in the future runs the risk of becoming a laggard. But it is impossible to have a stake in the future if one cannot imagine that future. This is why Microsoft established its Advanced Technology Group, which is charged with imagining and pursuing a host of new opportunities for Microsoft along the information highway.

Thus, a sense of possibility is just as important as a sense of foreboding in inducing a company to escape its past. However unappealing a company's present situation, it is unlikely to abandon the past for the future unless it has created for itself an alluring vista of future opportunities—an *opportunity horizon*—that presents a compelling alternative to simply reliving yesterday's successes. To give up the bird in the hand, a company must see a dozen birds in the bush. The future must become just as vivid and real as the present and the past. Senior management must help the organization build an intellectually compelling and emotionally enticing view of the future. The quest for industry foresight is the subject of our next chapter.

4

Competing for Industry Foresight

● ●

The goal of competition for industry foresight is, at one level, simple: to build the best possible assumption base about the future and thereby develop the prescience needed to proactively shape industry evolution. Competition for industry foresight is essentially competition to establish one's company as the *intellectual leader* in terms of influence over the direction and shape of industry transformation. Industry foresight gives a company the potential to get to the future first and stake out a leadership position. Industry foresight informs corporate direction. Industry foresight allows a company to control the evolution of its industry and, thereby, its own destiny. The trick is to see the future before it arrives.

THE NEED FOR FORESIGHT

Industry foresight helps managers answer three critical questions. First, what new types of customer benefit should we seek to provide in five, ten, or fifteen years? Second, what new competencies will we need to build or acquire to offer those benefits to customers? And third, how will we need to reconfigure the customer interface over the next several years?

Essentially, a point of view about the future is a point of view about benefits, competencies, and the customer interface. Motorola has such a point of view. Motorola dreams of a world in which telephone numbers will be assigned to people, rather than places;

where small hand-held devices will allow people to stay in touch no matter where they are; and where the new communicators can deliver video images and data as well as voice signals. For this world to become reality, Motorola knows that it will have to strengthen its competencies in digital compression, flat screen displays, and battery technology. Motorola also knows that to capture a significant share of a burgeoning consumer market, it will have to substantially increase the familiarity of its brand with customers around the world.

Apple Computer has often demonstrated substantial foresight. In the 1970s it looked forward to a world with "a computer for every man, woman, and child." This was at a time when computers were most often found in specially built rooms deep in the bowels of corporate office buildings, and the idea of a kid having a computer was laughable. The result was the Apple II, the first truly successful mass-market computer, which was introduced in 1977, four years ahead of the IBM PC.

A few years later, as individuals were struggling to become "computer literate," Apple had another burst of foresight—aided, it must be said, by pioneering work at Xerox. Apple engineers asked themselves, "If computers are so smart, why don't we teach them about people instead of the other way around?" Out of this unconventional thinking came first the Lisa, and then the Macintosh, and the world's enlightened computer users never again had to look at a C >.

General Magic, a consortium that counts Apple, AT&T, Motorola, and Philips among its members, has its own foresight. General Magic's founders dream of a world in which individuals can use a pocket-sized device to cruise the streets of a typical "downtown," visiting the virtual travel agent, bank, or library. Users will be able to send "information agents" zipping out into cyberspace to book airline reservations, retrieve a magazine article, check on a stock price, or review the menu of a local restaurant. As with most instances of industry foresight, General Magic's view of the future-to-be intertwines a sense of destiny, a deep understanding of technological trends, and a vivid dream of how life could be made better. Whether General Magic succeeds in turning this dream into reality is not yet clear. Foresight is not enough to guarantee a profitable journey toward the future. Yet without foresight, the journey cannot even begin.

We don't believe that any company can get along without a well-articulated point of view about tomorrow's opportunities and challenges. In recent years, some have questioned whether a company needs a "vision" at all. Adaptiveness, solid implementation, and basic blocking and tackling are increasingly regarded as more important than vision.[1] From former President George Bush to IBM's Lou Gerstner, a wide variety of leaders have pronounced themselves ill at ease with the "vision thing."

However, the subject of such antipathy is different from industry foresight. Visions that are as grandiose as they are poorly conceived deserve to be criticized, as do companies that seem to prefer rhetoric to action. All too often, "the vision" is no more than window dressing for a CEO's ego-driven acquisition binge. Chrysler's purchase of an Italian maker of exotic sports cars and its acquisition of a jet aircraft manufacturer were driven more by the ego and whim of the company's erstwhile chairman, Lee Iacocca, than by a solid, well-founded point of view about what it would take to succeed in the automotive business ten years hence. They were a side trip. Any vision that is simply an extension of the CEO's ego is dangerous. On the other hand, it is equally simplistic and dangerous to reject the very notion of foresight simply because some corporate leaders can't distinguish between vanity and vision.

Often, pundits criticize a company's vision when what is really at fault is the company's executional capability. Apple Computer has had more foresight than most companies in its industry, yet it has also committed its fair share of executional blunders. This doesn't take anything away from the quality of Apple's foresight, it just proves the point that foresight isn't enough. Industry foresight doesn't guarantee competitive success. The most foresightful firms aren't always the most profitable. All the foresight in the world, if not matched by a capacity to execute, counts for little. On the other hand, terrific executional ability, in the absence of industry foresight, is not enough to guarantee future success.

Today many companies seem to be convinced that foresight is the easy part, it's implementation that's the killer. We believe that creating industry foresight and achieving operational excellence are equally challenging tasks. Many times what are described as today's implementation failures are really yesterday's foresight failures in disguise. IBM's fat overheads were manageable when computers carried the gross margins of illicit drugs; IBM's overheads threatened to sink the company when computers became commodities with the margins of canned vegetables. An IBMer in the early 1990s might well have argued that "it's not a vision we need, it's a lower cost structure and faster development times." To this we would answer, "Of course you need to reduce costs—but why didn't you begin working on the cost problem a decade ago? Why did you so dramatically underestimate the downward pressure that open systems, clone makers, and the convergence of computing and consumer electronics would exert on margins?" Many of IBM's operational failures in the early 1990s could be traced to foresight problems in the 1980s.

The quality deficit, which cost U.S. automakers so much market share in the 1970s and 1980s, was more than just "poor execution." Detroit didn't suddenly get sloppy, and Japanese car makers didn't start out with a quality advantage. Japanese auto companies realized decades ago that new and formidable competitive weapons would be needed to beat U.S. car companies in their home market. The new weapons they set about developing were quality, cycle time, and flexibility. Twenty years later, Toyota's foresight had become GM's implementation nightmare.

For a variety of reasons we prefer the word *foresight* to *vision*. Vision connotes a dream or an apparition, but there is more to industry foresight than a single blinding flash of insight. Industry foresight is based on deep insights into the trends in technology, demographics, regulation, and lifestyles that can be harnessed to rewrite industry rules and create new competitive space. While understanding the potential *implications* of such trends requires creativity and imagination, any "vision" that is not based on a solid factual foundation is likely to be fantastical.

We're also wary of "visionaries." While Sony's Akio Morita, Bell Atlantic's Ray Smith, and Microsoft's Bill Gates have all been declared visionaries, a single-minded visionary may be just as likely to lead his or her company down a blind alley as toward the future. All too often, corporate leaders come to believe that they really are visionaries; that their forward view is more insightful and more accurate than everyone else's. A venture capitalist may be willing to bet a few million dollars on a visionary, but it would be foolhardy to bet the future of a multibillion dollar company on any single individual's reading of the future. As we will see, industry foresight is the product of many people's visions. Often, a point of view about the future, which is in fact an amalgam of many individual perspectives, is represented by journalists or sycophantic employees as the "vision" of one person. So while Mr. Kobayashi may have taken much of the credit for NEC's visionary concept of "computers and communication" ("C&C"), the idea of exploiting the convergence between the two industries wove together the thoughts of many minds in NEC, not just one. Senior executives aren't the only ones with industry foresight. In fact, as we'll see, their primary role is to capture and exploit the foresight that exists throughout the organization. They are responsible for ensuring the development of industry foresight, but the task is not theirs alone.

DEVELOPING FORESIGHT

Senior management teams compete in the acquisition of industry foresight. Senior management teams compete to develop a prescient, well-founded, and creative view of tomorrow's opportunities that will spur preemptive competence-building, provide focus to those efforts, ensure consistency in investment programs, and serve as a guide to decisions about strategic alliances and acquisitions and a brake on indiscriminate and tangential opportunism. Any top team that has not made a substantial investment in creating industry foresight will find itself at the mercy of more farsighted competitors.

Whether they knew it or not, Lou Gerstner and his team at IBM were competing, in the early 1990s, with Michael Spindler and his team at Apple, who were competing with Lewis Platt and his team at Hewlett-Packard, who were competing with Les Alberthal and his team at EDS, who were competing with George Shaheen and his team at Andersen Consulting to build a point of view about the future of the information technology industry. Arthur Martinez and his team at Sears were competing with David Glass and his team at Wal-Mart, who were competing with Joseph Antonini and his team at Kmart to build a farsighted perspective on the future of mass retailing. Roy Vagelos and his team at Merck were competing with Bob Bauman and his team at SmithKline Beecham, who were competing with Sir Paul Girolami and his team at Glaxo to imagine and prepare for a new and dramatically different health care environment. Ray Smith and his team at Bell Atlantic were competing with Bob Allen and his team at AT&T, who were competing with Richard McCormick and his team at US West to shape and profit from the future of "infotainment" services. Robert Crandall and his team at AMR were competing with Stephen Wolf at United and Colin Marshall at British Airways to create the world's first truly global airline. And in turn, all of these teams were competing against a myriad of newcomers and start-ups, eager to challenge the incumbents for leadership in tomorrow's radically transformed industries. At stake were billions of dollars in new opportunities, the chance to improve the lives of many of the world's citizens, and entry into the august company of history's farsighted business leaders.

We meet few senior management teams who seem to be fully conscious of their responsibility to develop industry foresight; who understand that, unless they first win today's battle for intellectual leadership, they will be unlikely to win tomorrow's battle for market leadership. When pushed on the point, managers will readily concede that success today doesn't guarantee success tomorrow; yet their behavior often seems to rest on an implicit assumption that the future will be, more or less, a replay of the past. How else can one explain, for example, why IBM was still devoting roughly one-third of its R&D budget to "big iron" in 1991? Although managers often point out to us just how different their industry is today from a decade ago, few seem to be alert to the possibility that their industry may be as different a decade hence. Fewer still have developed a broad perspective on *how* it might be different.

To get to the future first, top management must either see opportunities not seen by other top teams or must be able to exploit opportunities, by virtue of preemptive and consistent capability-building, that other companies can't. Again, we find few senior management teams that can paint an enticing picture of the new industry space their company hopes to stake out over the next decade. We find few senior management teams that have a clear agenda for competence-building. We find few senior management teams that spend as much time on opportunity management as they do on operations management.

Many companies rely on big, bold acquisitions and grass roots "intrapreneurship" for corporate regeneration. As potentially useful as these approaches may be, neither acquisitions nor skunk works are good substitutes for industry foresight. Top management often sees a major acquisition as the only escape route from a business that has become hopelessly mature. It's not news to anyone that few acquisitions actually benefit the shareholders of the acquiring company, yet acquisitions are, in many cases, an easy out for senior executives too intellectually lazy to think through the future of the firm's "core" business and too unimaginative to discover new ways of deploying existing capabilities. Thus, while Xerox was trying to "balance" its portfolio by acquiring financial services companies, it was unknowingly surrendering the "office of the future" to companies that better understood the potential of the technology created in Xerox's own Palo Alto Research Center.

Although skunk works, intrapreneurship, and thriving on chaos often do yield unexpected new product bonanzas, they aren't substitutes for industry foresight. Let us explain why. There is a common perception that it is almost impossible for large companies to be truly innovative. They are regularly described as "clumsy elephants" or "dinosaurs." In this view, any new business that successfully wriggles out from under the dead hand of corporate bureaucracy, conservatism, and short-termism will have been created despite the system rather than because of it. Yet even the fiercest critics of large, unimaginative companies seldom suggest that the employees of those companies are themselves any less imaginative than those who work for small companies. It's the bureaucracy, the multiple levels of approval, and the lack of personal freedom that bottle up innovation.

To protect imaginative individuals from overbearing corporate orthodoxies, several approaches have been tried: new venture divisions, skunk works, incubator projects, rewards for intrapreneurs, and so on. Although such efforts have been successful, notably at 3M, they are often treated as orphans, cut off from the very resources they need to succeed. Xerox, Eastman Kodak, and many other companies have had only modest success from their internal venturing and new business development programs.

One oft-quoted exception is the development of the IBM PC. IBM based the PC project in Boca Raton, a location that was farther from IBM's New York state headquarters than mere miles might indicate. The project was designated as an "independent business unit," with a direct reporting link to the chairman. All this allowed the PC team to crawl out from underneath IBM's suffocating blanket of corporate control and orthodoxy. The result was the speedy development of a new product that broke nearly every IBM rule. But there was a downside—a steep, slippery downside. The PC team didn't have direct access to IBM's substantial competencies in computer operating systems and semiconductors. Because these capabilities were locked up in IBM's traditional and hide-bound mainframe computer business, the PC team was compelled to turn to outside partners.

Microsoft and Intel profited mightily from the fact that IBM couldn't disentangle critical competencies from the old-line business in which they were buried. Today Microsoft and Intel are more IBM's competitors than its partners. The inability of the skunk works team to capture, reconfigure, and redeploy these capabilities meant that IBM was forced to concede much of the profit potential in the PC opportunity to its suppliers. Unfortunately, when the PC business was folded back into the traditional IBM structure, it lost much of its momentum, surrounded, as it was, by executives who saw PCs merely as "entry"-level systems (everyone's going to own a mainframe sooner or later) rather than an entirely new computing paradigm. So although a skunk works or intrapreneurial team can help a small group of people break out of the dominant managerial frame, the price they often pay for their freedom is an inability to fully leverage capabilities that reside elsewhere in the organization and are controlled by managers less eager to "boldly go where no one has gone before."

The goal of many new venture programs seems to be to create a greenhouse in which 1,000 flowers can bloom. But a lack of corporate conviction about the opportunities being pursued, and the inability of venture managers to access the firm's worldwide competence resources, give the greenhouse little more than six inches of headroom. Whereas new product "slush funds" and personal perseverance may be enough to create a new stand-alone product, such an approach is unlikely to propel a company into a complex systems business where the gestation period may be a decade or longer, and where critical resources may be spread across three or four divisions. There would seem to be almost an inherent contradiction between the need, on one hand, to protect new ventures from corporate orthodoxies, while at the same time ensuring that new business teams draw fully on the firm's stock of core competencies in creating fundamentally new markets. Yet a capacity to couple corporate imagination with access to worldwide resources, and to commit corporately to opportunities that, in their nascent stages, hardly seem worthy of top management attention, are all central to the capacity to create the future.

To create the future, an entire company, not just a few isolated boffins or "research fellows," must possess industry foresight. Top management cannot abdicate its responsibility for developing, articulating, and sharing a point of view about the future. What is needed are not just skunk works and intrapreneurs, but senior managers who can escape the orthodoxies of the corporation's current "concept of self."

THE FOUNDATIONS OF FORESIGHT

The obvious question at this point is where does industry foresight come from? Where do you find a crystal ball when they are in notoriously short supply? How is it possible to develop industry foresight when more and more industries seem to be in perpetual turmoil? How can one distinguish between foresight and fantasy? How is it possible to validate industry foresight when the future hasn't happened yet? The challenge in competing for industry foresight is to create hindsight in advance. This is not as impossible as it sounds. What prevents most companies from anticipating the future is not that the future is unknowable, though of course, in many respects it is, but that it is different. As Allen Kay, a pioneering researcher at Xerox's PARC facility, and now an Apple fellow puts it: "The future was predictable, but hardly anyone predicted it." The cues, weak signals, and trend lines that suggest how the future might be different are there for everyone to observe. There are little data critical to the development of industry foresight that are possessed by only one company.

How can it be, then, that so many companies fail to anticipate the future? What prevented DEC from seeing the opportunity for personal computers? Why did Canon see and commit to the opportunity for small, personal copiers rather than Xerox? How was it that an obscure Finnish company, Nokia, emerged as the number-two supplier of cellular telephones in the world, leaving European giants like Philips, Siemens, and Alcatel with mere crumbs? Why did the idea of combining pop art and timekeeping occur to the folks at Swatch rather than the top brass of Seiko or Citizen? How is it that, when facing the same set of environmental trends and conditions, some companies seem capable of weaving together a view of the future that is imaginative, compelling, and foresightful, and other companies seem merely confused?

Developing industry foresight requires more than good scenario planning or technology forecasting, though scenarios and forecasts are often useful building blocks. In competing for industry foresight the goal is not to develop contingency plans around a few "most likely" scenarios. In "unstructured" industries the number of future permutations are so multitudinous that any traditional scenario-planning process would be hard-pressed to represent the range of potential outcomes. Whereas scenario planning may be useful for considering the consequences of $50 per barrel of oil, it may not be much help finding the first five "killer applications" for interactive television or entirely new applications for genetic engineering. Scenario building and forecasting typically start with what is, and then project forward to what *might* happen. The quest for industry foresight often starts with what could be, and then works back to what *must* happen for that future to come about. It is this type of foresight that has been driving Motorola's commitment to satellite-based personal communicators. It is this type of foresight that underlay JVC's commitment to the VCR opportunity. It is this type of foresight that animates Bell Atlantic's view of a cornucopia of information, entertainment, and educational services made available to every home in its service area.

Industry foresight must be informed by deep insight into trends in lifestyles, technology, demographics, and geopolitics, but foresight rests as much on imagination as on prediction. To create the future a company must first be capable of imagining it. To create the future a company must first develop a powerful visual and verbal representation of what the future could be. To borrow from Walt Disney, what is required is "imagineering." Disney imagined an experimental city of tomorrow where run-down horse ranches existed. That dream became EPCOT—part of the world's number-one tourist destination. Interestingly, EDS, another foresightful company, hired Disney alumni to help the company put together an exhibit demonstrating how the information technology revolution will change the way we live and work in the next century. Motorola created a video presentation that brought its view of a "wireless" future to life. *The Daily Telegraph*, Britain's most-read quality newspaper, has put together a video representation of the newspaper of the future.

What is the secret to an enlarged sense of future possibilities? In our experience, industry foresight grows out of a childlike innocence about what could be and should be, out of a deep and boundless curiosity on the part of senior executives, and out of a willingness to speculate about issues where one is, as of yet, not an expert. Foresight is the product of eclecticism, of a liberal use of analogy and metaphor, of an inherent contrarianism, of being more than customer-led, and of a genuine empathy with human needs. We will consider each of these in turn, but we should first note that much of the future will be invisible to any firm that can't escape the myopia of its currently "served market" and the orthodoxy of current product or service concepts and existing price-performance relationships.

Escaping the Myopia of the Served Market

Many times what prevents companies from imagining the future and discovering new competitive space is not the unknowability of the future, but the fact that managers tend to look at the future through the narrow aperture of existing served markets. Thus, we often find that technical imagination in a company outstrips new product imagination, which, in turn, outstrips new business imagination. The result is substantially underleveraged technical and human resources.

If SKF saw itself only as a maker of roller bearings; if AMR, the parent of American Airlines, saw itself as only an airline operator; if Canon saw itself as no more than a manufacturer of cameras, copiers, fax machines, and printers; and if Motorola viewed itself as just a maker of cellular phones, mobile radios, and pagers, their view of future opportunities and threats would be severely truncated.

To successfully compete for the future a company must be capable of enlarging its *opportunity horizon*. This requires top management to conceive of the company as a portfolio of core competencies rather than a portfolio of individual business units. Business units are typically defined in terms of a specific product-market focus, whereas core competencies connote a broad class of customer benefits (e.g., "user friendliness" at Apple, "pocketability" at Sony, or "untethered communications" at Motorola). Canon has a camera business, a copier business, a printer business, and so on. But if Canon's view of itself is no more than a collection of market-facing SBUs, innovation will be limited to more cameras, more copiers, and more printers. Any company that defines itself in terms of a specific set of end product-markets ties its fate to the fate of those particular markets. Markets mature, but competencies evolve. Though Sony was one of the first companies in the world to apply solid-state electronics to AM radios, today it doesn't consider radios to be a big growth opportunity. On the other hand, Sony's competence in miniaturization, which had its roots in the pioneering use of transistors to produce pocket-sized radios, continues to be the wellspring for a rich stream of innovative new products. Though Honda had its start in the motorcycle business, it didn't tie its future to that particular business. Conceiving of itself as a world leader in engines and powertrains, Honda leveraged that competence into cars, lawn mowers, garden tractors, marine engines, and generators.

When one conceives of a company as a portfolio of competencies, a whole new range of potential opportunities typically opens up. We use the term *white spaces* to refer to opportunities that reside between or around existing product-based business definitions. One example of a white space opportunity was the video art tablet that Sony created for children. The art tablet is, in essence, a detuned workstation graphics pad. With it, kids can use a television as a virtual coloring book. Canon is another company where white space opportunities have taken the company far beyond its core camera business. The Canon *Handbook* attributes the company's success to its focus on core competencies. Success, it maintains, derives from the "synergistic management of the total . . . capabilities of the company, combining the full measure of Canon's know how in fine optics, precision mechanics, electronics and fine chemicals." While Canon searches for opportunities that leverage its core competencies and strong brand identity, it is not constrained in its search for new opportunities by existing business definitions.

The boundaries and definitions of a company's business units represent an administrative enactment of the firm's current industry view. But future opportunities are unlikely to correspond perfectly to today's business definitions. The risk, in the absence of a process for explicitly considering the shape of emerging opportunities, is that business unit managers end up mistaking the edge of their particular product-market "rut" for the outer limits of the opportunity horizon.

Most companies work hard to delineate precisely unit-by-unit ownership of existing market space, but shouldn't equal attention be given to assigning responsibility for white spaces? Too often white space opportunities are orphans. Eastman Kodak extended its opportunity horizon when it removed its traditional divisional blinkers and searched for markets that fell between, or more accurately, across its traditional competence areas of chemical imaging (film) and electronic imaging (copiers and so forth). One of the white space opportunities that emerged from this exercise was what insiders at Kodak referred to as an "electronic shoebox." Realizing that many family photographs sit in a shoebox, gathering dust in the attic, Kodak's chemical and electronic engineers dreamed of a medium that would allow customers to easily and safely store their photographs, view them on a standard television, and reorder and edit them at will. (Of course if people spent more time enjoying their photographs, they might buy more film, too!) The result was a process, available through photo developers, for turning chemical images on photographic film into electronic images that can be viewed via a video-CD player connected to a television—what Kodak calls "Photo-CD." The ultimate success of this product is less important than the lesson its managers learned about how a synthesis of skills residing in seemingly disparate businesses could be combined to create new competitive space.

Some companies, Sharp and Sony among them, have highly developed processes for exploring white space opportunities, and succeed in steadily pushing out their firm's opportunity horizon. Great pains are taken to ensure that both engineers and marketing staff have a good grasp of the range of competencies available to the company. Any employee who has an idea for a new business, be it the pocket organizer at Sharp or a CD-based book player at Sony, can make his or her case to the corporation and appeal for access to the firm's competence resources. If top management is convinced by the potential of the new product, it appoints a cross-company team that has the right to raid the company worldwide for the best resources (i.e., people).

Escaping the Myopia of the Current Product Concept

To see the future a company must be capable of escaping a narrow and orthodox view of "What business are we in?" and "What is our product or service?" Just as it is necessary to abstract away from business units to underlying core competencies, it is necessary to abstract away from traditional product and service definitions and focus on underlying functionalities.

Consider several examples of functionality thinking. Imagine that it's 1980 and a salesperson from a copier company is visiting a client—the manager of a big corporate duplicating department. Sitting in the midst of the company's copying facility, at five minutes to five in the evening, the salesperson sees a long queue of people lined up to use the one big copier open to individual use. Most of the people have only one or two copies to make, and are hoping to get them made before the copying center closes down for the night. What is the salesperson's interpretation of the "problem" of the impatient employees? Looking at the queue through the lens of the traditional product concept—a high-speed, high-priced, centrally located machine—the salesperson is likely to conclude that the client needs an even faster copier or, perhaps, a second copier. With an orthodox view of the product, it may never occur to the salesperson that what is really needed is a personal copier. What our mythical rep does know, from listening to the customer, is that approximately 25% of the people in the line are there to make "illicit" copies—of their car insurance claim, of their birth certificate, of a dog license, of just about anything. Being extremely customer-led, the salesperson reports back to headquarters that there's a need for a fail-safe security device that will help the manager stamp out illicit copying. So the company introduces copiers with "keys" and "codes" but, with its orthodox view of the product (something that sits in a sub-basement and costs $20,000) totally misses the bigger opportunity—personal copiers.

What's the functionality of a blackboard or flipchart? To share information, in real time, among a small group. But it is difficult to retrieve information off a blackboard or flipchart; neither can be put through a copying machine or stuffed in a briefcase. What's the solution? The obvious answer, if one conceives of the product in functionality terms, is an electronic whiteboard with a built-in scanner and copying system. It wasn't the blackboard manufacturers who came up with this idea, but Japan's Oki. Similarly, while many U.S. and European piano manufacturers have been dying a slow death—competing with Sega and Nintendo for the attention of nine-year-olds isn't easy—Yamaha reconceived pianos as keyboards, realized they could be made in a wide variety of sizes, coupled them with jazzy electronics, and launched a musical coup d'état on traditional piano makers.

Every product or service can be broken down into its functionality elements. Think of a record store. (They don't sell records anymore, but audio tapes, CDs, and videos.) Ask yourself, what is the difference between a good record store and a not-so-good one? The answer helps highlight the functionality elements of the store. In a good store there will be knowledgeable staff who can steer you to what's hot. Perhaps they'll even let you hear a sample of the music before you buy. The store will hold a large stock so you can find just what you want. The stock will be clearly laid out so you don't end up in opera when you want rhythm and blues. The price will be right, and the store will be located nearby.

Now imagine a world in which there is broad-band, two-way communication into the home. You can call up on a screen the top 1,000 or 10,000 pieces of music—song-by-song, symphony-by-symphony, aria-by-aria. You can read what the critics have said about the particular selection and listen to a 90-second sample to see if it suits your musical tastes. Once satisfied, you can have your chosen selections downloaded onto a digital recording device. At the end of the month, you get a bill. Take it a step further, and you can even imagine a "home juke box" where you could order up an evening's music—personally customized, of course—to accompany a 1960s rock-and-roll party, a romantic dinner for two, or a backyard Tex-Mex barbecue. The signal is scrambled so it can't be recorded, and you pay just for listening. Think what will happen to record stores as we know them—poof, they're gone!

Take a final example. It's entirely possible that in ten or fifteen years, the personal computer as we know it will be a relic. Having a PC at home is a hassle. Anyone who's had a hard drive crash, who's ever gotten a message that the computer doesn't have enough memory for a particular task, who's struggled with the byzantine installation procedures for a new piece of software or an expansion card, or who's worried about what would happen if a thief made off with the whole kit and caboodle in the middle of the night, knows that there are certain drawbacks to PCs. But what if there was an "information utility"? Instead of carrying an electronic organizer or cellular phone, one would carry an "InfoPort," a small device replete with a screen, telephone link, and data input device (stylus, keyboard, or microphone). The InfoPort would connect our happy user to his or her own small corner of the AT&T world, or British Telecom world, or Bell Atlantic world. In that little corner would reside all the user's files, quite safe from the neighborhood cat burglar, electrical surges, and other dangers. Anytime a new piece of application software was needed, it could be instantly accessed. Run out of hard disc space? No problem, more is immediately allocated. Instead of a finite and vulnerable PC, one has access to an almost infinite and much less vulnerable information utility. The example may be far-fetched, but any company that can't conceive of markets, both existing and potential, in functionality terms isn't likely to create the future.

One way to create the future is to wrap a traditional functionality in a fundamentally new delivery vehicle. One example is Yamaha's Disklavier, a digital reconception of old music roll pianos, which allows would-be Rubinsteins to hear a great pianist's performance, note for note and nuance for nuance. Other well-known functionalities that have been dressed up in new product clothing include Sharp's electronic organizers and automated teller machines. Further, one can add new functionalities to a well-worn product concept. Toto, a Japanese company, added biosensors and microprocessors to the lowly toilet. The result was an "intelligent" toilet that warms the seat, cleans and dries one's rear end, provides diagnostic medical information, keeps a record of the user's toilet habits and health, and can even relay a message to the doctor if something's seriously wrong. Finally, new space is created when an entirely new functionality is delivered via an entirely new product concept—for example, video games.

It is the marriage of core competence and functionality thinking that points a firm toward unexplored competitive space. It is core competence and functionality thinking that allows companies to move beyond what is to what could be.

Challenging Price-Performance Assumptions

Another way to escape orthodoxy is to challenge industry assumptions about price-performance trade-offs. A dramatic reduction in price can create a mass market where none existed. In 1979 Canon set itself the goal of producing a copier for $1,000. At the time Xerox's least expensive copier cost thousands more. A 200-strong design team coalesced around the challenge and the result was Canon's wildly successful line of "personal copiers."

In most companies, top management would never have had the courage to set such an ambitious target. Instead, developers would have been asked to "cost reduce" the current product concept. With a heroic price target, Canon engineers were encouraged to reconceive the product. The result was Canon's revolutionary cartridge-based toner system, a system that dramatically reduced the cost and complexity of producing the copier. It is interesting to speculate what result Canon engineers would have produced if they had been merely asked to "cost reduce" existing copier designs. With luck, they might have managed to bring the price down by 15 or 20%, but this wouldn't have been enough to open the potentially huge market for personal copiers. Other successful challenges to price-performance orthodoxy include the development of disposable 35mm cameras, Fidelity Investments' pioneering of mass market investment vehicles, and Virgin Atlantic's first-class airline seats priced at business-class rates.

Top management should ask itself, "What would happen to the shape and size of our markets if we could offer more or less the same functionality at 50% or even 90% off current price levels?"

JVC engineers saw the possibility of home video recording in a $50,000 Ampex machine. Toyota set itself outrageously ambitious goals in the development of the Lexus. U.S. car makers have seldom seemed interested in producing "the world's best car." "If it costs $3 billion per model to achieve mediocrity," they may well have asked themselves, "what would it cost for us to produce a world beater?" Taking a different tack, Mercedes-Benz focused on building the best car in the world—its S-class sedan—but ended up with a vehicle so expensive that only a millionaire could afford it. Toyota chose a third route. It set a specific price goal, one that would allow the company to undercut the price of German luxury cars, then worked backward from that to reinvent the very idea of a luxury car.

Lest Ye Be as Little Children . . .

Kids are naive. They don't know what's possible and what's impossible. So they ask innocent questions ("Why can't you touch the stars?") and hope for impossible things ("Why can't learning be fun?"). Adults are smart. They know what's possible and impossible. So they don't ask silly questions and they don't hope for impossible things. And they dismiss quizzical kids with a curt, "That's just the way it is." But anybody who really believes "that's just the way it is," anybody who is too lazy to ask, "Why couldn't it be different?" will never see the future. It is well known that personal creativity declines with age. As creativity falls, orthodoxy rises. The most precipitous fall in quizzicality takes place just after kids start school. (Every first grader knows that a dumb question gets you laughed at.) But occasionally a dumb question lifts the blinds of orthodoxy just long enough to let in a ray of light from the future.

Having watched her father snap a photograph, Dr. Edward Land's three-year-old daughter asked if she could see the results *right now*. This innocent question set Land off on a quest to create instant photography. Years later, at Polaroid, Land reflected that "we really don't invent new products . . . , the best ones are already there, only invisible, just waiting to be discovered."

Adults could equally well ask: Why can't one search a national video register of houses for sale when contemplating relocation? Why can't you see the person you're talking to on the telephone? Why can't manufactured materials match the strength, lightness, and flexibility of materials found in the animal kingdom? Why can't one simply replace a defective, disease-causing gene in a human being? Dumb questions like these are the keys that unlock new competitive space.

Nicolas Hayek, Swiss engineering consultant, asked a dumb question: Why couldn't Swiss watchmakers, with one of the world's highest-cost production bases, retake the "low end" of the watch market from Japanese competitors like Seiko and Citizen? By the early 1980s, the Swiss had virtually ceded that end of the watch business to the Japanese. Swiss companies had 0% of entry-level watches, 3% of medium-priced watches, and 97% of luxury timepieces. Essentially, they had been painted into a small, low-growth corner of the industry.

In 1985, Nicolas Hayek bought a controlling interest in the Swiss Corporation for Microelectronics and Watchmaking (SMH). The company had been formed two years earlier by a merger, on the advice of Hayek, between two of Switzerland's biggest watchmakers, both of which were insolvent at the time. The idea of the Swatch was born not out of careful financial analysis but a desire to rebuild the Swiss watch industry, a goal with obvious emotional appeal for any Swiss citizen or Europhile. With this as the goal, it was obvious that an inexpensive watch would have to be built around something Asian competitors couldn't easily duplicate—that something was a European sense of style and *savoir faire*. Initially, the banks were reluctant to lend money to the venture because they thought that it would be impossible for a Swiss company, operating in a high-cost labor environment, to compete successfully against Japanese rivals with low-cost Asian sourcing platforms. But Nicolas Hayek had a dream:

Everywhere children believe in dreams. And they ask the same question: Why? Why does something work a certain way? Why do we behave in certain ways? We ask ourselves those questions every day.

People may laugh—the CEO of a huge Swiss company talking about fantasy. But that's the real secret of what we've done.

Ten years ago, the people on the original Swatch team asked a crazy question: Why can't we design a striking, low-cost, high-quality watch and build it in Switzerland? The bankers were skeptical. A few suppliers refused to sell us parts. They said we would ruin the industry with this crazy product.[2]

Hayek's dumb question, "Why can't we compete with the Japanese?" needed a very smart answer. To produce a fashionable watch and sell it at an average price of $40, fundamental innovations were needed in design, manufacturing, and distribution. Swatch's highly innovative manufacturing process trimmed labor costs to less than 10% of manufacturing costs and to just about 1% of the retail price. Hayek boasted that the Swatch would turn a healthy profit even if Japanese workers donated their time for free. Swatch was not just a marketing innovation; it was a reconception of the entire Swiss watchmaking industry. The result: 25 million watches produced in 1992, a revitalized Swiss watchmaking industry, and incontestable proof that high European wage levels need not be a competitive death warrant. The examples of Polaroid and Swatch suggest that when it comes to creating the future, one wide-eyed innocent may be worth ten sophisticated scenario planners.

Developing a Deep and Boundless Curiosity

What makes the future difficult to anticipate is not that the future is inherently unknowable, but that the forces conspiring to produce the future often lie well outside top management's purview. To create the future of their industry, telecommunication executives have to learn something about how Hollywood works. To create the future of the cosmetics industry, its senior executives need to know more about pharmacology. To create the future of the video rental industry, managers may have to understand something about the arcane science of video compression. To create the future of publishing, its executives must learn about how individuals are using computer information services. To create the future of the construction industry, its bosses may need to comprehend the significance of virtual reality. Far-sighted corporate leaders may not be any better prognosticators than more short-sighted managers, but they are almost certainly more curious.

In one information technology company with which we work, we set up task teams to identify the dozen or so "discontinuities" that had the potential to dramatically reshape industry boundaries, customer expectations, price-performance relationships, delivery vehicles, value chains, and so on. One of the discontinuities identified was the role children would play in the development of information services in the future. At first, top management in this business-to-business, buttoned-down company was nonplussed by the suggestion that it should pay any attention to kids. But on further reflection it became obvious that the Nintendo/MTV generation might indeed have very different expectations about the form in which information should be presented, how "cuddly" and fun information should be, and how easy it should be to shape their own information environment. Unlike their parents, they might not be satisfied with information presented as strings of black and white text. And, of course, with the extension of information services into the home and the potential linking of home and school information technology systems, children might one day become a significant customer group. This insight sparked a concerted effort to gain a deeper understanding into the emerging expectations of the company's next generation of customers. The point here, and it's a crucial one, is that seeing the future first may be more about having a wide-angle lens than a crystal ball. In this particular example, the lens was widened to include kids.

Industry foresight requires a curiosity that is as deep as it is boundless. Gaining enough insight into potential discontinuities to actually draw conclusions about what to do—which alliances to form, how much to invest, what kind of people to hire—demands a significant expenditure of intellectual energy by senior management. The half-day or day-long planning review meetings that typically serve as forums to debate the future are totally inadequate if the goal is to build an assumption base about the future that is more prescient and better-founded than the competitors'.

Recently one of us spent a day with the top officers of a well-known U.S. company. The question put to these managers was simple: What are the forces already at work in this industry that have the potential to profoundly transform industry structure? A heated discussion followed, and a dozen discontinuities were identified. One of the potential drivers was picked at random, and the top team was asked, "Could you sustain a debate for a full day, among yourselves, about the implications of this trend to your company and the industry? Do you understand how fast this trend is emerging in different markets around the world, the specific technologies that are propelling it, the technology choices competitors are making, which companies are in the lead, who has the most to gain and the most to lose, the investment strategies of your competitors vis-à-vis this trend, and the variety of ways in which this trend may influence customer demands and needs?" The top team agreed that it simply didn't know enough about this critical driving force to answer these questions, and certainly couldn't keep a detailed, intelligent debate going for a full day. A few people suggested that these questions weren't really fair.

They were then asked, "Could you sustain a debate for eight hours on the issue of how you allocate corporate overheads, set sales targets, and manage transfer prices?" Now this was a fair question. "On this we could keep going for eight days, no sweat," replied a senior executive. Suddenly the point hit them: This group of managers was not in control of their company's destiny. They had surrendered control of that destiny to competitors who were willing to devote the time and intellectual energy necessary to understand and influence the forces shaping the future of the industry. The CEO's first response to this painful realization was typical: "I'll set up a couple of days when each of my divisional vice-presidents can come in and pitch their view of the future." Back came our argument: It takes more than two days to develop industry foresight; building foresight is not about "pitching" and "reviewing," but about exploring and learning. To really understand the future, to have the courage to commit, top management must get more than just a fleeting glimpse of the future. The required effort is measured in weeks and months, not in hours and days.

The outcome of this second painful realization was the establishment of a dozen or so "headlights" teams that worked for several months to refine and extend top management's initial list of industry drivers. The teams then proceeded to investigate each discontinuity in great depth. They sought answers to a variety of questions: How might this trend influence our current customers? How might it influence our current "economic engine"? What are the dynamics of this trend—how fast is it developing, and what are the factors that may accelerate or decelerate the trend? Who is moving to exploit this trend, or indeed, who is causing it—essentially, who is in the driver's seat, who is a passenger, and who is a bystander? Who has the most to lose and the most to gain from this discontinuity? What new opportunities—products or services—might be created by this discontinuity? What are our options for gaining further insight into this trend, influencing its direction and speed, or actually intercepting it? As tentative answers emerged, they were debated in marathon sessions involving business unit and corporate managers. At the conclusion of the exercise, top management felt confident that it had developed the most penetrating set of headlights in its industry. To see the future first, top management must have a curiosity that is as deep as it is broad.

Being Humble Enough to Speculate

To build industry foresight, senior management must be willing to move far beyond the issues on which it can claim expert status. It must admit that what it knows most about is the past. It must be willing to participate in debates about the future as equals, not as omnipotent judges. It must be willing to listen to voices in the company that are unconventional, that are less "experienced," and that raise questions for which there are no ready answers. Impatient, "results-oriented" senior executives must be willing to come back again and again to issues that are complex and seemingly indeterminable; they must be patient with open-ended discussions that yield no quick answers and produce no immediate decisions. They must recognize that building industry foresight is, at least initially, as much about discovering as deciding.

Take an issue that begs for thoughtful speculation: the impact of virtual reality (VR). Virtual reality is a technology with profound implications for almost every industry. VR is not about video games or cybersex, but about a capacity to model and simulate just about anything. VR is a powerful perceptual tool. Matsushita has used virtual reality to help people planning their dream kitchen "walk through" alternate layouts. NEC has experimented with a "virtual ski slope," where beginners can try out the sport. Virtual reality is used by physicists and chemists to climb inside complex molecular structures. Boeing is using virtual reality models in the development of new aircraft. As far-reaching as virtual reality's impact may be, how many senior teams have given any thought to how VR might influence their business? We were particularly pleased when the executive committee of one company we work with allowed itself to be led, by a 20-something savant, through an intellectually challenging series of meetings where the implications of VR were debated in depth. Concluding that it needed to better understand virtual reality, the top team set up an internal monitoring function to keep it informed of VR's development and suggest novel ways of exploiting the emerging technology.

Valuing Eclecticism

The future is to be found in the intersection of changes in technology, lifestyles, regulation, demographics, and geopolitics. For example, the opportunity for the "personal communicator," or "pocket office," being pursued by Apple, AT&T, Motorola, and several other companies lies at the juncture of lifestyle changes (incessant travel), technology changes (miniaturization, digitization, and digital compression), and regulatory changes (the freeing up of additional bandwidth). Yet it was Sharp that took an early lead in pocket organizers with its Wizard. As a Sharp executive recounted, "We saw that lifestyles were becoming busier. People had more information to manage." Introduced in 1988, and dismissed by competitors as a toy, sales amounted to $400 million in 1991.[3] Similarly, the opportunity that CNN found for global, 24-hour television news grew out of changes in lifestyle (ever longer and more unpredictable work hours), changes in technology (handicams and suitcase-size satellite link-ups), and changes in the regulatory environment (the licensing and growth of cable television companies).

Seeing the future first requires not only a wide-angle lens, it requires a multiplicity of lenses. Thus, any group charged with finding the future needs to encompass an eclectic mix of individual perspectives. No one functional group, no single geographic entity, and no one business unit can find the future on its own. Each is partially blind. Our experience suggests that companies possessed of extraordinary foresight are typically companies with rich cross-currents of interfunctional and international dialogue and debate. The future comes into view when technologists are imbued with marketing imagination and marketers have developed deep insights into technology trends; when product development staff located in one part of the world understands fully the implications of lifestyle trends on the other side of the globe; and when managers serving professional markets become familiar with the demands of consumer markets, and vice versa.

Companies that are functionally and geographically segregated are unlikely to discover the future. The goal is not just to put together multifunctional and multinational teams, but to create in every employee an eclectic set of perspectives, a set of interchangeable lenses. Sony pioneered a palmtop computer in Japan that could recognize written kanji characters. Where did the idea come from? A young Sony engineer, on a tour of duty in the United Kingdom, enviously noted the many ways in which British secretaries helped their bosses organize their time, prioritize their work, arrange meetings, and track down critical bits of information. Recognizing that personal secretaries were a somewhat rarer perquisite in his own and other Japanese companies, the young engineer came up with the idea of an "auxiliary brain" (perhaps not an altogether unflattering way of describing a secretary or administrative assistant). Thus was born Sony's palmtop computer and organizer, replete with character recognition software that allows the harried executive to write directly on the screen (in kanji) with a stylus.[4] The insight that led to this product was the result of that young engineer's eclectic experience base: a Japanese at work in Britain, an engineer looking at a problem through the customer's eyes.

Searching for Metaphors and Analogies

The future emerges at varying speeds and in different ways across different industries. Some industries (e.g., personal insurance) seem to be inherently less innovative than others (e.g., brokerage). Thus, it is often possible to steal a march on competitors simply by searching for applicable analogies from other industries. Let us share one with you that we tried out on a group of grocery retailing executives. Many people have a newspaper delivered to their home every day. This personalized service costs less than a dollar a day in most places. In nearly every U.S. city, of whatever size, a telephone call will bring a piping hot pizza to your door. Anyone wanting to order a piece of PC software can call an 800 number the afternoon of one day, and take delivery at home the next morning. In short, more and more services are available direct to your door. For $20 you can send a package across the country overnight. Why, we inquired of the grocery retailers, do we still have to fire up the car, fight traffic, hike across an expansive parking lot, search through miles of aisles, stand in a queue, and repeat the journey home to bring back a few loaves of bread, a jug of milk, and a couple of low-cal microwave dinners?

The average U.S. family spends $400 to $500 per month on groceries. Yet there is no other similar expense item that consumers can't get delivered to their homes. Why can't customers cruise through a virtual supermarket on a CD that is mailed out every month—just like they can cruise through a haunted house in a video game? Why can't consumers choose what they want and zap their order to the store's computer—like you can order airline tickets on CompuServe? Why can't consumers choose when the food should be delivered—the same way you specify when breakfast is to be brought to your hotel room? And come to think about it, why can't our electronic supermarket suggest a menu (for the kids' suppers this week, for an anniversary celebration, or for a dieter eager to shed a few pounds)? Why can't it produce a list of ingredients so you can order just what is needed? Why can't the darn thing make a wine recommendation as well? A supermarket executive's definition of "convenient" is 24-hour shopping and an express lane. That's not our idea of convenient!

Our example here draws on analogies from a variety of industries. It's really not much of a stretch to imagine the "supermarket" of the future, when so many other service industries have already moved far beyond supermarkets in the quest to make the customer's life easier. Of course, to create the supermarket of the future, one has to reconceive the very notion of what a supermarket is. A supermarket oriented to home delivery would need different physical facilities, a different information technology infrastructure, staff with different skills, a different location, and so on. We don't think home delivery will do away with the grocery store as we know it, but we bet some innovative retailer's going to make a lot of money "bringing the bacon home."

In setting goals for itself, General Magic, which aims to create a personal communicator replete with intelligent information "agents," has used the metaphor of a telephone. Says Bill Atkinson, one of the founders of General Magic:

> Imagine asking you today to stop using the telephone—never place another phone call. That's sobering, because it's probably more important than any other tool that you've got, more important than your personal computer. So here will be the measure of our success: What happens if I ask you ten years from now to stop using your personal communicator? The idea is that you will say, "This is core to how I live."[5]

In a very different context, executives in the insurance industry need to look to other areas of the financial services industry to understand the challenges they will confront over the next decade. They must seek to learn how other financial service companies have coped with and exploited the forces of consumerism, deregulation, disintermediation, commoditization, and so on. Executives who are alert to opportunities to learn from other industries, and who search for relevant analogies, often get a head start on the road to the future.

Oftentimes, one of the greatest difficulties in picturing the future is finding words to describe it. A metaphor based on something tangible and familiar can help describe something that is intangible and unfamiliar. "Knowledge navigator" and "personal digital assistant" are metaphors. They draw on familiar ideas—navigation, personal assistant—to describe unfamiliar product concepts. Not everyone is equally adept at thinking in terms of analogies and metaphors, but most people, if given a few examples, can come up with an idea that helps them span the chasm between what is and what could be.

Being a Contrarian

Companies that create the future are rebels. They're subversives. They break the rules. They're filled with people who take the other side of an issue just to spark a debate. In fact, they're probably filled with folks who didn't mind being sent to the principal's office once in a while. Foresight often comes not from being a better forecaster, but from being less hide-bound. Ted Turner was a contrarian—you don't need "superstar" news readers with their superstar salaries. Anita Roddick, founder of The Body Shop, was a contrarian. She believed, contrary to much of the cosmetics industry, that trying to seduce women into buying overpackaged, over-hyped, and overpriced cosmetics was an insult to their intelligence. Nicolas Hayek was a contrarian—you don't have to be based in Asia to make an affordable wristwatch.

Executives often like to believe that their industry is complicated and unique. On the other hand, we always tell senior managers, give us a couple of days to poke around your industry and we'll find the five or six fundamental conventions that underpin the industry. For many years, nearly every pharmaceutical company clung to the convention that drugmakers couldn't support innovative research without giant-sized margins. In the airline industry, conventional thinking held that a hub-and-spokes route structure was far superior to a point-to-point network. In banking, the convention was that customers were savers, rather than investors.

Once one discovers the conventions, then one can ask if there is any value in ignoring them. For example, Southwest Airlines became the most profitable in the United States by ignoring the hub-and-spokes convention. Contrarians find these conventions and use them as weapons against orthodox-ridden incumbents. To discover the future it is not necessary to be a seer, but it is absolutely vital to be unorthodox.

Beyond "Customer-Led"

It is much in vogue to be customer-led. From their bully pulpits, which today are likely to be worldwide satellite hook-ups, CEOs tell the troops that "everything begins with the customer." Companies claim to be reengineering their processes from the customer backward. Rewards and incentives are tied to measures of customer satisfaction. And it is almost impossible to check out of a hotel, pay for a restaurant meal, or hire a car without being asked to rate the vendor's customer service. While we are somewhat taken aback by the fact that some corporate leaders seem to find the idea of putting the customer first *novel*, we nonetheless applaud the sentiment and commend the ensuing effort. On the other hand, if the goal is to get to the future first, rather than merely preserving market share in existing businesses, a company must be much more than customer-led.

Customers are notoriously lacking in foresight. Ten or fifteen years ago, how many of us were asking for cellular telephones, fax machines and copiers at home, 24-hour discount brokerage accounts, multivalve automobile engines, video dial tone, compact disk players, cars with on-board navigation systems, hand-held global satellite positioning receivers, automated teller machines, MTV, or the Home Shopping Network? As Akio Morita, Sony's visionary leader puts it:

> Our plan is to lead the public with new products rather than ask them what kind of products they want. The public does not know what is possible, but we do. So instead of doing a lot of market research, we refine our thinking on a product and its use and try

to create a market for it by educating and communicating with the public.

The company's founder and honorary chairman, Masaru Ibuka, concurs, "Our emphasis has always been to make something out of nothing."[6]

One Detroit automaker introduced in 1991 a new compact that had been five years in development. The car's design and specifications grew out of the most intensive customer research ever carried out by the company. Yet when the car was launched, it turned out to be the perfect car to compete with the three-year-old models of Japanese competitors. The U.S. company was following its customers all right, but its customers were following more imaginative competitors. By way of contrast, Honda introduced in the early 1990s its mid-engined NSX sports car, a car that came close to matching the performance of a Ferrari but at a fraction of the price. In the print ad for the car, Honda claimed that the NSX was "not a car buyer's dream—no car buyer could have dreamt of this car." Instead, crowed Honda, the NSX is a "car maker's dream," which fulfilled the company's long-term ambition of producing a car that was both exotic and house-broken. Having achieved this goal, it is interesting to ask, who is Honda going to benchmark now? One gets the feeling that Honda is more interested in outpacing competitors than benchmarking them.

There are three kinds of companies. Companies that try to lead customers where they don't want to go (these are companies that find the idea of being customer-led an insight); companies that listen to customers and then respond to their articulated needs (needs that are probably already being satisfied by more foresightful competitors); and companies that lead customers where they want to go, but don't know it yet. Companies that create the future do more than satisfy customers, they constantly amaze them.

None of this is to argue that existing or potential customers can't play an important role in helping the firm stretch the boundaries of its current opportunity horizon. However, too often the questions asked of customers by market researchers—"Do you prefer a widget with a green strip or one with a red strip?"—provide little scope for fundamentally challenging traditional product concepts or creating real competitive differentiation. Although market research can be helpful in fine-tuning well-known product concepts to meet the demands of a particular class of customers (e.g., trying to discover just what diet cola formulation will appeal to European customers, which was the goal of researchers testing Pepsico's new Europe-targeted soft drink, Pepsi Max), it is seldom the spur for fundamentally new product concepts (such as IDV's Aqua-Libra, which created an entirely new category of sophisticated adult "health" drinks in Britain).

Listen to Hal Sperlich, the father of the minivan, who took the concept from Ford to Chrysler, when Ford balked at turning it into reality:

> [Ford] lacked confidence that a market existed, because the product didn't exist. The auto industry places great value on historical studies of market segments. Well, we couldn't prove that there was a market for the minivan because there was no historical segment to cite.
>
> In Detroit most product-development dollars are spent on modest improvements to existing products and most market research money is spent on studying what customers like among available products. In 10 years of developing the minivan we never once got a letter from a housewife asking us to invent one. To the sceptics, that proved there wasn't a market out there.[7]

Insights into new product possibilities may be garnered in many ways, all of which go beyond traditional modes of market research. Toshiba has a Lifestyle Research Institute; Sony explores "human science" with the same passion it pursues the leading edge of audiovisual technology. The insights gained allow these firms to answer two crucial questions: What range of benefits will customers value in tomorrow's products, and how might we, through innovation, preempt competitors in delivering those benefits to the marketplace? Yamaha gained insights into the unarticulated needs of musicians when it established a "listening-post" in London, chock full of the latest gee-whiz music technology. The facility offered some of Europe's most talented musicians a chance to experiment with the future of music making. The feedback helped Yamaha continually push out the boundaries of the competitive space it had staked out in the music business. Yamaha's experience illustrates an important point: To push out the boundaries of current product concepts, it is necessary to put the most advanced technology possible directly into the hands of the world's most sophisticated and demanding customers. Thus arose Yamaha's London market laboratory: Japan is still not the center of the world's pop music industry.

Being a perpetual follower is not the only risk from being customer-led. Being customer-led begs the whole question of who *are* my customers? As IBM, DEC, Xerox, and many other companies have learned, today's customers may not be tomorrow's. Folks buying Buick Roadmasters and Oldsmobile Ninety-Eights may be happy enough with GM service and quality, but if GM can't make a car that appeals to 30-something Benz and Bimmer owners, it will surrender its future. Recognizing this, GM has launched many self-proclaimed "import beaters," and its latest, the Oldsmobile Aurora, may finally prove to be a worthy contender. Although it is important to ask how satisfied my customers are, it is equally important to ask which customers are we not even serving. It was just this question that prompted Sony to introduce a line of products aimed at preschoolers. Branded "My First Sony," the brightly colored, simple-to-use radios, walkie-talkies, tape players, and video art tablets brought a whole new class of customers into Sony's catchment.

Think of a simple two-by-two matrix (see Figure 4-1). On one axis are needs—those that customers are capable of articulating and those that they can't yet articulate. On the other axis are classes of customer—those classes that the company currently serves and those that it doesn't. However well a company meets the articulated needs of current customers, it runs a great risk if it doesn't have a view of the needs customers can't yet articulate, but would love to have satisfied. And however content a company's existing customers may be, it may find its growth stymied if it can't reach out

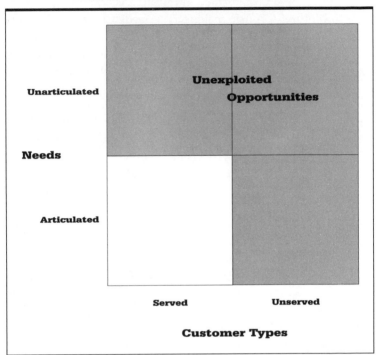

FIGURE 4-1 BEYOND "CUSTOMER-LED"

Unarticulated

Unexploited
Opportunities

Needs

Articulated

Served   Unserved

Customer Types

and appeal to fundamentally new customer groups. Any company that can do no more than respond to the articulated needs of existing customers will quickly become a laggard.

Empathizing with Human Needs
Industry foresight comes when senior executives in a company are able to empathize with basic human needs. When Raymond Smith, the chairman of Bell Atlantic, witnessed a demonstration of computer-based learning tools, he asked himself why those tools couldn't be made available to every kid in every classroom in the United States. Maybe Bell Atlantic will help provide an answer to that question. Cargill, a world leader in grain trading, constantly

asks itself what it can do to better meet the world's need for food. Companies that create the future are constantly striving to better the human condition. However exalted the role, and however generous the perquisites, corporate leaders must never lose the ability to identify with the individual stranded by a defective car, too busy to wait in a long bank queue, unable to "phone home" from a distant international locale, or trying to feed and clothe a family on a tightly stretched budget. If senior management isn't capable of empathizing with the needs of "ordinary" customers, it will be incapable of meeting those needs ahead of competitors.

To ensure that its product development staff empathize as fully as possible with potential customers, Honda matches the age of its design groups to the age of buyers targeted by a particular model. The youngest Honda car designers work on cars intended for young buyers. As designers age, they move along to cars oriented to older buyers. Again and again, Honda has worked hard to ensure that those charged with product development possess deep insights and real empathy for the customers they are seeking to serve. Robert Shook, the author of a book on Honda's American success,[8] provides a couple of illustrations.

> In the late 1960s, shortly after the company began manufacturing automobiles, Soichiro Honda announced that he wanted to make a "world car." To accomplish this, the company sent two teams of engineers to travel around the world to collect data about products and lifestyles of people in other countries. In conjunction with this program, Honda's R&D sent engineers to Europe to spend a full year there doing nothing but observing the relationship between the citizens of those countries and their automobiles. The engineers studied everything from road conditions to driving habits. Then they returned to Japan to report their findings. This information helped Honda to design the first Civic.
>
> A U.S. Honda design team, stalemated on a trunk design project, spent an afternoon in a Disneyland parking lot observing what people put into and took out of their car trunks and what kind of motion was involved. . . . Honda didn't hire an outside market research firm to provide stacks of data about trunk usage. They

took a more direct approach and ultimately came up with a new design.

One can only wonder how much insight car designers in Detroit have into the car driving habits of Japanese consumers, and how many have spent an afternoon in Tokyo's Disneyland doing first-hand customer research. The point is that many times the best foresight comes from deep-down customer insight—insight that comes from direct exposure to customers, not from second-hand market research.

The chairman of at least one European car maker has never bought a car in his life. Having joined his employer at a young age, this executive has never had to go through the experience of haggling with a dealer or taking a car in for service.[9] There is little chance that this manager can genuinely empathize with buyers who have to put up with poorly trained and poorly motivated dealer staff.

General Magic's ambition for its personal communicator is infused with human empathy:

> We have a dream of improving the lives of many millions of people by means of small, intimate life support systems that people carry with them everywhere. These systems will help people to organize their lives, to communicate with other people, and to access information of all kinds. They will be simple to use, and come in a wide range of models to fit every budget, need, and taste. They will change the way people live and communicate.[10]

As much as anything, foresight comes from really wanting to make a difference in people's lives.

Although potentially useful, technology forecasting, market research, scenario planning, and competitor analysis won't necessarily yield industry foresight. None of these tools compels senior management to reconceive the corporation and the industries in which it competes. Only by changing the lens through which the corporation is viewed (core competencies versus strategic business units), only by changing the lens through which markets are viewed (functionalities versus products), only by broadening the angle of the lens (becoming more inquisitive), only by cleaning off the accumulated grime on the lens (seeing with a child's eyes), only by peering through multiple lenses (eclecticism), and only by occasionally disbelieving what one actually sees (challenging price-performance conventions, thinking like a contrarian) can the future be anticipated.

The quest for industry foresight is the quest to visceralize what doesn't yet exist. The starting point is not the currently served market, but what Bob Galvin, the former chairman of Motorola, liked to term the "total imaginable market." Having imagined the future, a company must find a path that leads from today to tomorrow. Finding and mapping this path is the topic of the next chapter.

Crafting Strategic Architecture

. . . .

Not only must the future be imagined, it must be built; hence our term, "strategic architecture." An architect must be capable of dreaming of things not yet created—a cathedral where there is now only a dusty plain, or an elegant span across a chasm that hasn't yet been crossed. But an architect must also be capable of producing a blueprint for how to turn the dream into reality. An architect is both a dreamer and a draftsman. An architect marries art with structural engineering.

Every company has an information architecture (both hard-wired—the information technology infrastructure, and soft-wired—the prevailing patterns of interpersonal and interunit communication). To design an information architecture a company must agree on who should communicate with whom on what issues, how often, and in what ways. Every company has a social architecture (generally accepted standards of behavior and implicit hierarchy of values). To create a social architecture senior management must have a point of view on what values should predominate, what behaviors should be encouraged, and what kind of people should feel comfortable working in the company. Every company has a financial architecture (a particular structuring of the balance sheet, a financial-reporting process, and a capital-budgeting process). To build a financial architecture top management must have a point of view on the ideal balance of debt and equity, on how to finance acquisitions and disposals, on the criteria for making capital allocations, and so on.

We also believe that every company needs a strategic architecture. To build a strategic architecture top management must have a point of view on which new benefits, or "functionalities," will be offered customers over the next decade or so, on what new core competencies will be needed to create those benefits, and on how the customer interface will need to change to allow customers to access those benefits most effectively.

Strategic architecture is basically a high-level blueprint for the deployment of new functionalities, the acquisition of new competencies or the migration of existing competencies, and the reconfiguring of the interface with customers. For example, a textbook publisher that is alert to technology trends and is imaginative enough to envision their potential impact might dream of an "electronic textbook" that would one day allow teachers to customize their teaching materials to the unique interests and abilities of their students. To turn this dream into reality, the publisher must determine which competencies will have to be accessed, acquired, or strengthened to deliver the "customizable" functionality. To this end, the publisher may well have to learn more about multimedia technology, may have to develop automated textbook design tools for teachers, and may need to invest in new communication technologies. The publisher may also have to rethink how it takes textbooks to market: Will the identity of the purchaser change (school district versus school versus teacher)? What kind of selling tools will be needed? What kind of training will teachers need? Will the publisher need a physical distribution structure or only an electronic one?

Countries can have strategic architectures, too. Singapore's Economic Development Board has crafted a strategic architecture, laying out the national competencies to be developed to propel Singapore to the next level of industrial development. One senior EDB official in Singapore expressed his country's ambition as US = 2010, that is, matching U.S. per capita income levels by the year 2010.

Strategic architecture is not a detailed plan. It identifies the major capabilities to be built, but doesn't specify exactly how they are to be built. It shows the relative position of the major load-bearing structures, but not the placement of every electrical outlet and doorknob. Try a cartographic analogy: Strategic architecture is a high-level map of interstate highways, not a detailed map of city streets. It is specific enough to provide a general sense of direction, but doesn't detail every side street along the way. Imagine a couple of MBA students heading from London to Paris, by car and ferry, for a summer vacation. Their goal is to enjoy a sybaritic fortnight in the City of Lights. They are content to start the journey without having a detailed street map of their destination city; they'll get a map of Paris once they arrive. For now, it is enough to know that they have to head southwest toward Dover. They know the M20 runs toward Dover, so off they go. (Of course, they will have to figure out the precise routing from their apartment in central London to the relevant highway.) They know they will leave the ferry at Calais, but they can't know in advance the exact routing from the ferry terminal, through the streets of Calais, to the freeway that will take them toward Paris. This will all become clear once they get to Calais. Equally, our Francophile students know that they can't get to Paris on one tank of gas, but again they set off without knowing the precise location of every gas station between London and Paris. They will have to find these as they go.

Creating a detailed plan for a ten- or fifteen-year competitive quest is impossible. Planning assumes a degree of exactitude (which price points, which channels, where to source from, what merchandising strategy, what exact product features) that is impossible to achieve when one looks out beyond the next two to three years. Insisting on such exactitude before embarking on a new strategic direction is a recipe for inertia and incrementalism. Luckily, it is possible to create a broad agenda for functionality deployment and competence acquisition.

Komatsu long pursued a goal of "encircling" Caterpillar. In the mid-1960s, as Caterpillar entered Komatsu's home market, it would have been possible for Komatsu to identify the major hurdles it would have to overcome in pursuit of its ambitious goal. Clearly the first step had to be to improve the quality of Komatsu's line of small bulldozers. These products were the foundation of the company's product line in Japan, and unless Komatsu protected its base business from Caterpillar's encroachment, any further ambitions would be pure fantasy. It was also apparent that Komatsu would have to intercept Caterpillar's technology. Licensing arrangements with Cat's competitors were a short-cut to that end. Komatsu could also have concluded early on that, unless it captured a significant share of export markets, it would never have the volume necessary to match Cat's scale of manufacturing and R&D investment. Equally, it would have been clear to Komatsu that to challenge prematurely Cat head-on in sophisticated export markets like Europe and Australia would have been foolhardy. Hence Komatsu could have recognized a need to build up volumes first in markets where Cat was less of a threat, namely, in China and the countries of what was then the East Bloc. Of course, Komatsu's ultimate goal was still to gain a share of European and U.S. markets. To do this Komatsu would need a dealer network. To win over dealers, Komatsu would have to have a broad product line, so product development would be the next challenge. Raising quality, with an initial objective of protecting the home market; using Caterpillar's U.S. competitors to catch up with Cat's technology lead; capturing volume in export markets Caterpillar considered "peripheral"; and expanding the product line in anticipation of an assault on more sophisticated markets were major landmarks Komatsu could have seen from miles—or years—away. Not only could Komatsu have anticipated the broad competence-building agenda it needed to compete with Caterpillar, it could also have formed a logical judgment about the order in which those competencies would have to be built.

We often come across companies that have set an ambitious long-term goal, perhaps to double revenue and profits over five years, or to dramatically increase the proportion of revenues coming from new businesses, but have devoted almost no intellectual effort to thinking through the medium-term capability-building program that is needed to support that goal. In too many companies there is a grand, and overly vague, long-term goal on one hand ("Let's take a vacation" rather than "Let's go to *Paris*"), and detailed short-term budgets and annual plans on the other hand ("What route should I take home tonight, given the massive traffic jam along my usual route?"), with nothing in between to link the two together ("I need to schedule some time off and call my travel agent, and I need to read some guide books"). There seems to be, in many companies, an implicit assumption that the short term and long term abut each other, rather than being dovetailed together. But the long term doesn't start at year five of the current strategic plan. It starts right now! For example, though it will be many years before every man, woman, and child carries around a personal communicator, any company that is not working hard to extend its radio, digital, miniaturization, display, and battery competencies won't have much of a share in that particular future. Any company that says, "We'll hold off on this until it gets to be a significant market," is doomed to followership.

A strategic architecture identifies "what we must be doing right now" to intercept the future. A strategic architecture is the essential link between today and tomorrow, between short term and long term. It shows the organization what competencies it must begin building *right now,* what new customer groups it must begin to understand *right now,* what new channels it should be exploring *right now,* what new development priorities it should be pursuing *right now* to intercept the future. Strategic architecture is a broad *opportunity approach* plan. The question addressed by a strategic architecture is not what we must do to maximize our revenues or share in an existing product market, but what must we do today, in terms of competence acquisition, to prepare ourselves to capture a significant share of the future revenues in an emerging opportunity arena.

One of our favorite examples of a strategic architecture comes from the Japanese electronics company, NEC. Though NEC has recently been pummeled by the forces that are reshaping the world's computer and telecommunications industry, a strategic architecture the company assembled in the early 1970s helped turn the company into one of the world's global technology leaders. Initially a supplier of telecommunications equipment to NTT (Japan's equivalent of AT&T), NEC executives, under the leadership of Chairman Kobayashi, began to sense, in the late 1960s and early 1970s, that the communications industry and computer industry were converging in some important ways. Telecommunications, which had always been a "systems" business (telephones are tied together across the globe), was also becoming a "digital" business (telephone switches were becoming more and more like mainframe computers, based on semiconductors and complex system software). At the same time the computer business, which had always been digital, has become a complex systems business (companies wanted computers located in offices and factories around the world to be linked together in seamless data networks).

Starting with an understanding of these two industry discontinuities—systemization and digitalization—NEC built a strategic architecture that identified the competencies it would need to be able to exploit the opportunities that would emerge at the juncture of the computing and communications industries (see Figure 5-1). NEC's strategic architecture identified three interrelated streams of technological and market evolution. Computing would evolve from large mainframes to distributed processing (what is now called "client-server"), components would evolve from simple integrated circuits (ICs) to ultra large-scale ICs, and communications would evolve from mechanical cross-bar switching to complex digital systems. As this evolution took place, so NEC's thinking went, the computing, communications, and components businesses would begin to overlap in important ways (e.g., private corporate networks would need to handle voice, data, and image traffic simultaneously). NEC's ambition was to be a leader in "C&C," computing and communications.

While today one might be tempted to say "What's new?" about C&C, it represented a significant amount of foresight in 1977, when NEC first publicly articulated its strategic architecture.[1] Other companies, like GTE in the United States or the General Electric Co. in the United Kingdom, as equally well positioned as NEC in the early 1970s, lacked NEC's foresight and lost the opportunity to be leaders in C&C. Why would NEC publish its view of the future in its annual report—shouldn't strategic architecture be secret? Strategic architecture is of little value if it is not widely debated

FIGURE 5-1 NEC'S C&C

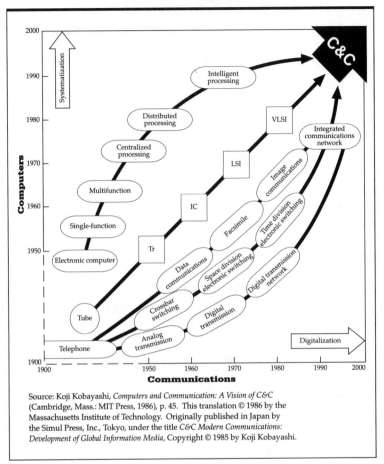

Source: Koji Kobayashi, *Computers and Communication: A Vision of C&C* (Cambridge, Mass.: MIT Press, 1986), p. 45. This translation © 1986 by the Massachusetts Institute of Technology. Originally published in Japan by the Simul Press, Inc., Tokyo, under the title *C&C Modern Communications: Development of Global Information Media*, Copyright © 1985 by Koji Kobayashi.

and ultimately understood by all employees. So keeping it secret is impractical. What appears in the annual report is a small fraction of the underlying thinking that went into the development of the architecture. The broad strategic architecture does not convey the particular meaning NEC attached to the terms and concepts used to lay out the map; nor does it reveal the breadth and depth of organizational consensus that was built around the concept of

C&C. The real value of the strategic architecture wasn't the uniqueness of the competence acquisition map, but the depth and consistency of corporate understanding that lay beneath it. NEC's strategic architecture, as described to outsiders, provided little insight into the unique operational meaning that C&C had for each NEC employee. Only when one asked employees across the company, "What does C&C mean?" and came away with a consistent and well-elaborated view, did one know that there was more going on than elegant conceptualizing.

Consistent with its strategic architecture, NEC worked unceasingly to strengthen its position in components (semiconductors) and central processors. Using collaborative arrangements to multiply internal resources, NEC was able to accumulate the necessary core competencies while investing less in R&D (both as a percentage of sales and in absolute dollars) than most of its major competitors. Our analysis of more than 100 such arrangements established by NEC between 1965 and 1987 demonstrated a remarkable consistency between the goals of each joint venture, alliance, or licensing deal and the overall logic of NEC's strategic architecture. In communications, where the company had strength, NEC's alliances were primarily oriented toward market access. In the computer field, its alliances focused on both technology and market access. Almost all the collaborative agreements in the component field were aimed at technology access. NEC's eagerness to learn from partners sometimes led to tensions and lawsuits, as in its relationship with Intel. Had NEC's partners understood how committed NEC was to its C&C goal, and the single-mindedness with which NEC pursued its competence-building agenda, some of them might have been a bit more reluctant to give NEC a helping hand.

Initially just a telecommunications equipment provider, NEC had sales of $3.8 billion in 1980, compared to IBM's $26.2 billion. By 1992 NEC was a global electronics powerhouse with $30.6 billion in sales. Even in the recession of the early 1990s and the disintegration of the computer industry, NEC could claim to be the only company in the world still among the top five computing, semiconductors, and telecommunications firms.

CREATING A STRATEGIC ARCHITECTURE

A strategic architecture doesn't last forever. Sooner or later "tomorrow" becomes "today," and yesterday's foresight becomes today's conventional wisdom. For NEC to prosper in the 1990s and beyond, it must invest anew in creating a prescient view of the future. One company that has done so is Hewlett-Packard. Interestingly, its strategic architecture builds on NEC's notion of C&C.

Hewlett-Packard has long been one of the most-admired U.S. companies. It is an entrepreneurial firm in which individual businesses have traditionally enjoyed substantial freedom and unit managers have jealously guarded their independence. It is also a company with a good measure of foresight. HP was one of the first companies to commit to reduced instruction set computing (RISC), a radically different paradigm for microprocessor design that supercharged its workstation sales. Foreseeing the rapid spread of personal computers, HP committed itself to becoming a leader in computer printers in the early 1980s. By 1993 it was closing in on $5 billion in annual revenues. As a result, HP was able to avoid much of the painful restructuring and downsizing that was the lot of its less prescient competitors.

Yet in the early 1990s, a few top HP managers began worrying that many of the new opportunities in the digital industry might fall between the cracks of HP's three autonomous sectors—computer systems, computer products, and test and measurement. Worse, some important competencies were becoming imprisoned within specific businesses, and the company was missing opportunities to create fundamentally new markets, particularly in the area of telecommunications. It was particularly clear to Joel S. Birnbaum, the director of HP labs, that HP needed to ask itself, "Given our unique portfolio of competencies as a corporation, what can we do better than anyone else in the world?" No other company in the world had HP's particular blend of computing, communications, and measurement competencies. He pressed his colleagues by asking, "What new opportunities lie at the juncture of these three capabilities?"

Slowly, Hewlett-Packard began to reconceive its sense of identity. It ultimately summarized itself as $HP = MC^2$, where M stands for measurement, and the two Cs stand for computing and communications. Early in 1993 HP's CEO, Lewis E. Platt, formed an $HP = MC^2$ Council, composed of top technical and marketing people from across the company. Its goal: to identify new multibillion dollar opportunities that would draw on the full range of HP competencies and would, in Platt's words, "turn markets upside down."[2] So far, the effort has produced a substantial menu of market-creating products. One is remote medical diagnostics. Marrying its medical instruments expertise with its computer skills, HP envisions a future when patients at home can be monitored by a physician miles away. Another idea is a home video printer that would allow couch potatoes to capture permanently any video image—be it product information on a home shopping channel or baby's first steps—from the camcorder.

Hewlett-Packard's first steps toward the future of MC^2 have been small but purposeful. It overhauled one of the company's oldest divisions, a maker of microwave components, and renamed it the Video Communications Division. It won a contract to supply Ford dealers with a diagnostic system that uses an innovative "flight recorder" to analyze car problems. It started supplying television set top controllers to a company experimenting with interactive television, and $300 color printers to another experimental television project. Each project cut across the business unit boundaries that traditionally defined and limited HP's view of its opportunities. The company also formed a cross-sectoral telecommunications committee to work for and coordinate HP's "cut-across" opportunities to develop innovative new products for telecommunications clients. As one senior executive put it, "HP's going to be an almost totally different company ten years from now."[3]

Another company that has been working hard to reinvent its industry and regenerate its strategy is Electronic Data Systems,[4] based in Dallas, Texas. EDS is one of a new breed of information technologies companies that have been remaking the information technology industry. With $8.2 billion in sales in 1992, EDS helps large corporations manage their enormously complex data and voice networks. For many of its customers, EDS has proven to be the Excedrin that relieves top management of its data-processing headaches. To support its business EDS built a worldwide infrastructure of mainframe-based information-processing centers. This network was enlarged dramatically when, in 1984, GM bought EDS and asked the company to take over all of GM's worldwide computer and telecommunication operations. By 1993 the company had more than 70,000 employees serving more than 8,000 customers in 31 countries. EDS owned and operated the world's largest private network, with more than 8,500 mips (millions of instructions per second) of computing power, 350,000 desktop computers, and 240,000 telephones. On any given day EDS handled more than 42.8 million computer transactions on behalf of its far-flung clients.

In 1992 EDS recorded its thirtieth consecutive year of record earnings. Looking forward to the ever-growing demand for outsourcing of computer services, EDS expected to be at least a $25 billion company by the year 2000. To most industry observers, EDS's position seemed unassailable. Yet in 1991, EDS had quietly launched a major exercise to reinvent the company and its industry. With its enviable track record, EDS seemed an unlikely candidate for a corporate renewal effort. But that success was exactly what made Les Alberthal, EDS's quiet-spoken chairman, nervous. He was keenly aware that whatever a company's past triumphs, future success is far from inevitable. In fact, he had asked one of his staff to calculate how many of the *Fortune* 500 companies in 1970 still existed in the same form in 1991. The answer—less than 40%—disturbed him. In 1990 Mr. Alberthal invited one of us to address the company's top officers, known collectively as the "Leadership Council," while they were visiting the United Kingdom. The subject of the presentation was "Why great companies surrender leadership." The top team was asked to consider the factors that undermine the success of industry leaders. As the EDS executives quietly pondered the antecedents of failure (Figure 5-2), they concluded that EDS was no more immune from "great company disease" than any other successful enterprise. Collectively they committed themselves to rebuilding industry leadership for the 1990s and beyond.

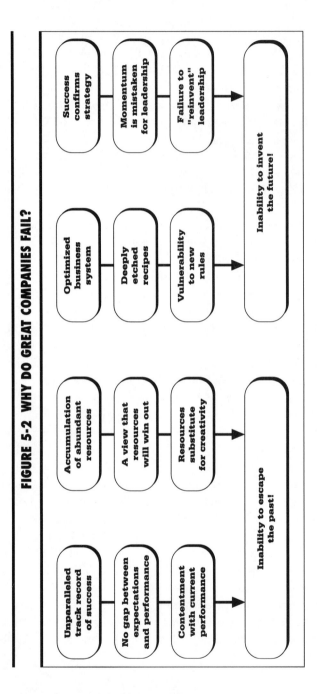

FIGURE 5-2 WHY DO GREAT COMPANIES FAIL?

Unparalleled track record of success

No gap between expectations and performance

Contentment with current performance

Inability to escape the past!

Accumulation of abundant resources

A view that resources will win out

Resources substitute for creativity

Optimized business system

Deeply etched recipes

Vulnerability to new rules

Inability to invent the future!

Success confirms strategy

Momentum is mistaken for leadership

Failure to "reinvent" leadership

While EDS was very profitable in 1992, there were a few warning lights blinking on the instrument panel. Margins in the outsourcing industry were under immense pressure from new competitors. Every major computer company, from IBM to DEC to UNISYS, concerned about yielding the high ground to EDS, was bent on entering the outsourcing business. Unconventional competitors like Andersen Consulting were increasingly successful in competing with EDS for big systems integration contracts, even though none of these competitors could match EDS's global information infrastructure. Some of the new competitors helped clients define their future information technology (IT) needs through high-level strategy consulting skills—skills in short supply at EDS. Customers were also becoming more sophisticated in their use of information technology. They knew that the price of computing power was on a steep downward slope and demanded hefty discounts in the outyears of long-term service contracts. It was costing EDS more to win deals. It was also getting harder to find customers among the ranks of U.S. leading-edge information technology users. Companies like AMR (American Airlines' parent), Federal Express, and Wal-Mart knew that information technology was central to the creation of competitive advantage in their industries, and they weren't willing to cede control to an outsider. In fact, many of these companies were setting up subsidiaries to sell *their* IT expertise. It was also becoming clear that, while the majority of computing power in the past had been located in central, mainframe-based data-processing facilities (a computing environment EDS well understood), the future of computing would be driven off the desktop. Looking further out, they realized that much of the world's computing power, and many of the most exciting new information network services, would focus on the home.

In 1990 EDS was a business-to-business company, heavily dependent on mainframe technology, not too interested in pursuing anything other than the next big megadeal, and largely uninvolved in consumer applications of IT. With its major business units defined in terms of the industries they served, the company had a reputation for being extremely responsive to customer's needs. Its development agenda, however, was driven more by the articulated needs of today's customers than by any particular foresight about the future of the information technology industry. Considering the exciting array of information-intensive industries visible on the horizon, some in EDS wondered if the company's conception of itself would be broad enough to encompass these new opportunities.

A few EDS executives were also concerned by the fact that revenue per employee, a broad measure of value added, which had coursed steadily upward for several decades, had recently gone flat, and in inflation-adjusted terms, had actually declined slightly. While EDS's economic engine still had a lot of miles left in it, it was clear that that engine might not be quite as efficient in producing profits in the future as it had been in the past. As one EDS executive put it, "Sometimes trying to tune up the old engine is like putting lipstick on a pig!" None of this suggested that EDS was a sick company. In fact, the only reason the story is worth telling here is because EDS realized that it needed to begin to regenerate its core strategies while it was still at the peak of its prosperity. That conviction was born out of a sense of opportunity, as much as a sense of anxiety.

Having returned from a short executive course at the London Business School, a small band of EDS managers, none of them yet corporate officers, set themselves up as the "corporate change team," and began meeting regularly. Despite the lack of an official charter, they were convinced that the company needed to rethink corporate direction, raise its aspirations, and develop a supporting strategic architecture. The team's first inclination, like that of the Leadership Council, was to hole up for a few days and crank out the company's new vision. Yet it soon realized that what was needed was not the product of "a few great minds in a small room," but a top-to-bottom challenge of the company's deepest assumptions about "who we are and what we do." It also realized that the task of developing a broad, deep, and foresightful view of EDS's future would require far more resources, both temporal and intellectual, than could be mustered by one small team. Accordingly it began to create the same sense of urgency it felt among a broader group of peers.

After much debate and dialogue with the Leadership Council, the corporate change team agreed on an approach to corporate renewal. One hundred and fifty EDS managers, from across the company and around the world, came to Dallas, thirty at a time, to begin the process of creating the future. They were the company's key "resource holders" as well as less senior managers who were known to be challenging, bright, and unconventional. The first step was to give these managers the intellectual tools needed to think about the future (what are core competencies, what is the basis for resource leverage, how can one discover the unarticulated needs of customers, and so forth). The objective was to demonstrate that getting to the future first is more about foresight and consistency than patient money and a propensity for risk taking. As each of the five "waves" joined the process, its members were asked to consider in detail the threats to the current economic engine and the new opportunities afforded by the "digital revolution." The goal was to create in these individuals the same blend of concern and hope that animated the efforts of the change team.

Each wave was given a "discovery assignment." The first wave dug deeply into the discontinuities that EDS might be able to use as levers to change the shape of the industry. The second and third waves tried to develop a view of the company's competencies that was substantially independent from the current definitions of "served market." Then they benchmarked those competencies against EDS's best "competence competitors." They also considered carefully the work of wave one: what new competencies EDS might need to build and how it might have to reconfigure existing competencies to grab hold of the levers of industry change. Drawing on the work of the previous waves, wave four pushed out the company's opportunity horizon. What were the "white space" opportunities that lay between the company's existing business units? What were the new information-intensive industries the company might wish to participate in? Wave five considered how to align company resources to give more impetus to competence building and opportunity management.

Wave participants involved their direct reports in the discovery process. Each wave appointed a few "linking pins" responsible for integrating the wave's work with that of the other waves. Change team members acted as coaches to each wave. The output of every wave was thoroughly debated by the other waves and with the Leadership Council. Finally, an "integration team," made up of some of the more "convergent thinkers" across the waves, boiled the work down to its essence and produced a draft strategic architecture that again was widely debated in the company.

The discovery process was full of frustrations, surprises, unexpected insights, and missed deadlines. It was recursive; answers were discovered by successive approximation. In the end, more than 2,000 persons participated in the creation of the company's new strategic architecture. Across the company nearly 30,000 person-hours were devoted to what was truly a high-involvement, high-drama exercise. (More than a third of the time investment was made outside normal business hours.) Most important, EDS had a view of its industry and its role that was substantially broader, more creative, and more prescient than it had been 12 months earlier. And it was not a view held by a few technical "gurus" or corporate "visionaries." It was a perspective and ambition shared by every senior EDS manager. Indeed, those who participated in the process thought it had contributed as much to leadership development as it had to strategy development.

To an outsider, EDS's strategic architecture appears deceptively simple. It is captured in three words: globalize, informationalize, and individualize. But it is more than a slogan; EDSers believe that these three words describe the "edges" of their "industry envelope." *Globalize* implies an ability to use information technology to span geographical, cultural, and organizational boundaries. *Informationalize* implies helping customers convert data into information, information into knowledge, and knowledge into effective action. *Individualize* refers to the mass customization of information services and products by and for individuals. EDSers think of this as "ize" on the future. They believe that any company that pushes the edges of the envelope faster than competitors is likely to be the "defining entity" in the industry.

EDS has a point of view on what new competencies will be required to push the envelope out along each of these dimensions.

It also envisions the new opportunities to be found in the interstices of globalize, individualize, and informationalize. EDS has made substantial progress in genetic reengineering; it is now busy on industry reengineering, including a series of trial projects, joint ventures, and experiments that would have been inconceivable a few years ago. Typical is EDS's deal with Spectradyne, which provides in-room movies to hotels. EDS will help the company convert to a digital system where movies will be plucked off of satellites. With US West and France Telecom, EDS is exploring the potential for interactive home banking. And in a deal with Apple Computer, EDS is hoping to put catalogs on CD-ROM so customers can browse at will and order from L.L. Bean, Tiffany & Co., or some other retailer over a computer network.[5] Although to outsiders the deals may appear unrelated, and although each is small in terms of investment and immediate revenue impact, insiders herald the deals as the beginnings of a new EDS. If EDS follows through on its strategic architecture it will be a very different company in ten years.

The ultimate test of whether a company has a strategic architecture is not fat notebooks full of graphs and matrices. The ultimate test is asking a random sample of 25 senior managers, "How will the future of your industry be different?" and comparing the answers. Try this in your own company. Ask a couple dozen senior managers to summarize the most important changes on a single sheet of paper. Give them a week or a month to formulate their answers. Don't tell them what you mean by "industry" or how far out the "future" is.

Pull together the answers and do a bit of content analysis. First, how did they interpret the word *future*? Did it mean next year, year five of the plan, or a decade hence? In other words, how far out do the headlights of your management team shine? How much foresight does it actually have? Second, how encompassing is its view of the future? How broad is its conception of the industry and of the forces that might reshape it? Is the team trapped in the myopia of currently served markets, or does it see a broad vista of new opportunities? Third, how competitively unique is its view of the future? Would it surprise competitors or provoke a yawn?

Fourth, what degree of consensus exists about how the future might be different? Without a fair degree of consensus, it's easy to spend money on everything, but not really commit to anything. And fifth, have the implications of potential industry changes been considered in enough detail so the short-term implications for action are clear? Is there agreement on what, precisely, must be done this year to prepare for the future? Are competence acquisition strategies and opportunity approach strategies in place? Foresight, breadth, uniqueness, consensus, and actionability—these are the criteria by which we judge whether a company really possesses a strategic architecture—whether it's really in control of its destiny.

COMMITTING TO THE FUTURE

EDS is committed to harnessing the forces of globalization, knowledge creation, and customization for the benefits of its current and future customers. In the same way, NEC was committed to the convergence of computing and communications. But commitment doesn't necessarily imply huge investments and bet-the-company risk-taking. IBM dropped a bundle with its failed Satellite Business Systems venture in the late 1970s, and then again on its acquisition and sale of Rolm in the late 1980s and early 1990s. AT&T lost millions trying to get into the computer business before it gave up and bought NCR. Coming from a starting point vastly inferior to that of AT&T or IBM, NEC made more progress in exploiting the C&C convergence while spending less. This illustrates an important point about competing for the future: The further out one is looking, the more careful one should be in making large, irreversible resource commitments. Whereas the broad direction of an industry's future evolution may be predictable, the precise routes along which it will evolve in terms of technology, standards, specific products, and services cannot be fully anticipated.

Getting to the future is a process of successive approximation. Just as there is a great risk in underspecifying the future—a company content with a vague and underdeveloped point of view about the size and shape of emerging opportunity arenas will find itself preempted by more clear-sighted competitors—so too is there a great risk in overspecifying the future—a company that fails to recognize the limits to what can actually be known about the future is likely to race off in the wrong direction.

Imagine having a foot on each of two parallel ladders—one ladder is called investment, the other industry foresight. The goal in competing for the future is to make sure that each foot never gets more than a rung or two above the other. As additional insight into the best route to the opportunity is gained, investment commitments are escalated. If the foot on the investment ladder gets many rungs higher than the foot on the insight ladder, a fall (misdirected investment) is as likely as it would be if the foot on an understanding ladder got too far ahead of the foot on a commitment ladder (being preempted by a competitor).

Too many companies, driven by an initial burst of enthusiasm, take a giant leap into the unknown and find themselves hurtling over a cliff. Not surprisingly, having taken a bad fall, managers are not enthusiastic about future opportunities. In this way, overcommitment often, and somewhat perversely, breeds undercommitment.

Risk-taking is the enemy of constancy. For example, prematurely abandoning a possible route to the future may be just as fateful as prematurely committing to a specific route. RCA, which experimented with a broad array of video-recording and playback technologies in the 1960s and 1970s, failed to fully appreciate the importance of timeshift to customers, and therefore prematurely abandoned its work on magnetic tape to concentrate on playback-only video technologies.

Earlier we argued that it is important to get to the future first. Perhaps now it sounds as if we're saying, "Wait for someone else to take a blind leap." We are not. We believe that every firm must proceed toward the future with all due haste. But the way to measure speed in the journey to the future is not how fast one is committing financial resources, but how fast one is gaining additional insight into the precise route that will get one to the future first—which technologies are most feasible, which product or service concepts are best attuned to customer needs, which channels should be used, what exactly do customers want in terms of product features, and where is the real mother lode of demand. In competing for the future, a key goal is to maximize the ratio of learning over investment. A disciplined approach to developing industry foresight can take a company only so far: It can set a basic direction and point out significant milestones. But to find the exact path to the future (which product concepts, which specific technologies, which channels, etc.), a company must learn as it goes—through small market incursions, through carefully targeted acquisitions, through alliances, and so on. The question every management team should ask itself is, "How do we learn about the future faster than competitors, while making fewer and smaller irrevocable commitments?"

One doesn't have to be a big risk-taker to get to the future first. Remember the bruising IBM got when it tried to take on Xerox in the copier business. But Canon succeeded in challenging Xerox while taking fewer risks. Canon entered the copier business by licensing technology from foreign partners. It distributed its first product, a coated paper copier, through a distribution agreement with Scott Paper Company in the United States. Using borrowed technology and borrowed channels, Canon was able to learn at low cost about that part of the copying market not served by Xerox. When Canon finally developed its alternative to xerography, it immediately licensed the new technology to many of Xerox's competitors. The license fees helped Canon bolster its own R&D spending, and the feedback from licensees helped Canon better target its development efforts. The goal in competing for the future is not so much to encourage enormous risk-taking, but to work to derisk one's ambitions.

We are not saying to hedge one's bets on the likelihood that the future opportunity will actually come to pass. Though the "when" and the "how" may be substantially indeterminable, the "what" should be clearly specified. There is no doubt that consumer electronics and computing will converge in some very important ways. There is no doubt that most of us will one day use wireless personal communication devices. There is no doubt that genetic science will dramatically alter the way diseases are treated. There is no doubt that most of us will be doing our banking over telephone wires rather than through drive-in windows in the future. There is no doubt that most of the world's information will be available in electronic form in the home.

Though JVC may have been unsure about how to squeeze six hours of recording time onto a half-inch tape, it was certain that "time shift" represented a real opportunity for any firm willing to fight its way through the thicket of underdeveloped and competing technological options. Knowing that most senior executives believe that there is a substantial gap between what their companies spend on information technology and the benefits actually derived, Andersen Consulting saw an opportunity in the early 1960s to help narrow that gap. At the time, however, Andersen could not have seen all the possible routes for accomplishing its goals (better training for internal staff, process reengineering, outsourcing the data-processing function, the introduction of automated software development tools, and so forth), and would have been ill-advised to commit irrevocably to just one path to the future.

Whereas a strategic architecture identifies broad competencies to be built—the potential highways to the future—the relative merits of specific routes emerge only as one moves forward. Where one hedges one's bets is on *how* to get to the future, not on the attractiveness of the destination. One must explore alternate service concepts, alternate channels and delivery mechanisms, and alternate technologies. Again, one doesn't want to prematurely commit to a particular route to the future. For example, although executives at Microsoft are convinced that there will be an explosion of information services in the home, they know that predicting whether, in the medium term, those services will be delivered primarily via the personal computer or television is impossible. Microsoft has begun to explore the option of partnering with cable television companies like Time Warner and TCI in the development of software standards for the delivery of television-based information services.

Ultimately, of course, tightly targeted investments in competencies, channels, brands, and product development are necessary to exploit and control an emerging opportunity. Experimenting with everything, and being committed to nothing, is as sure a way to miss the future as sitting on one's hands or betting it all on a single roll of the dice. Investing too little too late is as unwise as investing too much too early. Our point is simply that while an imaginative and unblinkered consideration of industry trends and drivers can help point a firm toward new opportunities and suggest likely routes for getting to the future, a significant degree of residual uncertainty is likely to remain. (We do feel that for most firms, that residual uncertainty is far higher than it need be because of a lack of sustained, deep, high-level thinking about the future.) This residual uncertainty can only be reduced as the company develops further insights into the size and shape of the opportunity.

Having exhausted what can be deduced analytically about the future, a firm must learn by doing: create alliances with leading-edge customers, perform prototype market testing, undertake joint development with potential competitors, study competing technologies, and so on. In this sense, a strategic architecture must be seen as work in progress. As one moves forward and acquires insight into the most attractive technologies, the best delivery vehicles, and the exact nature of customer needs, investment priorities become clearer and bets less equivocal. One then adds the wiring diagrams, the plumbing, the bricks and mortar, and the interior fittings to the broad structural architecture.

In extending industry foresight and crafting strategic architecture, top management competes for foresight. But getting to the future first takes more than a thoughtfully conceived strategic architecture. Strategic architecture is the map, but what about the fuel? As we will see, the fuel for the journey is not money alone. Many resource-rich firms have surrendered the future to poorer rivals. Ultimately, it is the emotional and intellectual energy of employees that provides the fuel for the journey. What is required is an ability to mobilize every ounce of emotional and creative energy in the company. This is the subject of our next two chapters.

Strategy as Stretch

· ·

I t is not cash that fuels the journey to the future, but the emotional and intellectual energy of every employee. Does this premise seem a bit farfetched? Well, think about this. Imagine you were an investor who, a decade or two ago, was asked to choose between the following pairs of firms as long-term investment opportunities:[1]

Volkswagen	versus	Honda
Upjohn	versus	Glaxo
CBS	versus	CNN
Xerox	versus	Canon
RCA	versus	Sony
Westinghouse	versus	Hitachi
Pan Am	versus	British Airways
IBM	versus	Compaq
Firestone	versus	Bridgestone
Sears	versus	Wal-Mart

Where would you have put your money? Without the benefit of hindsight, most investors would probably have been tempted to invest in the firms in the left column. Why? These firms had strong reputations, technological riches, and deep pockets. They could hire the most talented people in their industry, had sizable market shares, and, in most cases, had a worldwide distribution presence. In short, they had resources. Yet, in varying degrees, they lost much of their leadership to firms with far fewer visible resources.

Investors can be excused for having failed to anticipate the success of the challengers, but what about industry incumbents? What excuse do they have for, in so many cases, being unpleasantly surprised by the more vital and aggressive firms in the right-hand column? What would Volkswagen executives have concluded if they had trekked to Japan in 1970 for a close-up view of Honda? Honda's first attempt at a car was rather pitiful—certainly not up to the standards of German engineering—and Volkswagen managers would have been scornful. And what about RCA and Sony? RCA had almost single-handedly created the color television industry in the United States, and every competitor relied on RCA patents, products of one of the world's outstanding research laboratories. How could Sony out-innovate the United States' consumer electronics pioneers?

Incumbents tend to dismiss competitors with meager resource endowments. To the extent that challengers even register on the radar screens of leaders, they produce such small "blips" that they are easily ignored. Yet if there is one conclusion to be drawn from the endless shifting of competitive fortunes it is this: *Starting resource positions are a very poor predictor of future industry leadership.* A firm can sit atop mountains of cash and command legions of talented people, and still lose its preeminent position. Likewise, a firm can sometimes overcome enormous resource handicaps and successfully scale the heights of industry leadership.

The point here is that too often competitors are judged in terms of resources rather than resourcefulness. It was just such a misjudgment that led Manhattan's media mavens to label Ted Turner the "mouth of the South, all show and no go," at the very time the Atlanta-based firebrand was setting a torch to the cozy house of network news. Getting to the future first is more a function of resourcefulness than resources. Resourcefulness stems not from an elegantly structured strategic architecture, but from a deeply felt sense of purpose, a broadly shared dream, a truly seductive view of tomorrow's opportunity.

Komatsu's dream in the early 1960s was "Maru-C," to encircle Caterpillar by attacking in product and market segments where Caterpillar was underrepresented, with the goal of being the dominant challenger worldwide to Cat in the earth-moving equipment industry. For years Canon's dream was to "Beat Xerox." By the mid-1980s Canon had become the world's most prolific maker of copiers. An even earlier dream at Canon had been to "Beat Leica," the renowned German camera company. In a similar vein, one Japanese car maker launched its foray into the luxury car business with the cry, "Beat Benz." Less than a decade later, the line of cars spawned by this initiative were outselling both Mercedes and BMW in the crucial U.S. market.

STRATEGIC INTENT

The dream that energizes a company is often something more sophisticated, and more positive, than a simple war cry. The dream of British Airways, enunciated shortly after its privatization in early 1987, was to become "The World's Favourite Airline." Given BA's reputation for lackluster service (a bit of British understatement, that) customers could have been forgiven for regarding BA's aspiration with incredulity. Yet by 1992, *Business Traveler* was rating BA as the best transatlantic airline, and number-two worldwide only to Singapore Airlines. If not "the" world's favorite, BA had become one of those very few airlines that people would actually go out of their way to fly.

Strategic intent is our term for such an animating dream. Strategic intent is strategic architecture's capstone. A strategic architecture may point the way to the future, but it's an ambitious and compelling strategic intent that provides the emotional and intellectual energy for the journey. Strategic architecture is the brain; strategic intent is the heart. Strategic intent implies a significant *stretch* for the organization. Current capabilities and resources are manifestly insufficient to the task. Whereas the traditional view of strategy focuses on the "fit" between existing resources and emerging opportunities, strategic intent creates, by design, a substantial "misfit" between resources and aspirations.

As the distilled essence of a firm's strategic architecture, strategic intent also implies a particular point of view about the long-term market or competitive position that a firm hopes to build over the coming decade or so. Hence, it conveys a *sense of direction*. A strategic intent is differentiated; it implies a competitively unique point of view about the future. It holds out to employees the promise of exploring new competitive territory. Hence, it conveys a *sense of discovery*. Strategic intent has an emotional edge to it; it is a goal that employees perceive as inherently worthwhile. Hence, it implies a *sense of destiny*. Direction, discovery, and destiny. These are the attributes of strategic intent.

A Sense of Direction

Ask a third- or fourth-level employee in your company, "Where are we trying to get to as a company?" Our experience has been that few employees will be able to articulate anything more than vague ideals ("be market-led") or short-term operational goals ("improve profitability," "lower costs," or "achieve faster cycle time"). In most companies employees don't share a sense of purpose above and beyond that of short-term unit performance. Lacking a compelling sense of direction, few employees feel a compelling sense of responsibility for competitiveness. Most people won't go that extra mile unless they know where they are heading.

We've all heard, in one form or another, the familiar middle management lament: "We could be so much more successful if head office would just butt out and let us get on with the job." But the lament has a chorus: "We could be so much more successful if only we had a clearer sense of direction. We just don't seem to have a clear idea of where we're trying to get to."

How can we make sense of these seemingly conflicting demands? What are mid-level managers really saying about top management? We believe it's pretty simple: Most companies are overmanaged and underled. It is fair to say that in most corporate headquarters, far more effort goes into the exercise of control than into the provision of direction. What unit managers and their reports are rebelling against is the dead hand of corporate bureaucracy and the frustration of trying to make choices in the absence of an overarching sense of purpose.

A senior executive at Nissan remarked in 1992 that "GM is a powerful company, but they aren't clearly directing that power. If some [employees] turn left, and some turn right, a company cannot move forward." Not that Nissan doesn't have its own problems, but the point being made was that although GM was powerful in terms of resources, its lack of a unifying sense of purpose meant that individual efforts were unlikely to be cumulative. A lack of direction almost ensures that units will work at cross-purposes, that priorities will be set capriciously, and that consistency will too often be sacrificed on the altar of expediency. No wonder unit managers are frustrated.

Bureaucracy and its control over capital spending, financial rewards, planning, procedural guidelines, and organizational design is supposed to prevent people from turning left and turning right. It is supposed to be a system of checks and balances that prevents individuals from pursuing idiosyncratic and competing objectives. But without a point of view about corporate direction, bureaucracy is likely to be little more than an enforcer of corporate orthodoxies. Individual and unit freedom are circumscribed by measures of financial viability that are agnostic with respect to ends, and by the enforcement of operating traditions that are blind to the possibility of profound industry change. In reality, the bureaucracy works not so much to keep people from turning left or right, but to ensure that anyone who tries to do so has to walk through molasses to get anywhere.

Bureaucracy blocks initiative and creativity at every turn. Bureaucracy constrains the range of available tactics, but generally leaves open the question of ultimate goals. Hence, in many companies it is the means that are constrained rather than the ends. With no particular point of view about long-term corporate direction, the definition of "core" business changes every few years, acquisitions and divestments are made with no logic other than short-term financial expediency, and market and product development efforts are often hamstrung by a lack of constancy. At the same time, orthodoxies about which channels to use, the definition of the product concept, and where in the value chain to take profits constrain tactical freedom. Often the combination of directional ambiguity and tactical orthodoxy poses a substantial threat to future prosperity: "We don't know where we're going, but we're not going to stray from familiar paths."

Top management has not been deaf to the pleas of mid-level managers and first-line employees for more freedom. Decentralization is in vogue. "Devolve, devolve" is chanted like a mantra in corporate boardrooms. Bureaucracy bashing, delegation, and empowerment are strutting the catwalks of managerial fashion. It is right they should attract admirers. *Delegation* and *empowerment* are not just buzzwords, they are desperately needed antidotes to the elitism that robs so many companies of so much brain power. Thus, corporate staff groups, the guardians of conformance, have had their numbers slashed. Corporate vice presidents have been told they're "coaches" and should leave the "playing" to unit managers. Authority has been pushed down, capital spending limits have been raised, the number of reviews cut, and the rituals of planning and capital allocation simplified. Unit managers have been told to behave as if it's their business.

Although the principle of ceding responsibility for strategic decision making to those closest to customers and competitors is good medicine, like any other management wonder drug an overdose may prove toxic. Dismantling bureaucracy without putting in its place a clear and compelling sense of direction is a recipe for chaos. Empowerment without direction is anarchy.

Individual freedom and delegation often yield unexpected successes, but something more is needed if the goal is to position a company for leadership in complex systemic opportunities like interactive home entertainment systems (Time Warner's dream), the development of superjumbo aircraft (where Boeing is attempting to take the lead in an international consortium of airframe manufacturers), or the development of an electrically powered automobile (where Ford and GM are collaborating). These opportunities have 10- to 20-year time frames and require the integration of complex skills from both within and without the firm. Isolated and undirected entrepreneurial teams are unlikely to make much of a dent in them.

Brownian movement generates little forward progress. Better, we believe, is creativity in the service of a clearly prescribed strategic intent. Creativity should be unbridled, but not uncorralled. Strategic intent is more specific about ends than it is about means. Strategic intent ensures consistency in direction. Because every vale and hillock cannot be anticipated, strategic intent must be broad enough to leave considerable room for experimentation in how to reach the destination. Strategic intent broadly constrains the "where," but not the "how."

A Sense of Discovery

There beats in every person the heart of an explorer. The joy of discovery may be found in the pages of a new cookbook, in a brochure of exotic vacations, in an architect's plans for a custom-built home, in the trek to a remote trout stream, in the first run down a virgin-powdered ski slope, or in the birth of a child. We are all seduced, to one degree or another, by the opportunity to explore the unfamiliar. Thus, it's not surprising that when a company's mission is largely undifferentiated from that of its competitors, employees may be less than inspired.

Recently one of us made a presentation to the top 15 officers of a large multinational company. We showed them their company's mission statement. No one demurred; yes, that looked like their mission statement. Only what was there on the screen was actually the mission statement of their major competitor!

What value is a mission statement, we asked, if it is totally undifferentiated? What chance does it offer to stake out a unique and defensible position in an already overcrowded market? In fact, if we took the mission statements of 100 large industrial companies, mixed them up tonight while everyone was asleep, and reassigned them at random, would anyone wake up tomorrow morning and cry, "My gosh, where has our mission statement gone?"

Why should employees care about a garden variety mission statement? A strategic intent should offer employees the enticing spectacle of a new destination (as in Bell Atlantic's quest to bring a whole new range of information services to its subscribers), or at least new routes to well-known destinations (as in Toyota's foray into the luxury car business).

A Sense of Destiny

Strategic intent must be a goal that commands the respect and allegiance of every employee. The destination must not only be different, it must also be worthwhile. The intent of the Apollo program was as competitively focused as Komatsu's drive against Caterpillar, but it had a deep emotional appeal as well. In articulating the goal of reaching the moon before the end of the 1960s, John F. Kennedy reminded Americans of their destiny to explore new frontiers. Given Japan's long linguistic and geographical isolation, the emotional impetus behind that country's efforts to develop a translating telephone capable of bridging language gaps has been no less forceful. By the end of 1992 Japanese companies, in partnership with the government, had invested more than $130 million over seven years in this endeavor.[2]

Perhaps one of the most ambitious, and emotionally compelling strategic intents ever articulated was Christ's command to his tiny and impoverished band of followers to "Go into all the world and preach the gospel."[3] While few corporate intents are likely to invoke such lofty ideals, we believe that any strategic intent must contain pathos and passion. Too many mission statements fail entirely to impart any sense of *mission*. For this reason we prefer goals that are focused on making a real difference in the lives of customers. Apple's quest to develop truly user-friendly computers is one example. Undoubtedly, many of those who worked so feverishly first to bring the Lisa and then the Macintosh to market will look back on those endeavors as the most rewarding years of their professional lives.

In this sense, strategic intent is as much about the creation of meaning for employees as it is about the establishment of direction. We often ask managers, if we fast forward 10 or 15 years, what collective accomplishment would you like to point to as evidence that the last 15 years of your working life were the most exciting, rewarding, and purposeful of your entire career? In other words, what is the legacy you want to leave behind? We believe that every employee has the right to feel that he or she is contributing to the building of a legacy—something of value that is bigger and more lasting than anything that one could accomplish on one's own. Many companies are beginning to realize that all their employees have brains. How many companies, we wonder, understand that their employees have hearts as well? When queried as to his job, a journeyman stonemason at work on St. Paul's in London replied, "I build cathedrals." How many corporate stonemasons today feel they are building cathedrals, we wonder?

A few years ago one of us was advising the senior management team of a U.S. electronics manufacturer and visited its manufacturing facility "deep in the heart of Texas." Coinciding with a shift change, the visit provided an opportunity to chat with employees about their jobs and their company. We asked a group of about 30 employees who they thought were their major competitors. Surprisingly, very few could name their major global competitor in their particular product line. The question, in what respects are you more or less competitive than this rival, drew a complete blank. These reactions provided an excuse to share with these first-line employees the same competitive data (market share, growth, cost, innovation, productivity, and so forth) that had recently been the subject of discussion with senior management. The consequences of failing to remain competitive were also discussed, in terms of the disadvantage their customers would face if they were forced to buy the same components from more vertically integrated Japanese supplier/competitors. At the end of our discussion an outsized and gruff-looking employee remarked, in a very quiet voice, that

I have worked here for eight years. The pressure for yield improvement, quality improvement, cost improvement never goes away. But I never had any sense of being part of a worldwide team, fighting a worldwide war. And I never really understood the consequences of winning or losing.

This was sad to hear. This group of employees had been continually exhorted to do better, try harder, run faster, and kick more goals, yet there was no scoreboard that meant something to them. People just don't get interested in a game if there's no scoreboard. And the scoreboard of top management—shareholder returns—is likely to exert very little emotional pull on an employee several levels removed from the person defending himself or herself in front of shareholders.

Most human resource managers can tell you if employees are satisfied. In many companies, some form of a happiness index is used to measure employee satisfaction with pay and conditions. But strategic intent aims to create employee excitement, not just employee satisfaction. The more excited a worker is, the less are remuneration and hygiene the sole barometers of contentment. In high-drama, high-purpose organizations like Data General in the early years, described in *The Soul of a New Machine*, excitement often runs roughshod over satisfaction.[4] Bosses who impose impossible deadlines, 80-hour workweeks, and minimalist creature comforts may be willingly accommodated in the quest for greatness.

The responsibility of an employee to work diligently for the success of the firm, the cornerstone of a contract of employment, has a counterpart. It is senior management's responsibility to imbue that work with a higher purpose than a paycheck. The appeal to emotion as well as intellect must be based on more than the prospect of personal financial gain. It is impossible to create a financial reward system so finely tuned that the single-minded pursuit of personal gain will not, in the longer run, dilute firm success. In the absence of an overarching strategic intent, the establishment of profit-center accountability for every unit and performance-linked compensation for every employee may have significant and unexpected toxic side effects: interunit competition that fails to recognize the rewards of cooperation; fruitless debates about revenue sharing, transfer pricing, and allocation of overheads; and too much of a preference for the quick and the expedient. An emotionally compelling and broadly shared intent is a counterweight to these tendencies.

A goal simply to be the biggest or to reach a certain size is also unlikely to capture the imagination of employees. Becoming a $25 billion company or, as it was in the case of IBM, a $100 billion company is not a strategic intent for it implies no particular direction. The pursuit of growth for growth's sake is likely to end in, for example, unrelated acquisitions that don't pan out, costly share gains in inherently unattractive markets, or overspending on R&D in a business that is in permanent decline. While the quest for growth is intrinsic to almost any strategic intent, the real emotional *umph* comes when a company can articulate *what* it is growing toward. Creating new competitive space, taking on the best and winning, or delivering totally unexpected benefits to customers all have a deeper appeal than simply hitting some numerical milestone. It is, perhaps, a tautology, but only extraordinary goals provoke extraordinary efforts.

CORPORATE CHALLENGES

Direction, discovery, and destiny are the tests of any strategic intent. Turning strategic intent into reality requires that every employee understand the exact way in which his or her contribution is crucial to the achievement of strategic intent. Not only must everyone in the company find the goal emotionally compelling, each employee must understand the nature of the linkage between his or her own job and the attainment of the goal. In short, strategic intent must be *personalized* for every employee. The first task in personalizing strategic intent is to set clear corporate *challenges* that focus everyone's attention on the next key advantage or capability to be built. The precise nature of these challenges will be determined by the firm's strategic architecture.

Top management's job is to focus the organization's attention on the next challenge, and the next after that. The first might be quality; the next, cycle time; the next, entry into Asian markets; the next, mastery of a particular technology; and so on. In establishing the capability-building agenda, top management provides employees with a clear view of the next advantage to be constructed. In Komatsu this took the form of "management by policy." Each year the chairman, after extensive opinion taking, would enunciate the next key challenge. One year it was improving quality, the next it was dramatic cost reductions, then international expansion, and then product line development (see Table 6-1). Challenges are the

TABLE 6-1 BUILDING COMPETITIVE ADVANTAGE AT KOMATSU

Corporate Challenge	Protect Komatsu's home market against Caterpillar		Reduce costs while maintaining quality	
Programs	early 1960s	Licensing deals with Cummins Engine, International Harvester, and Bucyrus-Erie to acquire technology and establish benchmarks	1965	C D (Cost Down) program
	1961	Project A (for Ace) to advance the product quality of Komatsu's small- amd medium-sized bulldozers above Caterpillar's	1966	Total C D program
	1962	Quality Circles companywide to provide training for all employees		

Make Komatsu an international enterprise and build export markets		Respond to external shocks that threaten markets		Create new products and markets	
early 1960s	Develop Eastern bloc countries	1975	V-10 program to reduce costs by 10% while maintaining quality; reduce parts by 20%; rationalize manufacturing system	late 1970s	Accelerate product development to expand line
1967	Komatsu Europe marketing subsidiary established			1979	Future and Frontiers program to identify new businesses based on society's needs and company's know-how
1970	Komatsu America established	1977	¥ 180 program to budget companywide for 180 yen to the dollar when exchange rate was 240		
1972	Project B to improve the durability and reliability and to reduce costs of large bulldozers	1979	Project E to establish teams to redouble cost and quality efforts in response to oil crisis	1981	EPOCHS program to reconcile greater product variety with improved production efficiencies
1972	Project C to improve payloaders				
1972	Project D to improve hydraulic excavators				
1974	Establish presales and service department to assist newly industrializing countries in construction projects				

Source: Gary Hamel and C.K. Prahalad, "Strategic Intent," *Harvard Business Review* (May–June 1989): 68. Copyright © 1989 by the President and Fellows of Harvard College; all rights reserved. Reprinted by permission.

milestones on the path between today and tomorrow; they are the major structural members in the strategic architecture.

Corporate challenges are the operational means of staging the acquisition of new competitive advantages. Corporate challenges identify the focal point for capability-building in the near to medium term. As we will see, challenges are the means for allocating emotional and intellectual energy, energy that flows from enthusiasm for the firm's strategic intent. We believe that the task of focusing intellectual and emotional energy is as important for top management as allocating financial capital. Unless every employee feels a deep sense of responsibility for firm success, and has a clear channel for contribution, global leadership will remain elusive. In no company we know has capital been the critical hurdle standing between the firm and its aspirations.

If a company starts out as a laggard in some areas, the early challenges will focus on catching up, rather than getting out in front. But as with strategic intent, challenges are more prescriptive about ends (e.g., reducing development time to 24 months) than about means. It is up to employees to discover the specific "hows" that will enable the company to achieve its improvement targets. Also, like strategic intent, challenges are more concerned with what is desirable than with what is evidently obtainable.

When Komatsu set its goal to match Caterpillar's world-class quality, its product quality was less than half that of its exemplar. A more realistic goal for Komatsu might have been a 20% per year improvement in quality, but this would have left it far short of what was needed to wrest share from Caterpillar in export markets. Komatsu did achieve world-class quality levels and won the Deming prize a mere three years after announcing its quality quest. The enormous "reach" implied in such improvement goals forces the organization to abandon conventional wisdom. It is clear that the challenge cannot be met by doing more, better, faster. It can only be met by doing different—by fundamentally rethinking processes, roles, and responsibilities.

Every employee must have a personal scorecard that directly relates his or her job to the challenge being pursued in a particular time frame. This might be a quality benchmark, an indicator of timeliness, or a productivity number. It is undoubtedly true that you can't improve it if you can't measure it, but how many employees have a specific measure of their own performance that links individual achievement to the firm's overall strategic intent? In our experience, too few.

One approach that Ford used in the early years of its quality campaign was to videotape elements of the manufacturing process at Mazda, Ford's Japanese partner, and show these segments to Ford workers in Europe and the United States. In one sequence, involving the installation of the fabric "headliner" on the interior roof of the vehicle, a single Mazda employee successfully installed the component in less than a minute. At a typical Ford plant in Europe, it took four workers six minutes to perform the same operation. Obviously, such a 24:1 productivity gap was untenable. Just as obviously, the gap wasn't entirely the fault of production line workers. Mazda had only two different types of headliner while Ford had many; Mazda's headliners arrive at the production site appropriately sequenced to the types of vehicles coming down the line; the Mazda headliner snapped into place while Ford's required a cumbersome gluing operation; and so on. The message to workers was direct and inescapable: "You must help us improve in this area if we are to regain our competitiveness," and, "There is only one standard that matters and that is the world standard." This is a stellar example of how a broad strategic intent ("Quality is Job 1") can be personalized for individual employees.

Competitor and customer benchmarks may be the most underused motivators in management's administrative tool kit. One British manager, responding to our plea to provide every employee with a competitor benchmark, remarked, "We in Britain are just not that competitive minded. The killer instinct is a bit passé here." Yet anyone who's watched England play France at rugby knows that the competitive spirit is alive and well in England, as it is across Europe. Competitive drive and the will to succeed are not uniquely Japanese or American urges. But they are unlikely to be unleashed across the breadth and depth of a company unless every employee wakes up every morning knowing just what constitutes the world's best performance in his or her job. We've never met employees at any level who don't want to win. But it is senior management's responsibility to establish the sense of purpose ("Let's win the Super Bowl"), to identify the key capability-building challenges ("We gotta work on our passing game"), and then to help everyone understand just what role he or she plays in the pursuit of victory (be it the quarterback, the tight end, or the center).

In the absence of clearly specified challenges, employees are more or less powerless to contribute to competitiveness. As individuals they may work unstintingly, but advantages don't get built without sustained, firmwide effort. Similarly, without external benchmarks, it is all too easy for employees to believe that it is top management, rather than competitive reality, that is applying the pressure for improvement.

We are acquainted with one multinational that, for years, watched its market share decline against more efficient and fleet-footed Japanese competitors. Employees regularly received video-tapes from senior management, entreating them to do better, and berating them for substandard performance. But few first-line employees and middle managers had any job-related evidence of the exact nature and magnitude of the firm's competitive deficit. There was indeed a general consensus that the firm's costs were a bit inflated, and the product development times could probably be shortened a bit, but without specific data there was no highly focused sense of urgency about the improvement task.

For its part, top management was, at first, reluctant to acknowledge the enormity of the competitive problem. Few corporate staff members or divisional managers were impudent enough to present top management with painful and unequivocal data on competitive decline. How could the head of corporate R&D admit that his company spent 2½ times its major Japanese rival on development and yet launched many fewer successful new products, or that his firm had more development engineers yet took twice as long to bring new product ideas to the market? How could the director of worldwide manufacturing admit that his firm's defect rate was a dozen times higher than the world standard, or that a Japanese competitor could manufacture in Europe, at low scale, more cheaply than his firm could source from a plant in Taiwan? How could the head of corporate sales and marketing admit that selling expenses per dollar of revenue were half again as high as competitors with just half the revenue?

When such disturbing data did land in top management's lap, they were explained away by the "fact" that Japanese rivals obviously had some unique advantages that couldn't be duplicated in a European context. Yet even as this defense became less and less plausible (with Japanese competitors sourcing from European factories and with U.S. firms like Hewlett-Packard and Motorola successfully defending their turf against Japanese rivals), it was still difficult for the top brass to admit that their firm had fallen so far behind on a broad range of competitive parameters. Nobody at the top wanted to be the first to stand up and say *mea culpa.*

Nevertheless, every employee, of whatever rank, could easily see the dwindling shelf space commanded by the firm's products in local retail outlets. As the evidence of decline became more inescapable, confidence in top management throughout the company waned. "Why doesn't top management *do* something?" became the collective cry of the organization. Knowing this was a problem it couldn't fix on its own, yet too proud to go to the organization and ask for help, top management stonewalled it.

A way out of the impasse emerged only when the chairman was unceremoniously dumped, a new top team put in place, and a thorough and soul-searching review of the firm's competitive problems launched. With these data in hand, top management was in a position to set out precise improvement challenges for the company. Much additional work was done to give every employee a personal improvement goal, and with a deep sigh of relief, the organization set out to recapture the company's former glory. But the denial and the lost time cost tens of thousands of employees their livelihoods.

The lesson here is that setting corporate challenges requires great honesty and humility on the part of top management: honesty in portraying the magnitude of the task ahead; humility in admitting that it must bear its share of the responsibility for poor performance. Motorola is one of the most self-critical firms we know.

Motorola's refusal to ever be satisfied with "good enough" shows up in its results. Unfortunately, in some companies, honest criticism is, particularly when it comes from subordinates, more likely to raise hackles than standards.

Corporate challenges will engender more frustration than fresh thinking if employees don't have the right to challenge corporate orthodoxies in their pursuit of better performance. We find it paradoxical that the empowerment that counts the most—the freedom to challenge standard operating procedures, workflow design, and bureaucractic procedures—is the freedom that is most often denied to first-level employees. Although it is one thing to let a production employee bring the manufacturing line to a halt when a defect is found, it is quite another to let that factory worker have a significant say in task design and factory layout. It is sometimes said that the pursuit of total quality is the key to management innovation. To the uninitiated this must sound strange indeed. What has quality got to do with innovation in management methods? The connection is simple. The foundation of a quality program is a willingness to trace every quality problem back to its roots. The fact is that those roots usually reach far beyond the immediate vicinity of the problem. They reach into areas like supplier relationships, process design, information systems, physical infrastructure, and the like. And it is those closest to the quality problems who are best placed to offer real insight into how corporate processes and systems could be improved. Marginally enlarging the scope of authority for a first-level employee is not enough; every employee must be given the freedom to challenge anything that interferes with the pursuit of a company's strategic intent.

One of the salutary benefits of corporate challenges is that they focus the organization, top to bottom, on the same capability-building task. No single organizational level working alone can construct a new advantage or overcome a competitive deficit. Advantages like quality, cycle time, customer care, and flexible manufacturing are won by the efforts of every function at every level. Divisional presidents can no more build a competitive advantage in isolation than can front-line employees. Each level and function must understand the totality of the challenge, the interdependence of different roles, and the dimensions of their own responsibility.

Employees are unlikely to rise to a particular challenge if they don't believe they will benefit proportionately from the firm's success. For challenges to take root, an atmosphere of "shared pain, shared gain" must prevail. Such an atmosphere is not easily created when top management pays itself 75 or 100 times as much as front-line employees. Employees may be told that "you are the company's most valuable asset," or "you are responsible for our competitiveness," but such compensation levels send a more powerful and contradictory message. One can well imagine a low-level employee thinking, "If those guys at the top are so well paid, they darn well better have all the answers."

We believe that workers in many companies have been asked to take a disproportionate share of the blame for competitive failure. We consulted at one company where top management was beseeching workers to ameliorate their wage demands to help close a wage-cost gap with a foreign competitor. It turned out that the foreign competitor actually had higher wage rates, but was getting a higher output with a similarly sized employee base. The rival's productivity advantage came almost entirely from worker-inspired process improvements. You can imagine how eager the put-upon employees were to make similar contributions after finally yielding to a pay freeze. Contrast this situation with what often happens when a leading Japanese company runs into unexpected financial difficulties: Top management takes the biggest pay cut, and first-line employees take the smallest. This approach more accurately represents who really is at fault for failing to anticipate and respond to changed circumstances.

Finally, all employees must be given the tools they need to contribute to advantage-building efforts. The tool kit may include statistical analysis, general problem-solving techniques, benchmarking methods, systems modeling, and teamwork disciplines. Motorola established what was, in essence, a corporate university to embed these skills in its workforce. It realized that it was no help asking employees to build new advantages with their bare hands. Bare-handed empowerment is really no empowerment at all.

Corporate challenges are, then, stepping stones between the firm's present position and its strategic intent. Each challenge dares employees to do more than they thought possible. Each challenge is, in a sense, a mini-strategic intent. But it is the ability to focus an entire organization's attention on key challenges that determines the rate at which the future is built. Getting to the future first is not only about having a strategic intent, but also about building new capabilities faster than rivals. This is the ultimate competitive advantage. Whatever the particular stepping stone, the process of managing corporate challenges has the same elements: setting the challenge in the context of the strategic intent (e.g., why this is the next logical step in our quest for leadership); describing the nature and magnitude of the challenge with honesty and humility; specifying precisely the particular improvement to be sought in a given time frame; establishing measurements to link every employee's contribution to the overall challenge; and granting employees the freedom to contribute in ways that range far beyond the boundaries of their roles or organizational level.

FROM FIT TO STRETCH

A firm's strategic architecture and its overall strategic intent must be grounded in a deep understanding of potential discontinuities, competitor intentions, and evolving customer needs. Nevertheless, a firm's strategic intent should represent an ambition that stretches far beyond the current resources and capabilities of the firm. Unfortunately, planning and budgeting criteria often conspire to prevent the company from committing to a goal that lies beyond the range of currently available resources. What is immediately feasible drives out what is ultimately desirable. Let us explain.

Strategic planning is, in practice, a "feasibility sieve." It is a tool for ensuring that questions of feasibility are fully addressed. Do we have the resources? Is the market ready? Is the net present value positive? These are the concerns of strategic planning. Strategic planning and capital budgeting are, in essence, used to reject goals when the means for achieving those goals are not readily at hand. They require managers to "Be realistic," which is not a bad thing! These are legitimate questions—there are no excuses for poorly thought out, hare-brained strategies—but what happens if a firm tries to push an ambitious ten-year strategic intent through the sieve? It simply won't go through.

If JVC engineers had been "realistic" in the early 1960s, they would never have developed home videocassette recorders. If John Kennedy had been "realistic," he never would have committed the United States to going to the moon. If Torakuso Yamaha had been realistic back in the late nineteenth century, he never would have dreamed of turning Yamaha into the world's leading manufacturer of grand pianos and other musical instruments.

When what is feasible drives out what is desirable, an ambitious strategic intent becomes impossible. While politics may be the art of the possible, leadership is the art of making the impossible come true. Mahatma Gandhi, Martin Luther King, and Abraham Lincoln were leaders first, and politicians second. Similarly, strategic intent must take primacy over the *realpolitik* of planning. Although strategic planning is billed as a way of becoming more future oriented, most managers admit that their strategic plans reveal more about today's problems than tomorrow's opportunities. Plans seldom do more than project the present forward incrementally. The goal of strategic intent, the implicit task in developing a strategic architecture, is to fold the future back into the present. It forces the organization to ask, "What must we be doing differently today if we want to create this particular future—if we want to reach this particular future destination?"

While strategic intent may teeter on the brink of incredibility, it is not a quixotic quest. Ted Turner wanted to create a global news network, not wipe out the U.S. budget deficit. Strategic intent is a tangible goal; it is a destination that can be described. Remember, a firm's strategic architecture must be based on a deep and creative understanding of industry discontinuities, of the firm's core competencies, and of potential new customer needs. Industry foresight must be well grounded. It must point the company in the direction of genuine opportunities. At the same time, it must not put an arbitrary limit on just how far and fast the company can travel on the road to the future. Unless senior management is willing to commit to a goal that lies outside the planning horizon, there can be no strategic intent. The future will be discovered by someone else.

We believe that it is essential for top management to set out an aspiration that creates, by design, a chasm between ambition and resources. An explicit emphasis on the notion of "fit," and the way in which the idea of fit is embedded in strategy tools, often deflects managers from the enormously important task of creating a misfit between resources and ambitions. Of course, at any point in time there must be a loose fit between short-term objectives and near-at-hand resources. But even then the fit should not be too tight. Medium-term challenges should demand more of the organization than what it currently believes is possible. Perfect fit guarantees atrophy and stagnation. Thus, we need a view of strategy as *stretch* as well as *fit*.

A view of strategy as stretch, as we've outlined, helps bridge the gap that exists between those who see strategy as a "grand plan, thought up by great minds," and those who see strategy as a pattern in a stream of incremental decisions. Strategy as stretch is strategy by design in the sense that top management does have a relatively clear view of the goal line and a broad agenda of the capability-building challenges that lie between today and tomorrow. Strategy as stretch is strategy by incrementalism to the extent that top management cannot predetermine every single step of the journey to the future. Strategy as stretch recognizes the essential paradox that while leadership cannot be entirely planned for, neither does it happen in the absence of a clearly articulated and widely shared aspiration.

Where fit is achieved by simply paring down ambitions, there will be no spur for such ingenuity and much of the firm's strategic potential will remain dormant. Tests of realism and feasibility must not be prematurely applied. Stretch and the creativity it engenders are the engine and fuel for corporate growth and vitality. This is why the genesis of the strategy process must be a purposefully created misfit between where the firm is and where it wants to be.

Ultimately, one must find a way to close the gap between resources and aspirations that strategic intent opens up. Obviously, we don't believe the way to close this gap is by downsizing aspirations. Instead it is by leveraging resources, by traveling the maximum distance down the road to leadership, using the least possible amount of fuel. The goal is to challenge managers to become more ingenious both in multiplying the impact of the firm's resource base and enlarging it. This is the subject of our next chapter.

7

Strategy as Leverage

ogether Figures 7-1 through 7-5 tell a story. In Figure 7-1 we see evidence of the astounding employee productivity gains made by Japan's manufacturing firms. Nothing new here. Now look at Figure 7-2. Here we see that Japanese manufacturing companies not only possess a labor productivity advantage, their overhead costs have also been less, as a percentage of total costs, than is typical in the United States or Germanic countries. This is not labor productivity, but management and systems productivity. Go on. Figures 7-3 through 7-5 suggest that there is often little direct correlation between R&D spending and R&D output.[1] How is it that GM can spend more than four times as much as Honda on R&D and not be the undisputed world leader in powertrain chassis technology—at least as far as the customer is concerned? Where is the evidence that Philips's research budget, which in many years has been substantially larger than Sony's, has produced a proportionately higher number of new product winners? In these figures we see crude measures of research productivity. What does all this add up to? Here is a group of firms, Japan's leading manufacturers, that have demonstrated that it is possible to do more with less. That is the essence of resource leverage. It springs not from the sacred soil of Japan, but from an aspiration that takes little notice of current resource constraints. This isn't just lean manufacturing, it's lean everything!

Stretch and leverage are blood relations. We begin this chapter by exploring the relationship between stretch and leverage by way of a not-so-hypothetical example. Imagine two firms competing

FIGURE 7-1 MANUFACTURING LABOR PRODUCTIVITY (PER HOUR)

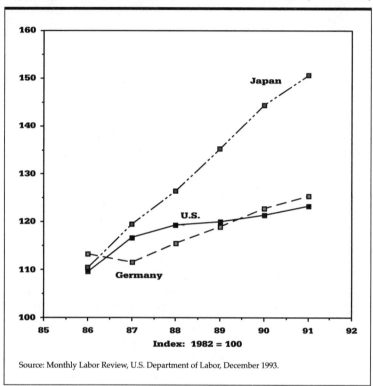

Index: 1982 = 100

Source: Monthly Labor Review, U.S. Department of Labor, December 1993.

in the same industry: Alpha has a wealth of resources of every kind—human talent, technical skills, distribution access, brands, manufacturing facilities, and cash flow. These resources, accumulated over decades, are the rewards of past and current industry leadership, not the guarantors of future leadership. Alpha has no particular aspiration other than to remain atop its present perch. This goal has been expressed by Alpha's senior management as "growing as fast as the industry." Alpha's resources can thus be described as substantial, and its aspiration as modest.

Beta is much smaller than Alpha and has far fewer tangible resources. It has no choice but to make do with fewer people, a

FIGURE 7-2 OVERHEAD COSTS

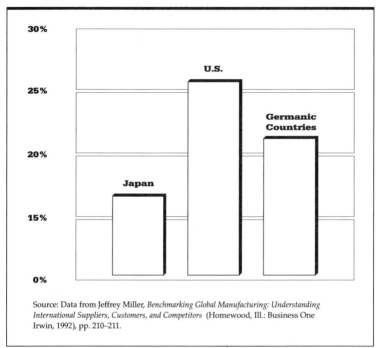

Source: Data from Jeffrey Miller, *Benchmarking Global Manufacturing: Understanding International Suppliers, Customers, and Competitors* (Homewood, Ill.: Business One Irwin, 1992), pp. 210–211.

smaller capital budget, more modest facilities, and a fraction of Alpha's R&D spending. But Beta is possessed of a grand ambition that belies its meager resource base. Beta has every intention of knocking Alpha off its leadership perch, though Alpha would mock any such intention. To accomplish this, Beta managers know that they must grow faster than Alpha, develop both more and better products, ultimately be present in all the world's major markets, build a credible worldwide brand franchise, and so on. Beta is the mirror image of Alpha: Beta is resource-poor, but aspiration-rich.

The gap between Alpha's resources and aspirations can be described as "slack"; the gap between Beta's resources and aspirations is what we have termed "stretch." Armed only with this knowledge, one can reasonably predict that the two firms will adopt

FIGURE 7-3 A COMPARISON OF R&D SPENDING IN ABSOLUTE TERMS ($ MILLIONS, 1993)

Siemens	5322	Philips	2079
Hitachi	3907	Sony	1809
G.M.*	5917	Xerox	922
Honda	1447	Canon	794
AT&T	2911	IBM	5083
NTT	2157	NEC	2274

Source: "R&D Scoreboard," *Business Week International,* 28 June 1993, pp. 54–57, and company reports.
*Includes engineering expenses.

FIGURE 7-4 A COMPARISON OF R&D SPENDING IN RELATIVE TERMS (R&D AS % OF SALES, FISCAL 1993)

Siemens	10.0	Hitachi	6.7
ABB	8.1	Mitsubishi	4.6
Thomson	8.3	Sharp	6.5
Philips	6.8	Sony	6.1
IBM	7.9	Matsushita	5.6
NTT	11.1	NEC	8.0
Bayer	7.5	Toray	3.4
Kodak	7.9	Fuji	6.6
Xerox	5.4	Canon	5.2

Source: "R&D Scoreboard,"*Business Week International,* 28 June 1993, pp. 54–57, and company reports.

FIGURE 7-5 JAPANESE COMPANIES TOPPING U.S. PATENT AWARDS, SEVENTH CONSECUTIVE YEAR (1992)

1. **Canon**

2. **Toshiba**

3. **Mitsubishi**

4. **Hitachi**

Source: U.S. Patent Office

fundamentally different approaches to competitive strategy, and each will exhibit different degrees of creativity in leveraging its resources.

Certainly Alpha is much better placed to behave "strategically," that is, to preempt Beta in building new plant capacity, to outspend Beta on R&D, to buy market share through aggressive pricing, to field the biggest salesforce, and so on. In fact, given its slack resources, this is precisely how Alpha will think about competitive battles with Beta. Alpha managers will find it hard to resist the temptation to take a World War I trench warfare approach to competitive strategy: "We have more bullets than the enemy has bodies." Alpha's approach to competitive warfare is to overwhelm the opposition by sheer weight of resources—however resource inefficient that may be.

Beta has no such luxury. Facing its wealthy rival, Beta is forced to adopt the tactics of guerrilla warfare, hoping to exploit the orthodoxies and complacency of the larger army. It must outmaneuver rather than overpower the enemy. This was the simple truth recognized by the North Vietnamese in their confrontation with U.S. military might. A story is told of an aging Western general who, while visiting Hanoi, took the opportunity to ask an old Vietnamese general a long-nagging question. How was it that the North Vietnamese had been able to move men and material so freely across rivers, despite the attempts of the U.S. military to locate and bomb their bridges? The simple answer was that the North Vietnamese had built their bridges just below the water line, where they would be practically invisible to airborne reconnaissance, yet usable by men and machines. One wonders how a resource-rich army would have responded to the challenge faced by the North Vietnamese—probably by committing more troops to the defense of the bridges, by constructing redundant bridges, by bringing in even more engineers and construction equipment, and establishing even more antiaircraft batteries. Subscribing to a goal that was as clear as it was daunting, North Vietnamese soldiers hid in tunnels, sabotaged enemy facilities, co-opted civilians, laid traps, and ambushed enemy soldiers with more verve and determination than could be mustered by U.S. forces.

Painful though it may be as a tutorial, the experience of North Vietnam in its conflict with the United States is as convincing a case study in resource leverage as can be found anywhere. Just as necessity begets invention, stretch begets resource leverage. There's no reason to expect this to be any less true in competitive battles than in battles of a more deadly nature. Tactical creativity is the child of resource scarcity. Although a galvanizing ambition and unconventional approach to resource deployment cannot be expected to compensate for any and all resource deficiencies, the annals of military history suggest that it is often the way to bet.[2]

Although an abundance of resources, or slack, enables firms to be strategic in an investment sense, it does nothing to enhance the wisdom of strategic decisions. Resource abundance and the attendant ability to make multiple bets and to sustain multiple failures too often substitute for disciplined and creative strategic thinking. Tens of billions of dollars later, no one can accuse GM of not being strategic in its pursuit of factory automation if, by "strategic," one means the willingness to make bold preemptive investments. Indeed, one could argue, as did many who worked in GM's Hamtramck plant, that GM was *too* strategic; that the firm's ability to make strategic investments totally outpaced its ability to absorb new technology, retrain workers, reengineer work flows, rejuvenate supplier relationships, and discard managerial orthodoxies. If there is no capacity for resource leverage, if a firm hasn't learned how to do more with less, if, in other words, the risks of being "strategic" are fully commensurate or more than commensurate with the potential rewards, there is no advantage to being strategic. Bigger bets sometimes bring bigger payoffs, but they're just as likely to bring bigger disasters. In the absence of an aspiration that outstrips a firm's resources and a capacity for resource leverage, abundance is likely to be little more than a license for carelessness in strategic decision making.

By way of contrast, what kinds of strategic decisions would be likely to emerge from Beta, whose aspirations run far ahead of its resources? First, Beta would eschew a "John Wayne" approach to competitive strategy. It would exploit opportunities to change the rules of the game rather than play by the rules of incumbents. It would search for "loose bricks" in Alpha's defenses rather than confront its competitor in well-defended market segments. Investments would be focused on a relatively small number of core competencies where the firm felt it had the potential to become a world leader. Beta would be compelled to invent lean manufacturing with its emphasis on doing more with less. With fewer product designers than its competitors, the firm would be forced to dramatically reduce product development times and therefore costs to develop a full product line. The need to accelerate product development would spur cross-functional communication. The growth of a vigorous and capable supplier base would be encouraged, and suppliers would be asked to share a significant part of the innovation burden. It goes without saying that Beta would be unable to support any superfluous corporate overhead or excess management layers. With a smaller human resource base, Beta would need to view every employee as a contributor. To avoid any diversion of effort, Beta's top management would seek a deep consensus on strategic goals.

A view of competition as encirclement rather than confrontation, a propensity to accelerate the product development cycle, tightly knit cross-functional teams, a focus on core competencies, close links with suppliers, programs of employee involvement, and so forth are elements of a managerial approach typically labeled as "Japanese." Yet each of these particulars can be logically induced when one views strategy as stretch. So-called Japanese management, as practiced in the past by companies such as Honda, Canon, Sony, and Sharp, may be less the product of groupthink, the subordination of the individual, and the pursuit of *wa* than it is the product of stretch.

It is this stretch—the fact that ambition forever outpaces resources—that fuels the engine of advantage creation. A firm that has a surfeit of ambition and a dearth of resources quickly discovers that it cannot merely imitate the advantages of more affluent competitors; it cannot match their spending dollar-for-dollar; it cannot afford the same entry costs; it cannot tolerate the same inefficiency and slack; it cannot risk playing by the leader's rules. For all these reasons, a few Japanese firms were compelled to create entirely new forms of competitive advantage (lean manufacturing and time compression management), and figure out ways of matching the existing advantages of competitors in more resource-efficient ways (for example, by initially relying more on third-party channels than on a direct salesforce).

We believe that companies like NEC, Charles Schwab, CNN, Sony, Glaxo, Canon, and Honda were united more by the unreasonableness of their ambitions and the creativity exhibited in getting the most from the least than they were by a common cultural or institutional heritage. If further evidence is needed, consider the less-than-sterling performance of Japan's largest banks and brokerages in world markets. Almost unique among Japan's multinationals, these firms possessed immense resource advantages when they entered world markets. Yet material advantages have proved to be a poor substitute for the strategic creativity engendered by resource scarcity. Further, the burst bubble of Japan's speculative economy in the early 1990s indicates that Japanese companies are no more immune to the strategic ill-discipline that arises from opulent success than the affluent corporate citizens of the West.

A view of strategy as stretch helps demythologize the success of those Japanese companies that have become world leaders despite initial resource handicaps. If the goal is to explain the success of Sony or Toyota or Yamaha, it is more honest to talk about the attributes of resource leverage rather than the attributes of Japanese management. The lesson for Western managers is not so much to become students of Japanese culture, but to ensure that there is sufficient stretch in their own firms to engender a relentless search for opportunities to better leverage resources.

One of us was attempting to explain the logic of stretch to the senior management of a large U.S.-based multinational. Through the 1970s and 1980s, this firm had been one of the world's most consistently successful firms. "Of course," interrupted one senior executive, "you must realize that we are number-one in our industry. Stretch only works if you're number-two." The manager was asked to name a single criterion, other than revenue, market share, or investment, on which his firm was still number-one in its industry. The point was made: This firm was living on the momentum of the past, and it had ceded intellectual leadership in its industry to hungrier, more ambitious rivals. What made stretch difficult for this firm was not that it was the biggest firm in its industry, but that it had not sought out a new definition of leadership more appropriate to its fast-changing industry, and had therefore failed to provide employees with a new, stretching ambition.

If Beta succeeds in reaching its grand goals, nothing guarantees that Beta will not fall into the same contented stupor that prevented Alpha from aggressively pursuing opportunities for better resource leverage. Within the fruits of success are the seeds of failure. A surfeit of resources may very well make Beta as uncreative as Alpha. The problem comes not because a company *is* the industry leader, but because employees *believe* the company is the leader. The arrogance of leadership and the tendency toward profligacy can be avoided only by periodically raising the collective aspiration level or recasting the criteria for leadership. The only vaccine for success is a renewed sense of stretch. Industry leadership is something to be aimed for; neither janitor nor sales rep nor chief executive should ever believe it has been achieved.

Stretch gives birth to the motive for resource leverage. However, much care and feeding is required to transform that newborn desire into a full-grown capability for resource leverage. Exploiting every possible opportunity for resource leverage takes creativity and persistence. A firm with an extraordinary ambition but an underdeveloped capacity for resource leverage will be dismissed as a dreamer. On the other hand, if a firm has developed a nascent capacity for resource leverage (e.g., a track record of successfully exploiting alliances, an ability to move skills across business unit boundaries, a creative approach to competitive tactics), but possesses no galvanizing ambition, it will be a "sleeper." A firm with neither aspiration nor a capacity for resource multiplication will be a "loser," and the "winners" will be those firms that have both.

STARTING PREMISES

Before considering the specific avenues for resource leverage open to companies, let us review our starting premises. The first is that the firm can be conceived of as a portfolio of resources (technical, financial, human, and so forth), as well as a portfolio of products or market-focused business units. A growing body of academic research and writing takes such a "resource-based view of the firm."[3]

The second premise is that resource constraints are not necessarily an impediment to the achievement of global leadership, nor are copious resources a guarantee of continued leadership. If it were otherwise, we wouldn't have witnessed the dramatic shifts in competitive position that have occasionally put seemingly invincible incumbents like GM, Volkswagen, Westinghouse, IBM, Xerox, and Texas Instruments on the defensive.

The third premise is that great differences do exist between firms in the market and the competitive impact they are capable of generating with a given amount of resources. Honda established leadership in its core competence area of engines and powertrains despite a much smaller R&D budget than General Motors. NEC succeeded in gaining market share against Siemens (telecommunications equipment), Texas Instruments (semiconductors), and IBM (computers) despite, for most of its history, an R&D budget substantially smaller than that of its rivals. Chrysler developed its small car, the Neon, for a fraction of the resources typically required by Detroit. IBM challenged Xerox in the copier business and failed, while Canon, a firm only 10% the size of Xerox in the mid-1970s, eventually displaced Xerox as the world's most prolific copier manufacturer. In its adolescence, CNN managed to provide 24 hours of news a day with a budget estimated at one-fifth that required by CBS to turn out an hour of evening news. Such differences beg for an explanation.

The fourth premise is that leverage-based efficiency gains come primarily from raising the numerator in productivity ratios (revenue and net profits) rather than from reducing the denominator (investment and headcount). With the goal of reducing the buck for a given bang rather than increasing the bang for a given buck, denominator-driven corporate restructuring programs are more about cutting resources than leveraging resources. An inefficient firm that downsizes, without improving its capacity for resource leverage, will find that productivity improves—for a while. Technological leadership, brand loyalty, distribution reach, and customer service won't deteriorate immediately, but unless a firm discovers new approaches to resource leverage (e.g., ways of preserving its technological leadership on a smaller R&D budget, building brand loyalty with fewer advertising dollars, deepening distribution coverage more cost-effectively, and improving customer service faster than the rate at which additional resources are committed to the task), it will find, in a few months or a few years, that the numerator has shrunk and another round of nonelective surgery is required. In such cases a firm will continue to ratchet down its resource base until investors locate a new owner with a proven track record of resource leverage.

What this also suggests is that while resource cutting is not an essentially creative activity, resource leverage is. It is about the continual search for new, less resource-intensive means of achieving strategic objectives. Slimming down the workforce and cutting back on investment are less intellectually demanding for top management than discovering ways to grow output on a static or only slowly growing resource base. Cutting the buck is easier than expanding the bang; thus, organizations prefer the former over the latter. Managers and operational improvement consultants must ask themselves just how much of the efficiency problem they're actually working on. If their view of "efficiency" encompasses only the denominator, if they don't have a view of resource leverage that addresses the numerator, they have no better than half a chance of achieving and sustaining world-class efficiency.

Our fifth premise is that the resource allocation task of top management has received too much attention when compared to the task of resource leverage. While numerous textbooks, courses, and consultants have sought to increase allocational efficiency (getting the right resources behind the most promising opportunities through the techniques of portfolio planning and capital budgeting), there has been relatively little emphasis put on top management's role in accumulating and orchestrating a firm's resources, particularly when the focus moves away from financial resources. If top management devotes more effort to assessing the strategic feasibility of projects in its allocational role than it does to the task of multiplying resource effectiveness, its value-added will be modest indeed.

Whatever the starting resource advantages of industry incumbents, and whatever the efficiency of resource allocation, sooner or later, in every industry, the battle revolves around the capacity to leverage resources rather than the capacity to outspend rivals. One crude measure of a firm's capacity to leverage resources is the ratio of its relative market share gain (or loss) to its relative share of investment or resources; revenue growth over resources would be another measure. Thus, while IBM and General Motors are highly rated in terms of their ability, and even willingness, to make strategic investments (where an investment's strategicness is measured by the number of zeros that follow the integer), they rate no better than "poor" in terms of resource leverage. Historically, Philips made so many "strategic" investments and was so poor at resource leverage that, despite the richness of its resource endowment, it went to the brink of financial catastrophe.

This points to the sixth and final premise: The capacity for resource leverage is the ultimate selection mechanism, sorting out the victors from the victims in prolonged battles for industry leadership. It's not enough to get to the future first, one must also get there for less.

ACHIEVING RESOURCE LEVERAGE

Resource leverage can be achieved in five fundamental ways: by more effectively *concentrating* resources on key strategic goals, by more efficiently *accumulating* resources, by *complementing* resources of one type with those of another to create higher-order value, by *conserving* resources wherever possible, and by rapidly *recovering* resources by minimizing the time between expenditure and payback. Let's consider some of the specific components of resource leverage within each of these broad categories.

Concentrating Resources

Converging　The pursuit of a single strategic intent over a long period of time ensures that the efforts of individuals, functional departments, and entire businesses converge on the same goal. In many companies with which we are acquainted there is no such convergence of long-term goals. We often ask managers to look back over the past six or seven annual strategic plans and test them for consistency in long-term direction. What these managers often find is that development trajectories, definitions of served market, investment programs, and even the definition of the firm's core competencies and core businesses get changed far more often than is justified by changing competitive circumstances. The goal of strategic intent is to ensure there is some "cumulativeness" to month-by-month and year-by-year decisions.

Almost as bad as having no clear aspirational goal is having multiple, competing goals. Where there are no shared, corporatewide priorities for growth and new business development, resource fragmentation and suboptimization is the likely outcome. This is not to argue that every multidivisional company can, or should, have an aspiration that encompasses the entire firm. Yet even in multidivisional companies competing within a single broad industry category, we often find that business unit managers possess radically different and sometimes mutually exclusive beliefs about future industry structure and the appropriate strategic intent of the firm. Too often divisional managers seem more interested in "fighting their corners" than in coming to a shared view. Managers become advocates for whatever point of view about the future poses the least threat to the continued funding of their individual businesses. In such an environment, it isn't surprising that the efforts of middle and lower-level managers are uncoordinated and often at cross-purposes.

Convergence requires an understanding of how all the resources of the firm can be orchestrated to achieve a stretch goal, one that firms with a more fragmented sense of corporate priorities cannot hope to achieve. Resource leverage comes only if the efforts of individuals, teams, functions, and businesses are additive across organizational units as well as through time. The principle is quite simple: One doesn't achieve resource leverage by going around in circles.

This fact also suggests that there may be a hidden cost when senior managers rotate across jobs every two or three years. What most often prompts a change in strategy in a large company is not a new competitor, new technology, or regulatory upheaval. What most often prompts change is a new executive in the corner office. It is all too easy for a succession of short-tenure executives to jerk the corporate tiller one way and then the other, confusing employees about corporate direction and slowing forward progress. We know of no company that has achieved a ten- or fifteen-year strategic intent with a succession of two-year executives in key jobs. When it comes to resource leverage, consistency counts. A revolving door in the executive suite frustrates the steady accumulation of insights about just where the future lies. Of course, there is no great merit to management continuity if those at the top are asleep at the wheel, but presuming a company has made the investment in building foresight and is intent on getting to the future first, it must then work hard to ensure that key executives stay in the saddle for some reasonable period of time.

Focusing If convergence protects against the divergence of goals over time, focus protects against the dilution of resources at a particular point in time. We believe that too many firms, finding themselves behind on cost, quality, cycle time, customer service, and other parameters, attempt to put everything right simultaneously, and then wonder why progress is so painfully slow. No single business, functional team, or department can attend to all these improvement goals at once, particularly if there is a sizable gap to be closed in each area. As a rule of thumb, no one group of employees can attend to more than two key operational improvement goals at a time.

The effort required to embed the quality discipline and to change the deeply entrenched work habits, processes, and management attitudes that are barriers to quality is monumental. So too is the effort required to establish just-in-time manufacturing, as that requires a complete rethinking of work flows, logistics, information systems, radical changes to plant layout, and the training of both staff and suppliers. Moreover, the advantages of just-in-time manufacturing are impossible to build without first having a solid foundation of total quality management. Cutting product development times by 50% or more or achieving fivefold and tenfold increases in customer satisfaction are similarly heroic tasks. Without focused attention on a few key operational goals at any one time, improvement efforts are likely to be so diluted that the firm ends up as a perpetual laggard in every critical performance area.

Consider once again Komatsu's quality drive. Many companies have been wrestling with quality for a decade or more and still cannot lay claim to world-class standards, Komatsu came from nowhere to win the Deming prize in three years. What accounts for the difference? When Komatsu initiated its TQC program, every manager was given explicit instructions: When it comes to a choice between cost and quality, vote quality. While quality may eventually be free, Komatsu managers realized that the pursuit of quality is certainly not free in the short run. It involves downtime, investment in better production equipment, training expenses, and so on. Thus Komatsu focused almost exclusively on quality for a period of time; then, having achieved world standards, it continued to keep a close eye on quality while focusing successively on value engineering, manufacturing rationalization, product development speed, and the attainment of variety at low cost. Each new layer of advantage provided the foundation for the next.

Focus is not an excuse to ignore everything else—that would be naive and dangerous. Rather, in providing operational focus, top management simply predetermines the trade-offs it expects operating employees to make when, inevitably, they must allocate scarce time and resources. Focus has brought Motorola a success as striking as Komatsu's. In 1987 Motorola established six sigma quality (3.4 manufacturing defects per million) as its paramount corporate goal—everything else came second. To date, defects have dropped from 6,000 per million to 40 per million, and the company expects to hit six sigma in the next couple of years.

As strategic capabilities, cost and quality are mutually supportive; as operational improvement goals, reducing costs and improving quality both compete for scarce management time and employee attention. At one time, it was assumed that product variety and cost leadership were mutually exclusive. They are not: When one thoroughly understands cost drivers, one can seek ways of cost-effectively accommodating greater product variety. Yet a firm that is far from the leading edge on both cost and variety must build the capabilities in sequence.

Dividing meager resources across a wide range of medium-term operational goals is a recipe for mediocrity across a broad front. Take a simple example. Suppose that someone standing three yards away suddenly hurls five golf balls at your head. What's your immediate reaction? Unless you're a world-class juggler, your first instinct is to duck. This is the same reaction middle managers have when top management attempts to push down five or six key improvement goals of undifferentiated priority. Now imagine someone throwing just one golf ball at you, waiting the few seconds it takes you to catch it, then throwing another and another. All five will be successfully caught in about half a minute.

Middle managers are regularly blamed for failing to diligently translate top management initiatives into action. On the other hand, middle management often finds itself attempting to compensate for top management's failure to sort out operational improvement priorities. Mixed messages and conflicting signals prevent a sufficient head of steam from developing behind any improvement task. Of course, once a firm is close to world standard on most key operational parameters and well understands the interaction of cost, quality, variety, cycle time, and so on, it can move forward on all fronts. Yet a challenge in a fundamentally new area requires a clear focus, predetermined trade-offs, and a critical mass of effort. Put simply, the bigger the improvement task and the smaller the resource base, the more critical is operational focus.

Focus is as important in research and product development as it is in setting operational improvement goals. In many companies, the fertilizer of corporate support is so thinly spread that growth is prematurely stunted in new business areas. 3M, with more than 60,000 separate products, has long prided itself on the breadth of its innovative efforts. Yet recognizing that without more focus big opportunities might remain small projects, the firm launched a "pacing program," in which each business picks one or two products that it thinks offers 3M the chance for a big win. The result, 3M hopes, will be a menu of perhaps 50 key future projects that will serve as magnets for R&D resources.[4] Following a similar logic, the British-based pharmaceutical giant SmithKline Beecham cut the number of drugs in its research pipeline by 26 percent and reduced the number of diseases it aims to treat from 100 to 58.[5]

Where there is convergence and focus, individual mediocrity may well sum up to collective brilliance. In their absence, individual brilliance may well sum up to collective mediocrity.

Targeting   The goal is not just to focus on a few things at a time, but to focus on the right things; to target those activities that will make the biggest impact in terms of customer perceived value. The trick here is to identify those areas where the ratio between value perceived by the customer and the cost of creating that value is as high as possible. Microsoft has targeted its resources on those things that make the biggest impact on the value someone derives from using a personal computer (i.e., the operating system, user interface, and core applications). Likewise, British Airways has worked to protect its margins and avoid deep discounting by targeting those aspects of the flying experience that make the greatest contribution to customer value on long, intercontinental flights. One British Airways innovation was an elegant arrivals lounge at Heathrow where passengers disembarking from overnight flights could shower, have their clothes pressed, and eat a quick breakfast before charging off to important meetings. For anyone who has had to cross the Atlantic and walk straight into a meeting, still gritty-eyed and rumpled, the arrivals lounge is heaven sent. Simply put, resources are leveraged when they are targeted in the areas that make the most difference to customers.

Accumulating Resources

Mining A firm is a reservoir of experiences. Every day employees come in contact with new customers, learn more about competitors, think up new ways to solve problems, and so on. What differentiates firms may be less the relative quality or depth of their experience stockpiles than their relative capacity to mine learning from out of those stockpiles. Put simply, some firms are capable of extracting greater learning from each additional experience than others. Some firms are just more efficient at learning than others. The capacity to mine ideas for improvement and innovation from each and every incremental experience is a critical component of resource leverage.

For example, Honda has launched a fraction of the number of new car models spawned by Ford or GM. How, then, can one account for the fact that, despite its relatively scanty experience base, Honda has often seemed capable of developing new car models in a fraction of the time, and at a fraction of the cost, of Ford or GM? Honda makes a mockery of the experience curve. There's no lockstep relationship between accumulated volume and productivity improvement; it's the relative efficiency with which a firm learns from each additional experience that determines the rate of improvement. The smaller a firm's relative experience base, the more systematic it must be in mining its experiences for any hint of where and how improvements could be made. A common saying in Japan is that an identified problem is a blessing in that it represents an opportunity for improvement. This is a different attitude from that observed in some companies, where problems are either camouflaged or shunted to someone else. The fundamental point is that each new experience, each success or failure, must be seen as an opportunity to learn.

Here's some hard data. Professor Hermann Simon, a German management professor, has reported on a study by the Institute of the German Economy that compared Japanese and German workers in terms of their contribution to productivity improvement.[6] Studying the number of suggestions made by Japanese and German workers, and the impact of those suggestions, Professor Simon judged the performance of Japanese workers to be 514 times better than that of German workers. In a company the size of Siemens, such a difference could add up to forgone efficiency savings of DM 2.2 billion per year. Such an approach to productivity is numerator driven—raising the number of ideas per worker—rather than denominator driven—reducing the number of workers.

The capacity to learn from experience depends on many things: having employees who are well schooled in the art of problem solving, having a forum where employees can identify common problems and search together for higher-order solutions, being willing to fix things before they're broken, and continuously benchmarking against the world's best practice.[7] Unlearning must often take place before learning can begin. What determines the capacity of a firm to mine learning from experience is, as much as anything else, the slope of its forgetting curve. The potential for leveraging the experiences of every employee in the quest for competitive advantage exists only when top management declares open season on precedent and orthodoxy.

Borrowing "Borrowing" the resources of other firms is yet another way of achieving resource leverage. Through alliances, joint ventures, inward licensing, and the use of subcontractors, a firm can avail itself of skills and resources residing outside the firm. At the extreme, borrowing involves not only gaining access to the skills of a partner but actually internalizing those skills by learning from the partner. Internalization is often a more efficient way of acquiring new skills than acquiring an entire firm. In making an acquisition, the acquirer must pay both for the critical skills it wants, as well as skills that it may already have or may deem less strategically valuable. Similarly, the problems of cultural integration and policy harmonization are much larger in an acquisition than in an alliance.

A senior manager in a Japanese firm expressed the simple logic of borrowing. Western companies, he remarked, "cut down the trees and we build the houses." In other words, our partners do the difficult, resource-intensive work of scientific discovery, and we exploit those discoveries to create new markets. It is interesting to remember that it was Sony that first commercialized the transistor and the charge-coupled device, both technologies pioneered by Bell Labs. Technology is increasingly stateless: It moves quickly across borders in the form of scientific papers, foreign sponsorship of university research, cross-border equity stakes in high-tech start-ups, international academic conferences, and so on. Tapping into the global market for technology is a potentially important source of resource leverage. In a sample of 74 small California high-tech companies in which foreign investors had taken a stake, a Japanese company was the foreign investor in 58% of the cases.[8] Harvesting the technology seeds planted in another nation is one method of resource leverage.

Borrowing can be used to multiply resources at any stage of the value chain. Firms such as Canon, Matsushita, and Sharp sell components and finished products on an original-equipment-manufacturer (OEM) basis to Hewlett-Packard, Eastman Kodak, Thomson, Philips, and others as a way of financing their leading-edge research in imaging, video technology, and flat screens. Almost every Japanese firm we know has a share of world development spending in key core competence areas and a share of world manufacturing in key components that is greater than its brand share in end markets. Even today, about half of the output of the Korean electronics company Samsung is sold to downstream partners on an OEM basis. One can think of this as borrowing market share from downstream partners to leverage up internal development efforts. The goal is to capture investment initiative from firms either unwilling or unable to invest in core competence leadership in order to gain control of next-generation competencies.

In such cases, upstream partners can be expected to work hard to internalize the understanding of customer needs, buying patterns, and distribution channels possessed by downstream partners. In this sense, alliances often represent a race to learn. If the upstream partner internalizes the unique skills of the downstream partner more rapidly than the reverse, bargaining power inevitably shifts to the upstream partner. More generally, whenever there is an asymmetry between partners in their relative capacity to learn from each other, bargaining power accrues to the partner that is most rapidly digesting the skills of the other. This partner may eventually be able to exit the relationship and regain its freedom, or it may choose to exploit its increasing control of its partner.

If the goal is to leverage resources through borrowing, a firm's absorptive capacity is as important as its inventive capacity. In our research on strategic alliances, it was obvious that some firms were systematically better at borrowing than others. In simple terms, some firms approached alliances and joint ventures with the attitude of a teacher; other firms did it with the attitude of a student. Suffice to say, arrogance and plenitude were not as conducive to borrowing as humility and hunger. Thus, for some firms, the ratio of total resources to internally developed resources was far more than one; for other firms it was less than one. Some companies were more likely to inadvertently surrender skills to their partners than they were to internalize partner skills. One might term this negative leverage!

Borrowing can take a myriad of other forms: welding tight links with suppliers to better exploit their innovation, sharing development risks with critical customers, borrowing resources from more attractive factor markets (for example, when Texas Instruments employs relatively low-cost software programmers in India via a satellite hook up), or participating in international research consortia (i.e., borrowing foreign taxpayers' money). Whatever the form, the motive is the same—to supplement internal resources with resources that lay outside the formal boundaries of the firm.[9]

Complementing Resources

Blending   Another form of resource leverage rests on a firm's ability to blend different types of resources in ways that multiply the value of each. This is the essence of the resource transformation process. Blending involves several skills: technological integration, functional integration, and new product imagination. Let's consider each in turn. It would be entirely possible for GM or Ford to outspend Honda in pursuing leadership in a set of discrete, engine-related technologies like combustion engineering, electronic controls, variable valve timing, advanced materials, fuel injection, and lean burn, and perhaps even attain scientific leadership in each area, but still lag Honda in terms of all-around engine performance.

What is critical is not just possessing the discrete skills, but one's capacity to blend those technologies to create a world-class engine. This requires technology generalists, systems thinking, and the optimization of complex technological trade-offs. Absolute leadership in a narrow range of technologies may count for little, and the resources expended in that quest may remain substantially underleveraged, if the firm is not as good at the subtle art of blending as it is at brute force pioneering. When it comes to leveraging resources, a capacity for technological integration and harmonization may be just as important as a capacity for invention and may represent a more resource-efficient route to best-in-class product performance.

A second form of blending is the ability to successfully integrate diverse functional skills—R&D, production, marketing, and sales—to produce a successful product. In firms where narrow functional specialization and organizational chimneys prevent such integration, functional excellence rarely gets fully translated into product excellence. In such cases a firm may outinvest its competitors in every functional area, but reap smaller rewards in the marketplace.

Sometimes the issue is less a firm's ability to integrate disparate skills than its ingenuity at dreaming up new permutations of existing skills. Sony has often demonstrated great imagination in blending core technologies in novel ways. Sony's Walkman was a product of headphone and tape recorder skills and created a huge new market. Yamaha combined a small keyboard, a microphone, and magnetically encoded cards to create a play-along piano-karaoke system for children. Resource leverage comes not just from better amortizing of past investments or a particular skill set, but from creating entirely new forms of functionality and, thereby, value-added.

Balancing   Blending and balancing are different—one involves the creative interweaving of disparate skills, the other involves taking ownership of resources that multiply the value of a firm's unique competencies. Yet both are forms of resource complementation.

Let's start with an example. In the early 1970s the British company EMI invented computerized axial tomography (i.e., the CAT scan). Despite having a ground-breaking product, EMI lacked a strong international sales and service network and adequate manufacturing skills. With such an unbalanced resource profile, EMI was a bit like a one-legged stool—long on technology but short on distribution and manufacturing. Because of this, EMI could not capture and hold on to what it thought was its fair share of the CAT scan market. Much of the financial bonanza created by EMI's innovation ended up in the pockets of General Electric and other competitors that, once having figured out a way around or through EMI's patents, used their distribution clout and manufacturing excellence to squeeze EMI out of the market.

To be balanced, a company, like a stool, must have at least three legs: a strong product development capability, a capacity to produce its products or deliver its services at world-class levels of cost and quality, and a sufficiently widespread distribution, marketing, and service infrastructure; in short, a capacity to invent, make, and deliver. If any leg is much shorter than the others, the firm will be unable to fully exploit the investment it has made in its areas of strength. The leverage impact comes when, by gaining control over complementary resources, the firm is able to multiply the profits it can extract out of its own unique resources.[10]

Many small high-tech firms are unbalanced the way EMI was. A firm that has a strong product development capacity but is relatively weak in terms of brand or distribution or lacks the disciplines of cost and quality is unlikely to gain much of the profit stream that will ultimately accrue to its innovation. Although it can enter partnerships with firms that do possess critical complementary resources, the innovator is likely to find itself in a poor bargaining position with such firms when it comes to divvying up profits. This explains why every Japanese company we know, though willing to borrow temporarily the downstream resources of foreign partners, has also worked diligently to establish its own global brand franchise and worldwide distribution infrastructure. These companies realize that they cannot fully capture the economic benefits of their innovation if they rely entirely on others for market access. Thus, they have sought to control critical complementary resources. A similar logic drove Sony's purchase of CBS records and Columbia Pictures. Sony's software enhances the customer value of its hardware, and vice versa.

In the international drinks industry, IDV, Seagrams, and Guiness once saw themselves as primarily brand creators and managers. Yet they now realize that to leverage fully the equity of brands like Smirnoff, Johnny Walker, and Chivas Regal, they must control distributors around the world. This realization has set off a frenzied competition to buy up and consolidate distributors around the world.

Whatever the nature of the imbalance—whether strong on distribution and weak on product development, strong on manufacturing and weak on distribution, or another combination—the logic is the same. A firm cannot fully leverage its accumulated investment in any one dimension if it does not control, in a meaningful way, the other two dimensions. Control doesn't have to mean ownership, but it typically requires something more than temporary, arm's length contracting. Rebalancing leads to leverage when the additional profits captured by gaining control over critical complementary assets more than covers the cost of acquiring those resources.

Conserving Resources

Recycling   The more often a given skill or competence is reused, the greater the resource leverage. Canon applies its optics expertise in cameras, copiers, ophthalmic testing equipment, semiconductor production equipment, camcorders, and more. Canon's cartridge-based imaging system, which first made its appearance in a line of personal copiers, migrated to laser printers and plain paper faxes. Sharp exploits its LCD competence in calculators, electronic pocket calendars, mini-TVs, large-screen projection TVs, and laptop computers. Honda has recycled engine-related innovations across motorcycles, cars, outboard motors, generators, and garden trac-tors. It is little wonder that these firms have unmatched R&D efficiency. It is said that in Japan no technology is ever abandoned, it's reserved for future use. These firms are proof of that maxim.

Unless senior managers across a firm have reached agreement on key development priorities, the potential for recycling will be severely limited. Divisional managers will be more likely to hoard scarce resources than loan them to sister businesses. We sometimes ask divisional vice presidents to rank what they believe are the company's top-ten opportunities. When rankings differ substan-tially across divisional managers, there is no agreed-on basis for recycling scarce resources across unit boundaries.

Of course recycling isn't limited to technology-based competen-cies. A brand can be recycled as well. Again, it is not surprising that resource-constrained Japanese firms have almost universally elected to use "banner" brands rather than individual product brands to capture the economies of scope of banner brands. Famil-iarity with a high-quality banner brand creates a strong predisposi-tion on the part of customers to at least consider purchasing new products that bear the "maker's mark." Think of the leverage Sony gets when it launches a new product; consider the relatively modest cost that faces Sony in building credibility for a new product with retailers and consumers; consider the amount of goodwill with which a new product is imbued simply because it carries the Sony brand.

The ability to quickly switch a production line from making widgets to making gadgets, known as flexible manufacturing, is another form of resource recycling. Some Japanese car producers can make up to seven models on a single production line; U.S. producers seldom manage more than one model per line. Such flexibility means less downtime as production shifts from one model to another, and therefore, better resource utilization.

Opportunities for recycling hard-won knowledge and resources are manifold: sharing merchandising ideas across national sales subsidiaries, migrating operational improvements from one plant to another, reusing a subsystem across a range of products, quickly disseminating ideas for better customer service, and lending experienced executives to key suppliers. Gaining leverage through recycling requires a view of the corporation as a pool of widely accessible skills and resources; it requires that unit managers realize that they are stewards rather than "owners" of key human resources; it requires deeply etched patterns of lateral communication about which resources are located where; and it requires a cooperative spirit among unit managers. These are the organizational foundations for resource recycling.

Co-opting   Sometimes it is possible to entice a potential competitor into a fight against a common enemy. Sometimes it is possible to work collectively to establish a new standard or develop a new technology. Sometimes a group of firms can coalesce around a particular legislative issue. In these cases and others the goal is to co-opt the resources of other firms and thereby extend one's influence and power in one's industry. In co-opting resources, one can enroll others in the pursuit of a common objective.

A firm that seeks to co-opt other industry players must first identify a common objective—that's the carrot. The process of co-option begins with the question: How can I convince other firms that they have a stake in my success? Co-option is often driven by the logic that my enemy's enemy is my friend. This may suggest that being slightly Machiavellian is no disadvantage when it comes to co-opting resources. Their common interest in rebuilding a U.S.-based semiconductor production equipment industry motivated a group of U.S. semiconductor companies to form Sematech with government help.

Sometimes co-option requires a stick as well as a carrot. Typically the stick is control over some critical resource that other players in the industry are forced to rely on. The unstated logic is, "Unless you play the game my way, I'll take my ball and go home." A good example of co-option has been Fujitsu's relationship with its partners in the computer business: ICL in Britain, Siemens in Germany, and Amdahl in the United States. Each partner shared a common objective—challenging the dominance of IBM. That is the carrot. Fujitsu's stick is the substantial, in some cases almost total, dependence of its partners on Fujitsu's semiconductors, central processors, disk drives, printers, terminals, and components.

Co-option doesn't require an equity stake. Although Fujitsu acquired a majority of ICL shares, Fujitsu was not eager to take over the company. Its hand was forced by the risk that ICL's parent company, STC, might sell Fujitsu's long-time partner to a competitor. In many ways, Fujitsu already controlled ICL through ICL's technological dependence. An equity stake was, to some degree, redundant. This is not to argue that Fujitsu had a deep, dark plot to undermine ICL's independence. It was ICL, in the early 1980s, that instigated the partnership with Fujitsu. ICL, more than Fujitsu, recognized that it could not hope to take on the industry giants without a strong friend.

Protecting A wise general ensures that his or her troops are not exposed to unnecessary risks: One doesn't attack a heavily fortified position, one disguises one's true intentions, carefully reconnoiters the territory before advancing, diligently studies the enemy's weaknesses, feints to draw the enemy's forces away from the intended point of attack, exploits the element of surprise, and so on. The greater the numerical advantage held by an enemy, the greater the incentive to avoid a frontal confrontation. The goal is to maximize the losses inflicted on an enemy while minimizing the risk to one's own forces. This is the notion of "protecting."

Attacking a competitor in its home market, attempting to match a larger competitor strength for strength, accepting the industry leader's definition of market structure, or becoming a prisoner of "accepted industry practice" are akin to John Wayne's taking on all the bad guys single-handedly. This works better in Hollywood than in global competition. Judo may be a better approach to resource leverage than a two-fisted brawl. Judo's first principle is to use the opponent's weight and strength to one's own advantage: Deflect rather than absorb the energy of your opponent's attack, get him or her off balance, and then let momentum and gravity do the rest.

Dell Computer, one of the fastest-growing computer companies in the United States, couldn't have hoped to match Compaq's dealer network or IBM's direct salesforce. Instead, Dell chose to sell its computers by mail. Industry incumbents, with big stakes in their existing distribution arrangements, found it difficult to quickly match Dell—not because they didn't have the resources, but because they faced powerful constituents (i.e., dealers) who had a big stake in the status quo. Critical success factors become orthodoxies when a competitor successfully changes the rules of competitive engagement. Such competitive innovation is an important way of shielding resources.

Searching for underdefended territory, or "loose bricks," is another approach to protecting resources. Honda's success with small motorbikes, Komatsu's early forays into Eastern Europe, and Canon's entry into the "convenience" copier segment all failed to alert incumbents, whose attention was focused elsewhere. Understanding a competitor's definition of its served market is the first step in the search for underdefended competitive space. The goal is to build up one's forces just out of sight of stronger competitors.

Recovering Resources

Expediting Success   Another important determinant of resource leverage is the elapsed time between the expenditure of resources and the recovery of those resources, in the form of revenues, via the marketplace. A rapid recovery process acts as a resource multiplier. A firm that can do anything twice as fast as competitors, with a similar resource commitment, enjoys a twofold leverage advantage. This rudimentary arithmetic explains, in part, why Japanese companies have been so intent on accelerating product development times.

In the early 1990s it was estimated that Detroit's Big Three require an average of 8.0 years to develop an entirely new model line; the figure for Japan was 4.5 years, with individual model variants developed in about half that time. This allowed Japanese car makers to recoup their investments more quickly, have more up-to-date products, and give customers more opportunities to switch allegiances. A disciplined approach to agreeing on product development priorities (focusing), seamless functional integration (blending), and tight integration with a network of capable suppliers (borrowing and co-opting) also means that Japanese car companies were capable of developing a new model with 1.7 million person-hours of effort, rather than the 3.0 million person-hours typical of U.S. manufacturers. Not only do Japanese auto firms get a much quicker payback, they need a much smaller payback to reach the black on a particular model.[11]

We have made no attempt here to present an exhaustive list of possible strategies for resource leverage. The goal is simply to challenge managers to be more imaginative in thinking up ways to get the most from the least. Table 7-1 summarizes the aspects of resource leverage we have just discussed. A firm's capability for resource leverage can be calculated, at least in part, in terms of this inventory. We challenge our readers to discover other routes to resource leverage. However, we believe the five broad arenas of resource leverage outlined in Figure 7-6 encompass the range of potential leverage opportunities. By sufficiently *concentrating*,

TABLE 7-1 ASPECTS OF RESOURCE LEVERAGE

Converging	Building consensus on strategic goals
Focusing	Specifying precise improvement goals
Targeting	Emphasizing high-value activities
Learning	Fully using the brain of every employee
Borrowing	Accessing resources of partners
Blending	Combining skills in new ways
Balancing	Securing critical complementary assets
Recycling	Reusing skills and resources
Co-opting	Finding common cause with others
Protecting	Shielding resources from competitors
Expediting	Minimizing time to payback

FIGURE 7-6 CATEGORIES OF RESOURCE LEVERAGE

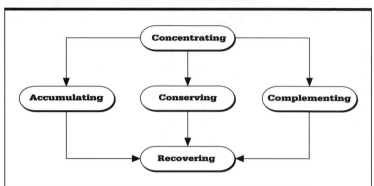

efficiently *accumulating,* creatively *complementing,* carefully *conserving,* and speedily *recovering* resources, firms close the gap between where they are and where they want to be.

ENLARGING THE STRATEGY FRAME

The dominant strategy frame pays much attention to the task of resource allocation. Resources, it is rightly assumed, are scarce; top management must apportion them with care. But isn't it equally top management's job to effectively multiply the firm's resource base through creative approaches to resource leverage? Is leverage any less important than allocation? If not, why the almost exclusive preoccupation of managers and strategy researchers with the allocational task?

"If only we had more resources, we could be more strategic," is an opinion frequently voiced by managers. Yet with a view of strategy as stretch and leverage, it is apparent that the real issue for many of these managers is not a lack of resources, but too many priorities, too little stretch, and too little creative thinking about how to leverage resources. It's no wonder that many of these managers feel they are resource-constrained: In a sense they are. But showering them with more resources, in the absence of a fundamental improvement in their capacity to leverage resources, would provide no more than temporary relief of their frustrations.

Foresight and strategic architecture provide the map, and stretch and leverage provide the fuel. Yet even with these critical ingredients in place, the voyage to the future can be long and tortuous. In the next several chapters we consider what senior management must do to navigate between today's markets and tomorrow's.

Competing to Shape the Future

. . . . .

GETTING TO THE FUTURE FIRST

A finely crafted strategic architecture is worth little without an ability to turn intellectual leadership into market leadership, and to do it ahead of rivals. In this and the next two chapters, we will discuss what must be done to turn foresight into reality and outpace competitors on the road to the future.

There are substantial rewards for getting to the future first—provided, of course, that the risks of pioneering are recognized and managed. Getting to the future first may allow a company to establish a virtual monopoly in a particular new product category, as Chrysler did in minivans and Sony did in portable audio products. Getting to the future first may allow a company to set standards and capture the royalties that flow from owning critical intellectual property rights, as Matsushita did in VCRs and Intel has done in microprocessors. Getting to the future first may enable a company to establish the rules by which other companies will have to compete.

Brokers and mutual fund companies are struggling to come up with a response to Charles Schwab's innovative "Street Smart" software that lets individual investors trade stocks and track their portfolios with a modem and a user-friendly program. Schwab fooled competitors a second time when it negotiated to offer hundreds of competitors' mutual funds through a single, no-load investment account, "OneSource." Not included among the funds on offer were those of Fidelity Investments, the leader in mutual funds. Fidelity faced the uncomfortable choice of either letting Schwab steal a march or bringing competitive funds in under Fidelity's distribution umbrella, and thus, potentially, losing market share. In the end, Fidelity followed Schwab's move.

Getting to the future first may allow a company to build an infrastructure or "installed base" not easily duplicated by latecomers. For example, when AT&T decided, in the early 1990s, to enter the cellular telephone business in the United States, having missed the opportunity to do so in the early 1980s, it had no option but to buy, at a substantial premium, the infrastructure and customer base of McCaw, a company that had entered the business at its inception. In a very different industry setting, many of the sites where Wal-Mart preemptively built its retail outlets cannot support more than one store of such brobdignagian proportions. Getting to the future first may allow a company to amortize more quickly its past investments in competence building, and may force competitors who are denied early revenues to downscale or abandon investment programs.

Companies that fail to get to the future first may end up dependent on those that do. Until its takeover by BMW, Rover, the British car company, was substantially dependent on Honda. It was Honda's engineering and manufacturing skills that saved Rover. Companies that fail to get to the future first often lose control over their destiny. Even when companies succeed in "catching up," their success may be less than complete. Samsung and Goldstar, which entered the VCR business on the back of technology agreements with the Japanese pioneers, have captured a much smaller percentage of life-cycle profits than Matsushita. Likewise, in entering the laptop computer business half a decade after Toshiba and Compaq, IBM effectively ceded millions of dollars of profits to its rivals.

Notwithstanding all this, there is, in many companies, an implicit assumption that it is better to be a quick follower than a pioneer. This belief rests on two assumptions, both of which need to be carefully tested before one willingly surrenders the pioneering role to rivals. The first assumption is that the pioneering role is inherently risky. The second premise is that the pioneer will, inevitably, stumble, creating an opportunity for an alert follower to snatch away the prize of the new market. Let's consider each assumption in turn.

Whereas getting to the future first brings substantial rewards, it can, of course, carry significant risks. The goal is to ensure that those risks are less than commensurate with the potential rewards. While pioneers often do end up with arrows in their back, many companies are not as creative as they might be in seeking out ways to contain the risks of pioneering, and many underestimate the equal or greater risks of failing to lead. The risk that matters most to companies is financial risk: the risk that a large, irrevocable investment fails to produce the intended revenues and profits. Yet getting to the future first is not about "heroic," bet-the-company investments. Getting to the future first is not about outspending rivals, for the race to the future is seldom anything so simple as an investment race. Creativity in leveraging scarce resources can help a company minimize the risks of pioneering new competitive space.

There is often a presumption that it is better to be a follower; that it is more prudent to "let the other guy make the mistakes." The goal of the follower is to let brash competitors rush in where angels fear to tread. The follower lets the impetuous pioneer take the risk that the timing is not right, or the product isn't sufficiently well-developed, or customers don't really need or want the new service. But being first carries a risk of failure disproportionate to the rewards of leadership only when the pioneering firm permits its financial commitment to race ahead of its understanding of the precise nature of the emerging opportunity. The objective is to learn as quickly and as inexpensively as possible about the precise nature of customer demand, the suitability of the new product or service concept, and the need for adjustments in market strategy. This can be done by involving key customers early on in the development phase, by regularly testing emerging product concepts and prototypes with employees and / or with customers in small-scale market experiments, by sharing investment risk with alliance partners, or by using a partner to gain insights into a new and unfamiliar class of customers or set of technologies.

In any case, the goal is not to be first in any absolute sense (i.e., the very first in the world to introduce a path-breaking new product), but to be first with the product that finally— because of its ideal blend of price and performance—unlocks the emerging mega-market. Failed pioneers often claim that "the market wasn't ready." But the market is always ready; what wasn't ready was the product or service in that it was too expensive, too difficult to use, too unreliable, or lacking in some other dimension of performance. A failed pioneer is a company that, having overcommitted to an emerging and underformed market opportunity, compounds the error by failing to learn from its experiences and is ultimately forced to retreat or forgo the opportunity entirely. GE's ill-fated foray into factory automation is one example. Japan's multibillion dollar experiment with high-definition television, and its premature attempt to get the Japanese HDTV standard adopted by U.S. broadcasters and regulators, is another.

Being a successful follower also rests on the assumption that it is possible to waltz in at the last minute and steal an opportunity out from under the nose of the pioneer. There are several unstated premises here. The first is that the pioneer will stumble so badly that its grasp on the opportunity will be significantly loosened. Of course, this doesn't always prove to be the case, and any company that bets the pioneer will slip up is itself taking a giant gamble. IBM willingly surrendered leadership in microprocessors to Intel in the early 1980s, and Intel took full advantage of the opportunity afforded it by IBM. Although IBM soon realized that it had surrendered a good share of PC profits to its partner/competitor, it wasn't until 1994, thirteen years after the launch of the PC, that IBM was able to mount a credible challenge to Intel's dominance in PC microprocessors. In an alliance with Motorola and Apple Computer, IBM hoped to rally PC makers and users around its "Power PC" chip, a direct competitor to Intel's Pentium chip.

Undoubtedly it is sometimes possible to overwhelm a small, less capable early entrant, just as it is sometimes possible to overtake a corporate giant that is less than fully committed to an emerging opportunity. But any company that knowingly surrenders the pioneering role to rivals in the hope of scoring a decisive second strike must be confident in its judgments about competitors' relative capabilities and commitments. Allowing a competitor to take the lead because one is absolutely certain the competitor is overcommitting financially or investing prematurely is one thing; surrendering leadership to a rival simply because one doesn't have a point of view about the future is something entirely different.

A preference for following typically rests on an unstated and often erroneous premise that the follower has in place the skills and competencies necessary for a quick follow-up. Given the ten plus years it often takes to build a world-class competence, this is unlikely unless the follower has previously committed to the new opportunity and has been diligently building up its competencies. Having let Japanese competitors take the lead in camcorders, Philips, Thomson (RCA), and Zenith have found it essentially impossible to catch up. The only sizable consumer electronics business where Philips can claim absolute leadership is color television—a business where almost no company has made any money over the past decade. If one is slow to stake one's claim to future market territory, one may find the most fertile land already occupied.

The lesson is that it is difficult to overtake a pioneer who hasn't overcommitted financially, who has built up the requisite core competencies, and who continues to pursue opportunities for low-cost, low-risk market learning. This is not to argue that a company should mimic or preempt a competitor's hopelessly premature or overfinanced development or market investments. Rather, it needs to decide when to let a competitor rush ahead down a road of folly, and when to redouble its efforts in an attempt to head-off a well-directed competitor at the pass. To make such a distinction, one must have developed one's own point of view about the most likely route to the future and the most likely time frame for the maturation of technologies, evolution of the regulatory environment, and development of complementary capabilities. Simply sitting back and betting the company's future on the possibility that the pioneer will trip up is irresponsible.

Having an independent and prescient point of view about the road to the future is important for another reason. Even when the leader does trip up, a meaningful follow-up may require a company to have begun building needed competencies years before. For example, Sony's home-stretch tumble in the VCR business was of benefit only to those companies—principally JVC—that had been working for nearly two decades to perfect videotape competencies. Once the market took off, the only choice for those consumer electronics companies that had not been in the race from the beginning (Zenith, Thomson, General Electric) was from whom to source (usually JVC and Matsushita).

MANAGING MIGRATION PATHS

To get to the future first, a company must find the shortest path between today and tomorrow. Dreams don't come true overnight, and many years may elapse between the conception of a radically transformed industry and the emergence of a real and substantial market. The goal is to minimize both the time and investment required to turn foresight into genuine market opportunity. You will recall that we identified three stages in competing for the future. Stage 1 is competition for intellectual leadership— developing industry foresight and crafting strategic architecture. Stage 2 is competition to shape and foreshorten the migration paths between today's markets and industry structure and tomorrow's. Stage 3 is competition for market power and position once the new opportunities "take off" and the new industry structure begins to form. Competition in the first stage is competition to *conceive* of an alternate industry structure or a new opportunity arena. The goal is to out-think and out-imagine competitors. Competition in the second phase is to actively *shape* the emergence of that future industry structure to one's own advantage. The goal here is to out-flank and outdistance competitors.

Competition to shape migration paths is, like competition for intellectual leadership, *premarket* or *extramarket* competition in that there is little or no direct, product-to-product rivalry between firms. The preoccupation of most managers (and strategy professors) is with Stage 3 *market-based* competition, where much of the technical uncertainty has been resolved, there is a tangible product or service to offer, the value chain has taken a definite form, and the complementary roles of buyers and suppliers are more or less clear. Yet understanding this final stage of competition for the future, after many contestants have already fallen by the wayside and industry structure has begun to solidify, is a bit like observing the last 100 meters of a marathon: One knows who won but has gained little insight into the training and mental preparation that went on before the race or into the race tactics employed over the 26 miles that positioned the winner for the finish.

Consider a brief example of *premarket* competition. In 1994 the dream of ubiquitous, fully interactive television was still a decade or more away from being a true mass market reality. Nevertheless, a variety of firms were experimenting with interactive TV services in test communities in Orlando, Florida, Castro Valley, California, and other sites. Many firms, including Hewlett-Packard, General Instruments, AT&T, Microsoft, Silicon Graphics, and Philips, were already competing, and sometimes collaborating, to create the set-top signal converters, video servers, and software standards for interactive television. This competition revolved around coalition building, competence accumulation, standards setting, and market experimentation. Each company was hoping to chart for itself the shortest possible course from product concept to market reality, and position itself to capture the biggest possible slice of future revenues.

Thinking in terms of shaping and managing a migration path makes sense because there is almost always more than one possible path to the future. Apple, AT&T, Compaq, Tandy, Motorola, and Hewlett-Packard all have different approaches to producing hand-held computers and communication devices. Typically, several firms hope to find future treasures in more or less the same opportunity arena. Companies that may share the same broad vision of a future opportunity may, at the same time, envision very different routes for getting there in terms of the technologies they are betting on, the standards they are hoping to create, and the configuration of the product or service itself. The "ideal" migration path will be different for different companies, depending on the unique starting point of each firm in terms of skills, resources, and present market position, and on each company's particular and somewhat idiosyncratic view of just where tomorrow's opportunities lie. For example,

Sony has one view of an ideal multimedia future, Nintendo another, Apple another, Philips another, and Microsoft yet another. In some respects these views may be complementary. The revenues each firm ultimately garners from the multimedia opportunity will depend in large part on which product concept wins out, which technical standards are adopted, which applications predominate, and which channels prove to be most important.

In their quest to develop VCRs, Sony and Matsushita (JVC) took different routes to the future. Similarly, Philips and Sony have chosen different routes to digital audio recording as well—with Philips's digital compact cassette (DCC) representing one road and Sony's minidisc representing another. The United States, Europe, and Japan have been on different roads to the future of high-definition television (HDTV). Japan's major broadcaster, NHK, and Japanese manufacturers supported an analog standard called MUSE; the European Community sponsored, to the tune of hundreds of millions of ECUs, a competing analog standard known as D-MAC; and U.S. companies raced to create digitally based standards, one or more of which was to be chosen by the FCC as the new U.S. standard for HDTV. Likewise, a number of computer companies—IBM, Sun, Hewlett-Packard, and DEC among them—have competed to establish new computer architectures based on RISC (reduced instruction set computer) technology.

Just as each company is trying to discover the shortest possible migration path between today and tomorrow, it is trying to force its competitors onto paths that are longer and more expensive, or co-opt them into helping make its own particular view of the future come to fruition. In its many battles with Japanese competitors, Philips has often come up short in the final stage of competition, when the criteria for success are rapid product enhancement and cost reduction. Nevertheless, Philips has often demonstrated an instinct for pushing competitors onto longer and more tortuous migration paths. When Sony threatened to take an early lead in digital recording with digital audio tape (DAT), Philips succeeded in using the influence it had over the recording industry through its Polygram subsidiary to erect hurdles in Sony's path. Philips also worked to ensure that Matsushita would not support the proposed

Sony standard. DAT died a premature death, and Philips gained the time it needed to develop and promote its alternative to DAT—DCC (digital compact cassette). Likewise in the battle for HDTV leadership, Philips, through its membership in a coalition of European and U.S. companies, helped slow down and ultimately derail Japan's attempts to get the MUSE standard adopted in the United States. This forced Japanese companies off their desired migration path and brought Philips, and U.S. companies as well, much needed time to develop a digital alternative to MUSE. The "anti-MUSE" coalition succeeded in restarting the clock on the race to high-definition television. Though of course Japan's consistent competence accumulation in video displays means that whatever HDTV standard prevails, Japanese companies can be expected to capture a sizable share of the economic benefit.

MAXIMIZING SHARE OF INFLUENCE

We have argued that because the ideal migration path for one company is seldom the ideal migration path for another, companies often compete to influence the trajectory of industry development. Depending on which product or service concept ultimately "wins out," a company's investments in pioneering are more or less fully rewarded. Thus, the goal for any company intent on capturing a significant share of future profits in a new opportunity arena is to maximize its *share of influence* over the trajectory of industry development.

Competition to maximize share of influence is part of the broader competitive battle to maximize one's *share of future profits.*

A company's share of influence and share of future profits is determined by four factors: (1) its capacity to build and manage coalitions (accessing and harmonizing complementary resources residing in other companies); (2) its success in building core competencies central to the provision of customer value in the new opportunity arena (only by possessing a critical or "core" competence can one hope to profit from the future); (3) its ability to rapidly accumulate market learning (racing to identify just where the "mother lode" of demand is in an emerging market); and (4) its global "share of mind" (i.e., worldwide brand presence) and distribution capacity (a preexisting worldwide share of mind and distribution infrastructure that ensures one is able to preempt competitors when a new product or service concept finally "takes off"). In many industries there are additional and increasingly vital determinants of a company's ability to manage migration paths and capture future profits: the ability to shape the regulatory environment, influence the emergence of technical standards, and control intellectual property rights (see Figure 8-1 for a summary of key issues in managing migration paths).

If a company is particularly adept in one or more of these arenas of premarket competition, it may gain for itself a share of influence disproportionate to its size. In managing migration paths the goal is, in fact, to maximize the ratio of influence over size. Every company hopes to punch more than its weight and cast a shadow bigger than its actual size. One can easily think of examples of companies whose "influence ratio" has been more than 1, and other companies where the ratio has been less than 1. General Instruments, a relatively small company that possesses unique competencies in video compression (packing a lot of video signal into a relatively small amount of transmission bandwidth), has played a role in the development of interactive television and high-definition television significantly out of proportion to its size. By contrast, in the evolution of the computing industry over the past ten years, DEC's influence ratio has been less than 1. The company was late to exploit the personal computer revolution, late to build critical competencies in RISC architecture computing, and late to recognize the shift in the industry away from hardware and toward services.

A company that constructs and leads a coalition of firms, all focused on the same end product goal, may be able to substantially increase its share of influence. In the remaining pages of this chapter we will consider the challenges involved in assembling and managing the coalition of firms that is often required to create the future, and will briefly consider the challenge of standards setting. We will take up the challenges of core competence leadership, market learning, and global brand building in subsequent chapters.

FIGURE 8-1 MANAGING MIGRATION PATHS

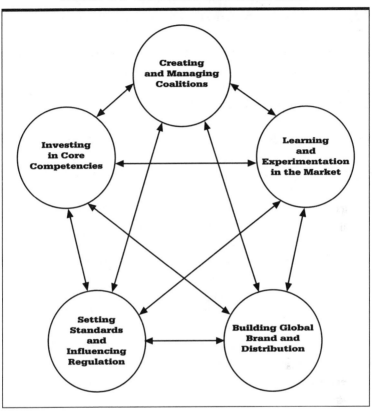

Coalitions—Becoming a Nodal Company

Many of tomorrow's most intriguing opportunities—interactive television, on-board navigational systems for cars and trucks, cell therapy, remote at-home medical diagnostics, satellite-based personal communication devices, a national video register of homes for sale, an alternative to the internal combustion engine—will require the integration of skills and capabilities residing in a wide variety of companies. Competition for the future often takes place between coalitions as well as between individual firms. Sometimes these coalitions are cemented by substantial share holdings, as in the case of US West's investment in Time Warner Entertainment. Sometimes they involve the creation of a new joint venture company, as when IBM and Apple formed Kaleida to exploit multimedia opportunities, or when Warner-Lambert formed joint ventures with Wellcome and Glaxo Holdings to develop and market over-the-counter versions of its partners' popular prescription drugs. And some coalitions simply involve close, collaborative development work such as Apple's cooperation with Sharp for the production of the Newton.

Coalitions may be required for several reasons, the most obvious being the fact that no one firm possesses all the requisite resources to bring the new product or service to fruition. Nestlé and Coca-Cola are collaborating to distribute hot, canned drinks through vending machines, a business largely unknown outside Japan. This alliance combines Nestlé's strength in soluble coffee and tea with Coca-Cola's powerful international distribution and vending machine network. There have recently been a spate of alliances and minority investments linking local telephone companies in the United States (e.g., Bell South, Southwestern Bell, and US West) with cable television companies. Each participating company envisions a world of interactive television-based services in the home, bringing together telephony, entertainment, and on-line retailing. Each company also realizes that it doesn't have all the necessary skills to turn that vision into reality. Cable companies recognize that they need access to the complex billing and signal-switching competencies of the telephone companies, and the telephone companies know that they need access to the broad-band transmission and programming competencies of the major cable operators.

Another reason coalitions form is to assuage political concerns. European consumer electronics companies like Philips and Thomson believed that they needed U.S. partners not only to access technology, but to participate fully in the FCC-sponsored HDTV standard-setting process. A coalition may also be useful in co-opting potential competitors and thereby reducing the threat of future rivalry, or in denying the resources of a partner to a competitor. In signing Matsushita up to support its digital compact cassette efforts, Philips hoped to access Matsushita's global distribution power, as well as preempt any deal Matsushita might make with Sony to develop an alternative to DCC. Finally, coalitions may also help partners share risk. This was an important consideration for the national aerospace companies that came together to form Airbus Industries. Risk-sharing was also an important factor in Motorola's decision to invite partners from around the world to share in the task of launching "Iridium," a $3.4 billion satellite-based wireless communication system capable of reaching portable telephones and pagers anywhere on the globe. The system would rely on more than 60 satellites circling the globe, and even Motorola, with its substantial resources, can't launch the system single-handedly.

Almost every large company has today a spaghetti bowl of alliances, but there is seldom an overall logic to the set of partnerships in that there is no distinctive, underlying point of view about industry futures and no conscious attempt to assemble the companies that have the complementary skills to turn that conception of the future into reality. Thus, although many companies have a wide variety of partnerships, the individual partnerships are often disconnected, each serving an independent and unrelated purpose.

By way of contrast, what we have in mind are multilateral partnerships that possess a clear "cumulative logic." For example, the Japanese video game company, Sega, which is intent on joining the first ranks of the world's entertainment companies, has put together deals with AT&T, Time Warner, TCI, Pioneer, Yamaha, Hitachi, and Matsushita. Sega's partners give the company access to the technologies that will be needed to download computer games over a cable television network, to imbue video games with lifelike graphics, to create "virtual" amusement parks, and much more.[1] Take another example: Whatever the ultimate fate of the product, Apple's Newton integrated the skills and capabilities of several partners: Pacific Bell, Random House, Motorola, Bellcore, SkyTel, as well as Sharp.[2] Some of these relationships were essentially arm's length and some were intimate, but each allowed Apple to access an important competence outside its field of expertise, and all were part of a broad plan to create a new product category. Figure 8-2 shows a variety of other coalitions aimed at creating new competitive space.

In the Newton coalition Apple was a *nodal company* in that it sat at the center of the coalition with a commanding share of influence within it. Influence within a coalition is largely dependent on the relative importance and uniqueness of a company's competencies versus those of other partners. To a great extent, a company's ability to shape the evolution of emerging opportunities depends on its having built unique and valuable core competencies. General Instruments' competencies in video compression have propelled it into a broad array of relationships aimed at creating the future of interactive television. Because Apple may have a broader choice of partners in its quest to access world-class component development and manufacturing skills than do Japanese companies in their search for a company that understands the future of the person-machine interface and user friendliness, Apple has a disproportionate share of influence within its coalition. Competence leadership is the magnet that attracts partners, and is a large contributor to a company's power within a coalition.

Over time the relative importance of different competencies or capabilities may shift, provoking power realignments within the coalition. This occurred in the IBM-Intel-Microsoft coalition that created the personal computer business. IBM's distribution and brand power, so important in the early years of the industry, became less important as other competitors entered the fray, and IBM's "share of market" declined accordingly. While IBM had the whip hand in the early years, by the early 1990s Microsoft felt confident enough to launch an operating system—Windows—that was, in many respects, a direct competitor to IBM's O/S2 architecture, to which Microsoft had earlier pledged its support.

Companies that were partners in the early stages of market evolution frequently become competitors in the final stage of market evolution. Sony and Philips collaborated in the development of audio CD, and then competed vigorously for market share in the market for CD players. The partners of General Magic (Apple, Sony, Motorola, Philips, AT&T, France Telecom, NTT, Fujitsu, and

FIGURE 8-2 COALITIONS TO CREATE NEW COMPETITIVE SPACE

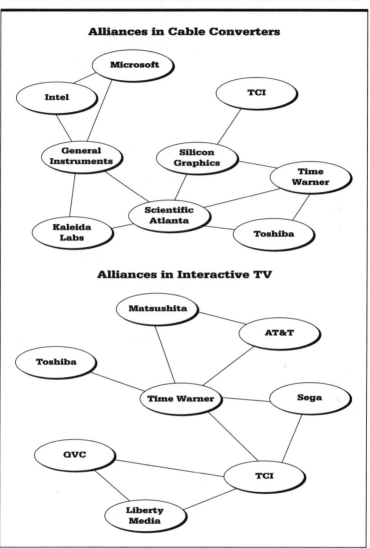

Alliances in Cable Converters

Alliances in Interactive TV

FIGURE 8-2 CONTINUED

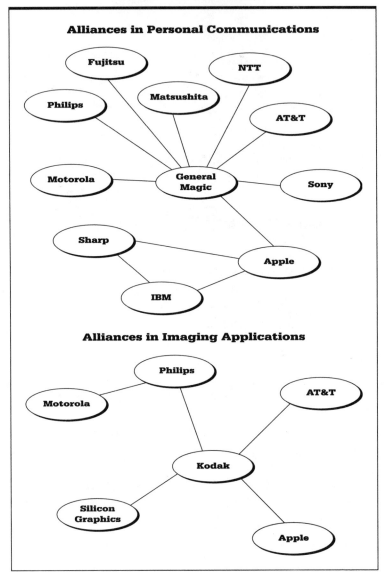

Alliances in Personal Communications

Fujitsu

NTT

Philips

Matsushita

AT&T

Motorola

General Magic

Sony

Sharp

Apple

IBM

Alliances in Imaging Applications

Philips

AT&T

Motorola

Kodak

Silicon Graphics

Apple

Matsushita) are collaborating to create the communication and software standards for hand-held communicators. Yet the partners will become competitors once the market for such devices begins to take off. Each company will offer consumers its own particular version of a personal communicator.[3] In fact, the joint venture has been structured so that each partner has only a partial window into the development efforts underway. "Chinese walls" within the joint venture prevent one partner from learning too much about the future product plans of another.

Managing coalitions thus often entails a careful balancing of competitive and cooperative agendas over time. Coalition members must be careful to keep their competitive instincts in check or run the risk of undermining the partnership prematurely. Companies with a long history of bitter competition may find it almost impossible to work with others to create the markets of the future. Professor Walter Kumerth, executive vice president at Siemens, makes this point when talking about the proliferation of alliances in electronics:

> The future shape of our industry will be much more complex. . . .
> The same companies will compete in one field and cooperate in
> another. This is only possible if you have mutual trust and common
> business ethics. If you have been hitting someone on the head for
> years, cooperation is very difficult.[4]

Sony and Matsushita have often found it easier to cooperate individually with Philips than with each other, given the intense and sometimes personal rivalry between the two Japanese giants. Detroit's "Big Three," which have formed a joint venture to develop electrically powered vehicles, will no doubt face similar tensions.

Nodal firms must accept that all coalition partners may not have the same level of commitment to the concept. Partners exhibit a wide variety of interests and varying levels of commitment. Some of them see their involvement in the coalition as just a "listening post." They want to be involved in monitoring the progress of an idea and see how it is catching on with customers. Their goal is not to make a big one-time commitment to the "intellectual agenda" proposed by the nodal firm or make big investments to support it. At the other extreme are firms willing to make a significant commitment to developing the market and investing in the idea. It must be understood at the outset that all partners will not have the same commitment to building the future. Nodal firms need to have this perspective and understanding in order to manage each partner appropriately.

Influence within a coalition is also a function of the relative "seductiveness" and prescience of the various views different partners possess about the future and their relative commitment to making that future a reality. While there must be, at a broad level, a shared view of the particular future the coalition is seeking to create, and some minimum level of commitment from each partner, one or two partners will typically have a more developed or more compelling view than the others and a greater sense of urgency in creating the future. Such a partner typically understands more about technology trends, has greater insight into lifestyle issues, or is better connected to the regulatory process than its partners. In such cases the foresight of this nodal firm provides much of the connective tissue for the coalition, and its undeniable commitment puts it in a central role. These reasons, more than a disparity in capabilities, placed Aerospatiale as the nodal company in the Airbus consortium.

Assembling and managing coalitions aimed at creating new markets takes a broad range of subtle political skills. One must develop great insight into the motives of all the involved players. Every management team must ask itself: How can we create a situation in which other companies will have a stake in our success? How can we isolate competitors who would like to see us fail? How can we "tie-up," through alliances or equity stakes, companies that possess critical complementary resources (part of the motive for Sony's and Matsushita's buying U.S. movie studios and record companies) and thus deny their resources to competitors? How can we co-opt our enemies' enemies? What companies are dependent on us, and how can we exploit that dependency? Where are the areas of "common cause" between ourselves and others in the industry? In short, with whom and where should we compete, collaborate, and/or contain and control?

Influence within the coalition comes also from an ability to recognize and then exploit, or redirect and frustrate, the differing agendas and concepts of self-interest possessed by the various partners. Managing a coalition requires a Machiavellian sense of the personal agendas of senior executives and of the relative power of each partner. It also requires an enlightened self-interest. Managing the coalition to extract the maximum possible benefits for oneself at every stage is likely to destroy the goodwill and sense of give and take that is critical to a coalition's survival.

Standards Setting

Facing complex, multiyear development challenges, companies are recognizing that it is impossible to "go it alone." Vertical integration, and a concern for keeping all components and competencies inside, no longer makes sense. "Virtual integration" is replacing vertical integration. The relationships among the partners are not transaction oriented; they are long term. One often sees in these relationships interdependence without ownership or legal control. Any one company's capacity to motivate, direct, and manage the coalition derives not from legal control and unilateral dependency, but from political skills, possession of critical competencies, a clearly articulated and inspiring point of view about the future, and a track record of honoring commitments to partners.

Competition for the future often involves competition to establish new standards for the interworking of products and services supplied by a number of different vendors. Standards setting is important in two fundamental ways. First, lack of a common standard can dramatically slow the arrival of the future. With NEC, Fujitsu, and IBM Japan all offering different PC operating systems in Japan, the Japanese personal computer market has been much slower to take off than the U.S. market. In the absence of one or two dominant standards, vendors of complementary products can't capture economies of scale because they must design different products for different standards. The result is diminished potential for economies of scale, higher prices for consumers, and a market much slower to take off. Competing standards confuse customers and make them less apt to buy; many will prefer to wait until a clear winner emerges. When an industry finally coalesces around one or two primary standards, market growth spurts ahead.

For the most part, therefore, companies competing for the future are keen for standards to emerge as early as possible. Not only does this accelerate market development, it also reduces the risk of committing resources to a technology or approach that ultimately fails to become the dominant standard. There are, of course, many factors that work against the early emergence of a standard. Two such factors are technology and market uncertainty. Although competitors may all sign up to a particular standard, as happened among Japanese firms early in the development of the HDTV, the standard will not survive if the technology is still underdeveloped and the nature of customer demand not yet well understood.

Another substantial factor that typically inhibits the emergence of a standard are competing interests of contestants. Herein lies the second way in which standards battles are often central to competition for the future. Put simply, whose standard ultimately wins out often largely determines who makes money from the future and who doesn't. Although each company prefers to see a standard emerge earlier rather than later, each would like to see its particular technical approach to the opportunity emerge as the standard. As individual companies embark on the future, with eyes set on a broad new opportunity arena like RISC-based microprocessors or interactive home video, each possesses a somewhat different conception of the ultimate product configuration and starts out from a different point in terms of technical strengths and other competencies. The result is that each company goes down a somewhat idiosyncratic path to the future; the farther they get down that path (i.e., the more resources they've expended in developing their particular approach to the new opportunity), the greater the negative consequences if their approach fails to become the standard.

The rewards that accrue to a winning standard can be high. Microsoft receives $13 to $14 for each copy of its DOS (disk operating system) shipped by PC makers. With an 81% share of the more than 20 million PCs shipped every year in the United States alone, that adds up to a tidy sum. Microsoft's control of the operating system standard, in the form of DOS and Windows, also gives Microsoft an advantageous position from which to develop application programs. The income that derives from having one's technology adopted as a standard also enables a firm to fully recoup its research investment. Whether you're Motorola or Intel, each new generation of microprocessors costs a fortune to develop, but in recent years Intel has been able to recoup its investment in PC-oriented microprocessor development much faster than Motorola because Intel's "X86" family has been the de facto standard for PCs. Once customers have made significant investments in a particular standard (e.g., all that DOS-based PC software), they are likely to demand that new products be compatible with the existing standard. This, of course, gives the owner of the current standard a significant advantage in future battles for standards leadership. Just such an advantage enabled Microsoft to take its customers from DOS to Windows without dropping the ball. Likewise, Intel has maintained its lead while moving customers from 286 to 386 to 486 to its latest Pentium chips, and Matsushita has remained the world leader in videotape as it has developed VHS into Super VHS and VHS-C (a camcorder standard).

In the next two chapters we consider another critical task in shaping the future of an industry—building the core competencies that will spawn the products and services of the future.

Building Gateways to the Future

. . . .

We have repeatedly used the term *core competence* to describe the capabilities that underlie leadership in a range of products or services. In this chapter we will argue that a key challenge in competing for the future is to preemptively build the competencies that provide gateways to tomorrow's opportunities, as well as to find novel applications of current core competencies.

Any company that wants to capture a disproportionate share of profits from tomorrow's markets must build the competencies that will make a disproportionate contribution to future customer value. Because building world-class leadership in an important core competence area may take five, ten, or more years, a company intent on capturing a substantial share of profits from tomorrow's opportunities must possess a point of view today about what core competencies to build for the future. In our experience, few companies understand how to leverage existing core competencies beyond the boundaries of current business units to create new competitive space. Fewer still have a clear, well-articulated agenda for building entirely new core competencies. Any company that lacks such a point of view is likely to be preempted in the markets of the future.

GATEWAYS TO THE FUTURE

Core competencies are the gateways to future opportunities. Leadership in a core competence represents a potentiality that is released when imaginative new ways of exploiting that core competence are envisioned. For example, Sharp and Toshiba have invested hundreds of millions of dollars in building leadership in flat-screen display competencies. This investment was not predicated on a product-specific "business case," but was driven instead by a sense of the broad *opportunity arena* that might be accessible to a firm with a near-monopoly in flat screens. Potential markets could include everything from pocket diaries to laptop computers to miniature televisions to LCD projection televisions to video telephones. Sharp and Toshiba were committed to building competencies in flat screens long before it was possible to write a business case for every potential application; before, in fact, every specific application could be envisioned. Likewise their early financial commitment could not be justified on the basis of the then-existing market for LCD displays—principally calculators. Yet to have waited until it was possible to construct a convincing product-specific business case would have meant losing competence leadership to firms that were quicker off the launching pad. By 1992 Sharp had a 38% share of the $2.1 billion dollar market for LCD displays—a business that was expected to grow to more than $7 billion by 1995.[1]

Preemptive investment in a core competence is not a leap into the dark nor a megabet on the unknown. For while one can't write a business case for end-product markets that may not emerge for another five or ten years, one doesn't have to be a genius, or even an MBA, to know that if one controls a good part of the world's capacity to produce low-power consumption, portable high-resolution displays, one will have access to dozens of end-product opportunities. It is the simple desire to build world leadership in the provision of a key customer benefit, and the imagination to envision the many ways in which that benefit can be delivered to customers, that drives the competence-building process. Today Sharp and Toshiba are reaping the financial rewards of their prescient investments. And any company hoping to enter a product-market category where portable displays are important (whether IBM in laptop computers or Apple in personal digital assistants), will wind up, sooner or later, talking and doing business with either Sharp or Toshiba.

Clearly, the competencies that are most valuable are those that represent a gateway to a wide variety of potential product markets. To take a financial analogy, investing in core competence leadership is like investing in options. A core competence leader possesses an option on participation in the range of end-product markets that rely on that core competence. Hewlett-Packard's competencies in measurement, computing, and communications give it the option of participating in a broad array of markets that require excellence in those skill areas. Sony's unrelenting pursuit of leadership in miniaturization has given it access to a broad array of personal audio products. 3M's core competencies in adhesives, substrates, and advanced materials have spawned tens of thousands of products. Of course, the flip side is that if a company fails to build core competence leadership, it may be foreclosed from not just one product market, but from a broad range of market opportunities.

A core competence is a bundle of skills and technologies that enables a company to provide a particular benefit to customers. At Sony that benefit is "pocketability," and the core competence is miniaturization. At Federal Express the benefit is on-time delivery, and the core competence, at a very high level, is logistics management. Logistics are also central to Wal-Mart's ability to provide customers with the benefits of choice, availability, and value. At EDS the customer benefit is seamless information flows, and one of the contributing core competencies is systems integration. Motorola provides customers with the benefits of "untethered" communications, which are based on Motorola's mastery of competencies in wireless communication.

The commitment a firm makes to building a new core competence is a commitment to creating or further perfecting a class of customer benefits, not commitment to a specific product-market opportunity. Sony's commitment to pocketability preceded the invention of the Walkman, the portable CD player, and the pocket television. The commitment to core competence-building is based less on a detailed financial pro forma for a particular new product or service than on a deeper understanding of the benefits that accrue to a company that controls, more or less uniquely, the ability to provide that broad class of customer benefits.

An investment in core competence leadership often cannot be justified by the contribution the competence makes to leadership in a single product category. For example, in stark contrast to the early and sustained commitment to flat screens demonstrated by Sharp and Toshiba, U.S. companies tended to be interested in flat screens only to the extent that they were a necessary component of current products, such as laptop computers or small televisions. Most Western companies, concentrating on leadership within a specific end-product market, were for years happy to buy flat screens from Japanese manufacturers. Belatedly, U.S. companies began to realize that flat screens had a multitude of applications, many of them military, and that if they continued to rely exclusively on Japanese suppliers they would not only give away a substantial proportion of the value-added on current products, but would also allow their Japanese suppliers and competitors preferential access to a broad range of new markets. This finally prompted the U.S. Department of Defense to grant $110 million over three years to more than two dozen U.S. firms for research into flat screens.[2] As of early 1994, proposals for as much as $500 million in government support for would-be American flat screen producers was under discussion in Washington. Only time will tell whether this commitment will kick start U.S. competence-building in flat screens or prove to be another case of too little, too late.

It is difficult to get on board the competence-building train once it's left the station. It would be exceedingly difficult for any company, starting from scratch, to quickly match Motorola's wireless competencies, the skills of Goldman Sachs in financial engineering, or the distribution reach of Charles Schwab. Because competence-building represents more cumulative learning than great leaps of inventiveness, it is difficult to "time compress" competence-building. Product cycles may be getting ever shorter, but the quest for core competence leadership is still more likely to be measured in years than in months.

Thus competition for competence leadership typically antedates competition for product leadership. Although AT&T began working on video telephones several decades ago, a critical core competence—video compression—is still not sufficiently advanced to allow the transmission of full-motion, television-quality images over a single telephone line. As we saw in the case of the VCR, it took JVC almost 20 years to perfect the videotape competencies that contributed to its success with VHS; Philips worked just as long to establish its leadership in optical media storage and playback.

INTERCORPORATE COMPETITION

For the most part, the unit of analysis for competitive strategy has been a particular product or service. Issues of positioning, experience curves, order-of-entry, pricing, cost and differentiation, competitive signaling, and barriers to entry are typically discussed in the context of a single product or a closely related line of products. Likewise, competitive battles are usually described in product terms: Diet Coke versus Diet Pepsi, Apple's Powerbook versus IBM's ThinkPad, or the first class transatlantic services of American Airlines versus British Airways. But companies compete in a more fundamental way as well. American Airlines competes with British Airways to develop competencies in fleet management, cabin service, and reservation systems. Ford's competition with Honda goes deeper than Taurus versus Accord; it includes decades-long battles for leadership in powertrains, vehicle electronics, and styling excellence.

Competition for competence is not product versus product, or even business versus business. It is corporation versus corporation. In competing to build leadership in competencies like electronic imaging and printing and fine optics, Canon competes with a broad array of "competence competitors," including Toshiba, Kodak, Nikon, and Hewlett-Packard. Wal-Mart competes with Kmart and Sears in developing world-class logistics. Glaxo competes with Merck to develop new drug-discovery competencies. There are several reasons it makes sense to conceive of competition for competence as intercorporate competition.

First, as we've already argued, core competencies are not product-specific. They contribute to the competitiveness of a range of products or services. In this sense, core competencies transcend any particular product or service, and indeed may transcend any single business unit within the corporation. Core competencies are also longer lasting than any individual product or service. While the constituent skills that go into Sony's miniaturization competence have changed markedly since the company first licensed the transistor from Bell Labs, and while the range of products where Sony exploits that competence has grown and changed, miniaturization has been at the heart of Sony's competitiveness for decades. Likewise, Motorola's core competence in wireless communications has outlived many of the specific technologies that have contributed to that competence, and many of the products that have embodied it.

Second, because a core competence contributes to the competitiveness of a range of products or services, winning or losing the battle for competence leadership can have a profound impact on a company's potential for growth and competitive differentiation, a much greater impact than the success or failure of a single product. If Motorola lost its leadership position in wireless competencies, a broad spectrum of businesses would suffer—including pagers, two-way mobile radios, and cellular telephones.

Third, because the investment, risk-taking, and time frame required to achieve core competence leadership often exceeds the resources and patience of a single business unit, some competencies will not be built in the absence of direct corporate support. Senior management can't leave it up to individual business units, each of which is interested primarily in protecting its position within a preexisting product or market, to identify and sustain investment in core competencies that will secure the firm's position in the markets of the future.

Most important, only by building and nurturing core competencies can top management ensure the continuance of the enterprise. Core competencies are the well-spring of future product development. They are the "roots" of competitiveness, and individual products and services are the "fruit." Every top management team is competing not only to protect the firm's position within existing markets, but to position the firm to succeed in new markets. Hence, any top team that fails to take responsibility for building and nurturing core competencies is inadvertently mortgaging the company's future.

WHAT IS A "CORE COMPETENCE"?

In our experience, many companies are confused over just what is, and is not, a core competence. Having introduced the concept, it may be useful to provide a somewhat more specific definition of core competence before going on to consider the nature of "competition for competence."

An Integration of Skills

A competence is a bundle of skills and technologies rather than a single discrete skill or technology. As an example, Motorola's competence in fast cycle-time production (minimizing the time between an order and the fulfillment of that order) rests on a broad range of underlying skills, including design disciplines that maximize commonality across a product line, flexible manufacturing, sophisticated order-entry systems, inventory management, and supplier management. The core competence Federal Express possesses in package routing and delivery rests on the integration of bar-code technology, wireless communications, network management, and linear programming, to name a few. It is this integration that is the hallmark of a core competence. A core competence represents the sum of learning across individual skill sets and individual organizational units. Thus, a core competence is very unlikely to reside in its entirety in a single individual or small team.

The dividing line between a particular skill and the core competence to which it contributes may be difficult to define. As a practical matter, if in defining the core competencies of a medium-sized company or business unit a team of managers comes up with 40, 50, or more "competencies," they're probably describing constituent skills and technologies rather than core competencies. On the other hand, if they list only one or two competencies, they're probably using too broad a level of aggregation to yield any meaningful insights. The most useful level of aggregation is typically one that yields somewhere between five and fifteen core competencies. If, however, a team has a good understanding of the entire hierarchy of competencies—from metacompetencies (logistics in the case of Federal Express), to core competencies (package tracking), to constituent skills (bar coding)—the question of just where to draw the line between contributing skills and competencies is primarily a question of convenience. In any case, to actually manage a firm's stock of core competencies, top management must be able to disaggregate core competencies into their components, all the way down to the level of specific individuals with specific talents.

Core versus Noncore

Whether one uses the term *competence* or *capability,* the starting premise is that competition between firms is as much a race for competence mastery as it is for market position and market power. Of course, there is nothing very novel in the proposition that firms "compete on capability." The subtlety comes when one attempts to distinguish between those competencies or capabilities that are "core" and those that are "noncore." If one produced an inventory of all the "capabilities" that are potentially important to success in a particular business, it would be a long list indeed—too long to be of any great managerial usefulness. Senior management can't pay equal attention to everything; there must be some sense of what activities *really* contribute to long-term corporate prosperity. The goal, therefore, is to focus senior management's attention on those competencies that lie at the center, rather than the periphery, of long-term competitive success. To be considered a "core" competence, a skill must meet three tests.

Customer Value　A core competence must make a disproportionate contribution to customer-perceived value. Core competencies are the skills that enable a firm to deliver a fundamental customer benefit. The distinction between core and non-core competencies rests, in part, on a distinction between core and non-core customer benefits. It is this distinction that leads us to describe Honda's know-how in engines as a core competence, and its management of dealer relationships as a secondary capability. Whereas the experience a potential buyer has in a Honda dealership is important to the sales process, it does not constitute a core customer benefit. Very few customers choose Honda over competing marques because of some unique capability on the part of Honda's dealers. Nor would Honda argue that its dealer network provides customers with a substantially better experience than the dealer network of Toyota, BMW, or some other first-rate competitor. On the other hand, Honda's ability to produce some of the world's best engines and powertrains does provide customers with highly valued benefits: superior fuel economy, zippy acceleration, easy revving, and less noise and vibration. It is interesting to note that in the advertising that supported the U.S. launch of Honda's updated Accord, the car's engine received several column inches while the dealer network got scarcely a mention. This is not to say the sales mechanism can never be a core competence. For years, IBM's extraordinarily well-trained salesforce was a significant factor in the company's ability to intermediate between customer needs and the company's technological capabilities.

That a core competence must make an important contribution to customer perceived value does not imply that the core competence will be visible to, or easily understood by, the customer. Few customers could express in words exactly why the Honda driving experience may be better than that experienced in, for example, a Chevrolet Lumina. Likewise, few computer users could tell you much about the competencies that support the user-friendly interface of a Macintosh, but they do know that the computer is refreshingly easy to use. What is visible to the customers is the benefit, not the technical nuances, of the competence that underlies that benefit.

Customers are the ultimate judge of whether something is or is not a core competence. In attempting to identify its core competencies, a company must continually ask itself if a particular skill makes a significant contribution to "value perceived by the customer." Although most companies possess detailed cost breakdowns on their products or services, few possess similarly detailed value breakdowns. Questions to answer include: What are the "value elements" in this product or service? What is the customer actually paying for? Why is the customer willing to pay more or less for one product or service than another? Which value elements are most important to customers and thus make the biggest contribution to price realization? Such an analysis ensures that a company focuses its efforts on core competencies that do, indeed, make a real difference to customers.

There is an important exception to the rule that a core competence must make a substantial contribution to customer value. Process- and manufacturing-related competencies that yield sizable cost benefits to the producer may also be considered core competencies, even though little or none of the cost benefits are passed on to the customer. A chemical company, for example, may have a process competence that enables it to produce a certain kind of plastic 20% cheaper than any other firm in the world. The plastic may very well be a commodity and have a world price that reflects the cost structure of the least efficient producer in the business. The more efficient producer, with its process competence, may well choose to "bank" its cost advantage rather than pass it on to customers. Thus, any bundle of skills that yields a significant cost advantage in the delivery of a particular customer benefit may also be termed a core competence.

Competitor Differentiation   To qualify as a *core* competence, a capability must also be competitively unique. This does not mean that to qualify as core, a competence must be uniquely held by a single firm, but it does mean that any capability that is ubiquitous across an industry should not be defined as core unless, of course, the company's level of competence is substantially superior to others. Thus, you could argue that while powertrains have truly been a core competence at Honda, they have not, over the past decade or two, been a core competence at Ford.

In any industry there will be a number of skills and capabilities that are prerequisites for participation in the industry, but do not provide any significant competitor differentiation. We term such skills "table stakes." Just as one may need $100 or $500 to belly up to a high stakes gaming table in Las Vegas, a company will need to have some minimum set of capabilities simply to participate in a particular industry. Table stakes in the package-delivery business include well-trained, courteous drivers. Although no delivery company would last long without competent drivers, the attitudes and capabilities of the drivers have not, thus far, been a differentiating feature among the major delivery companies. In short, there is a difference between "necessary" competencies and "differentiating" competencies. It makes little sense to define a competence as core if it is omnipresent or easily imitated by competitors.

In some cases, managers may believe that a particular competence, while ubiquitous within an industry, has remained substantially underdeveloped. Such a competence might be targeted as a potential core competence if managers believe that there is scope for dramatic improvement and that customers would value highly such improvements. British Airways' efforts to provide a level of cabin service significantly above the mediocre average in its industry is one example.

Again, just as customers provide a reality check on what is and isn't a core competence, so do competitors. In our experience, companies often define a particular skill set as a core competence, even when that skill is more or less common currency within the industry, or when the firm's own level of accomplishment in the skill area is significantly below the industry's best. Benchmarking a company's competencies against those of competitors helps guard against a natural tendency to overstate the uniqueness of one's own capabilities.

Extendability   At the outset we argued that core competencies are the gateways to tomorrow's markets. While a particular competence may be core in the eyes of a single business, in that it meets the test of customer value and competitive uniqueness, it may not be a core competence from the point of view of the corporation if there is no way of imagining an array of new products or services issuing from the competence. As a practical matter, this means that in defining core competencies, managers must work very hard to abstract away from the particular product configuration in which the competence is currently embedded, and imagine how the competence might be applied in new product arenas.

For example, while SKF, the world's leading manufacturer of roller bearings, might be tempted to define its core competence as bearings, such a definition would be unnecessarily limiting in terms of providing access to new markets. No doubt, SKF engineers and marketers have searched diligently for every possible opportunity to apply the company's roller-bearing expertise, but there are only so many places one can put a roller bearing. The company's growth need not be totally dependent on finding new uses for roller bearings because, when SKF moves away from a product-based view of its competencies to a skill-based view, new opportunities quickly emerge. SKF has competencies in antifriction (understanding how different materials work together to either generate or reduce friction), in precision engineering (it is one of a very few European companies that can machine hard metals to incredibly tight tolerances), and in making perfectly spherical devices. One can speculate whether SKF might be capable of manufacturing the round, high-precision recording heads that go inside a VCR, most of which are now manufactured by Japanese firms. Perhaps SKF could make the tiny "balls" that go into roller-ball pens—another component often made by Japanese firms. A core competence is truly core when it forms the basis for entry into new product markets. In assessing a competency's extendability, senior management must work hard to escape a product-centric view of the firm's capabilities.

What a Core Competence Is Not
Just as it's important to know what a core competence is, it's important to know what it is not. We often encounter substantial confusion over the distinction between assets, infrastructure, competitive advantages, critical success factors, and core competencies. First of all, a core competence is not an "asset" in the accounting sense of the word. Core competencies don't show up on the balance sheet. A factory, distribution channel, brand, or patent cannot be a core competence—these are things rather than skills. However, an aptitude to manage that factory (e.g., Toyota's lean manufacturing), channel (e.g., Wal-Mart's logistics), brand (e.g., Coca-Cola's advertising), or intellectual property (e.g., Motorola's ability to protect and exploit its patent portfolio) may constitute a core competence.

Unlike physical assets, competencies do not "wear out," although a core competence may lose its value over time. In general, the more a competence is used, the more refined it gets and the more valuable it becomes. As Honda has extended its engines competence across motorcycles, cars, generators, and the like, Honda's overall understanding of combustion engineering has multiplied. The breadth of applications allows Honda to take a competence element developed in one product market and extend it to another. It is not by accident that Honda has a capability for making very compact, yet very powerful car engines. In making motorcycles, Honda has long understood the need to maximize an engine's power-to-weight and power-to-size ratios.

A core competence is, most decidedly, a source of competitive advantage in that it is competitively unique and makes a contribution to customer value or cost. But whereas all core competencies are sources of competitive advantage, not all competitive advantages are core competencies. Likewise, every core competence is likely to be a critical success factor, but not every critical success factor will be a core competence. A firm might have a licensing agreement that allows it unique access to a particular technology; a company might be granted an exclusive import license for a particular product; a business's factories might be preferentially positioned close to raw material supplies; a firm's plants might be located in a low-wage cost location; customers may prefer to buy from the company because its products are locally produced, as in "Buy American," or because they're produced abroad, as in "real" (i.e., French) champagne. All of these are examples of competitive advantage and each is a critical success factor, but none is a core competence.

A core competence is just what the name implies: an aptitude, a skill. A business may possess many advantages vis-à-vis competitors that don't rest on skills and aptitudes. This doesn't make these advantages any less valuable or critical to success, but it does mean they will be managed in quite a different way than people-embodied competencies.

One of the reasons it is important to distinguish between core competencies and other forms of competitive advantage is that it is too easy for a company to rest easy on an asset or infrastructure-based advantage and underinvest in building unique competencies. For example, for years, Porsche had a sterling reputation among technically sophisticated car buyers based on its world-class engineering skills. Unfortunately, Porsche's brand strength and its ability to command a premium price blinded the company to the relative erosion of its unique engineering skills. It's not that Porsche's skill base deteriorated, but that the automotive engineering skills of competitors, principally Japanese competitors, improved at a faster rate than did Porsche's. By the early 1990s Japanese competitors were producing world-beater sports cars (the Nissan 300ZX, Honda NSX, and Toyota Supra) that could often be purchased for a lot less than a top-end Porsche 911, and that sometimes delivered superior performance as well. Through the 1980s Porsche raised its price with seeming abandon, riding the wave of yuppie brand envy. Inevitably, buyers came to realize that the Porsche's brand premium wasn't always backed up by a competence-based performance advantage. The result was that Porsche's sales in the United States plummeted from a high of 30,741 in 1986 to only 3,728 in 1993.

We distinguish between the endowments (brands, assets, patents, an installed base, distribution infrastructure, and the like) that have been inherited from the past and the competencies that will be required to profit from the future. One gets an accurate reading of a company's capabilities when one subtracts from a company's profits the percentage of the profits that derive from its historical endowments. The remaining profitability is a measure of a company's ability to manage and exploit its unique capabilities.

Intel provides an interesting example. With profits of $2.3 billion in 1993, Intel was the world's most profitable semiconductor company. But Intel's profits are not an entirely accurate barometer of the company's competencies. Buried in Intel's profits are two significant "endowments." First are its intellectual property rights. There is no doubt that Intel is an innovative firm and produces elegant and parsimonious microprocessor designs. On the other hand, if there were as few legal barriers to copying a semiconductor design as there are to copying a retailing concept, much of Intel's profits would be shared with competitors capable of reverse engineering and then manufacturing Intel-designed chips. Intel's intellectual property rights, created by patent legislation and enforced through the courts are, in essence, a tax levied on every Intel customer. A second endowment is Intel's installed base. The fact that Intel's X86 chip became the standard in the PC world owes much to the enormous distribution power of IBM. IBM made the X86 architecture the *de facto* standard. The installed base of X86 microprocessors has given Intel a substantial advantage in migrating customers from 286 to 386 to 486 to Pentium-based PCs.

What every Intel manager must wonder is just how profitable Intel would be if these two endowments disappeared. How, for example, would the competition between Intel's Pentium chip and the Power-PC chip of IBM, Motorola, and Apple turn out if there were no legal constraints on cloning chip designs, and if no competitor had the advantage of a preexisting installed base? Intel's profitability would be substantially reduced. In fact, intellectual property rights are under threat around the world and at some point, as microprocessor technology shifts, it will be impossible for Intel to continue to simply extrapolate on past chip designs or to count on its installed base for forward momentum. A new phase of competition will eventually open up where the only advantages Intel will be able to count on will be its own design, manufacturing, and distribution competencies. Ultimately, what sustains competitiveness is not a firm's endowments, but its competencies. Managers must be able to distinguish between the two.

Core competencies are not just another way of describing vertical integration. In the concept of core competence there is no suggestion that a company must make everything that it sells. For example, although Canon has a very clear sense of its core competencies, it buys more than 75% of the components that go into its copiers. What a company should seek to control are those core competencies that make the biggest contribution to customer value. Nike may not stitch together the shoes that bear its famous name (it outsources that task, just as insurance companies outsource the production of paper for their forms), but Nike does control competencies in logistics, quality, design, product development, athlete endorsement, distribution, and merchandising.

There is a trend in many industries away from vertical integration toward *virtual integration*. In a coalition or network, each firm specializes in a few core competencies. Although managers must understand the range of competencies needed to compete in any particular product or market, they need not have the total complement within their firm. Apple understood this when it assembled a group of firms to help it develop and launch the Newton Message Pad. But one must be careful not to overhype the so-called networked or modular company. The influence, power, and profits of any firm within a virtual corporate network depend on the uniqueness and relative importance of that firm's core competencies. Some competencies, which are core and uniquely define the firm in the minds of customers and provide access to new markets, need to be kept in-house. One can hardly imagine Sony outsourcing its video competence, or Cargil outsourcing its competence in commodity buying, or UPS outsourcing its critical wireless communications competencies, or Swatch its innovative low-cost manufacturing skills. Decisions on what to own and what to outsource are aided by a deep understanding of what is and isn't a "core" competence. Nevertheless, in no case should the idea of core competence provide a license for vertical integration into noncore activities.

The Changing Value of Competencies

What was a core competence in one decade may become a mere capability in another. For example, in the 1970s and 1980s quality, as measured by defects per vehicle, was undoubtedly a core competence for Japanese car companies. Superior reliability was an important value element for customers and a genuine differentiator for Japanese car producers. It took more than a decade for Western car companies to close the quality gap with their Japanese competitors, but by the mid-1990s quality, in terms of initial defects per vehicle, had become a prerequisite for every car maker. There is a dynamic at work here that is common to other industries. Over long periods of time, what was once a core competence may become a base-line capability. Quality, rapid time to market, and quick-response customer service—once genuine differentiators—are becoming routine advantages in many industries.

Sometimes a dramatic structural change in an industry can substantially reduce the value of a company's core competencies. Consider, for example, defense contractors. All of those who worked with the Department of Defense (DOD) acquired a unique competence—specialized contracting skills that were based on specific bidding protocols, long development cycles, unique accounting procedures, adherence to security guidelines, and so on. With the "ending" of the Cold War and the dramatic scaling down of U.S. defense procurement, U.S. military contractors have found some of their competencies to be of less value than they were a decade or two ago. Although DOD suppliers have enormous technological capabilities, they are unable to make rapid breakthroughs in commercial markets in part because many of their historic competencies are of little value in non-defense markets.

MULTIPLE LEVELS OF COMPETITION FOR COMPETENCE

In Chapter 2 we argued that competition for the future takes place in three stages (competition for intellectual leadership, competition to shape migration paths, and competition for market share and position). Competition for competence takes place at four levels (see Figure 9-1). Understanding the nature of competition at each level is critical to winning the race to establish core competence leadership. In most companies and strategy textbooks, competition for brand share, Level 4, receives 99% of the attention. We believe that this is inappropriate because much of the battle for the future takes place at Levels 1 through 3, as we now describe.

Level 1: Developing and Acquiring Constituent Skills and Technologies

The goal of Level 1 competition is to acquire or develop the constituent skills or technologies that make up a particular core compe-

FIGURE 9-1 COMPETITION FOR COMPETENCE

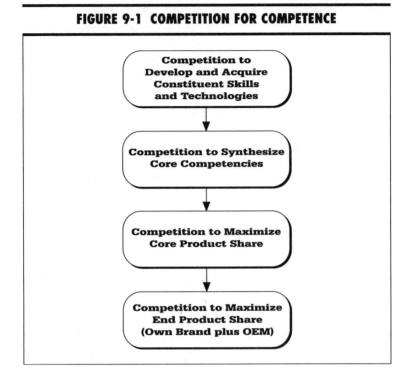

tence. This competition takes place in the markets for technology, talent, alliance partners, and intellectual property rights. Far-sighted companies compete for access to the individual skills and technologies that comprise a more general core competence. For a pharmaceutical firm this may take the form of competing to "tie-up" leading-edge professors and university departments in long-term research contracts. For a Japanese electronics company it may mean taking preemptive equity positions in or licenses from small California start-ups. For a leading brokerage company it may mean competing to hire the best finance Ph.D. graduates each year.

Companies intent on building core competencies in new areas may also compete to establish preemptive, and perhaps exclusive, relationships with other interested parties. This could mean competing for access to government research contracts, competing to form a joint venture with a company that possesses related skills, or competing to entice a potential customer into a long-term development contract. Another way in which companies compete for competence leadership is by competing to be first to register patents protecting their particular approach to providing customer benefits from imitation.

Resource leverage at this stage of the battle comes principally from an ability to access and "absorb" skills and technology from outside. Japanese companies in particular, and Asian companies in general, have been adept at importing science and ideas from the West and combining them into world-class competencies. Western technology has been imported via strategic alliances, licensing agreements, the repatriation of students who have attended U.S. universities, and equity investments in entrepreneurial start-ups.

Often, long-term alliances allow companies insight into competencies that are deeply buried within the fabric of a partner. Thomson, the French consumer electronics firm, learned much from JVC, its partner in VCR production, about the subtle interplay of hard technology and process improvement skills that combine to produce a world-class manufacturing competence. When the relationship began, Thomson knew next to nothing about how to make a VCR—at that time the most complex consumer electronics product in existence. Five or so years later Thomson was able to start production of VCRs in Singapore, more or less free of JVC's help.

Japanese companies have been especially adept at learning. NEC, a company that has had significant strategic alliances with Hughes, Intel, and Honeywell, as well as with dozens of other companies, learned much from its foreign partners. In a similar fashion, General Motors has used its joint venture with Toyota—NUMMI—as a window on Toyota's comparatively low-tech, high-touch approach to manufacturing. The point here is that if the goal is to import something that is closer to a fully developed competence, rather than a specific skill or technology, a long-term relationship with a very capable partner may be required.

Level 2: Competition to Synthesize Competencies

Whereas companies may compete directly to hire key people, secure an exclusive license, or tie up a partner, the competition to turn discrete skills into competencies is much less direct, though no less important. Earlier we argued that a competence represents the synthesis of a variety of skills, technologies, and knowledge streams. A portfolio of discrete skills does not a competence make. A core competence is a tapestry, woven from the threads of distinct skills and technologies. A car company could hire the best engineers and technologists, and lavish billions on R&D, and still not produce the best engines. A competence in powertrains requires the integration of knowledge about combustion engineering, electronic engine management systems, advanced materials, and so on. What is critical is an ability to harmonize a wide variety of disparate skills and technologies. What is required are generalists, not just narrow specialists. Experts who are sympathetic to other disciplines, and who can overcome the parochial perspectives of their specific technical or functional background, are rare. Just as absorption may be as important as invention, integration may be as important as invention. If the inventive capacity of Japanese companies has, in years past, not been as highly developed as that of some Western competitors, Japanese firms have more than compensated by excelling at absorption and integration.

Many companies have had difficulty blending the multiple streams of science or technology that comprise their heritage into new, higher-order competencies. Kodak has been attempting just such a feat by trying to blur the line between its experts in fine chemistry and its experts in digital imaging and electronics. One early success for Kodak was a product called Tele-Cine, which allows a movie maker to transfer an image from film into a digital format, manipulate that image through the use of computers, and then return the image to film with no distortion in color standards and no loss of clarity. Kodak won an Oscar for the product.

At this stage of competence building, leverage comes not from borrowing from outside, but from reusing a competence in multiple applications. For example, EDS applies its understanding of scheduling, reservation systems, and tracking in vertical markets as diverse as auto rentals, airlines, and trucking.

Level 3: Competition for Core Product Share

The third level of competition occurs around what we call *core products* or, in the case of services, *core platforms*. A core product or platform is most typically an intermediate product somewhere between the core competence and the end-product. Many companies seek to sell core products to other companies, even to competitors, on an original equipment manufacturer (OEM) basis, as a way of capturing "virtual market share." Leverage here comes from "borrowing" the distribution channels and brands of downstream partners. This virtual market share, and the revenues and experience it brings, allows the company to accelerate its core competence–building efforts.

For example, Canon sells laser printer engines to Apple, Hewlett-Packard, and other companies that make laser printers. The engine is the heart of the printer, and Canon is, by far, the world's most prolific producer of such engines. Canon's core product share is far higher than its brand share in laser printers. Canon is content to rely on the distribution power of its partners and to concentrate its investment on building leadership in laser and bubble jet printing competencies.

Directly measuring Canon's competence share would be difficult, but by looking at its share of "core products"—intermediary products or services that lie between the competence and the end product—one can gain some appreciation of Canon's competence share. Japanese companies in particular have concentrated on building core-product share as a way of supporting their core competence–building efforts. Almost every Japanese company and all the major Korean multinationals have used OEM relationships to bolster core-product share. Sometimes core products are sold as components, and sometimes they are packaged inside finished products that will be sold under another company's brand name. Examples include making microwaves for GE, videotape recorders for RCA, computers for ICL, engines and powertrains for Ford, airframe components for Boeing, and flat screens for Apple. Asian companies have typically had a ratio of core-product share to brand share greater than 1. Fully one-third of what Samsung makes is sold as a component in someone else's product or under someone else's brand name.[3] Thus, Samsung's manufacturing share is substantially higher than its brand share. Although Taiwanese companies are virtually unknown outside their own country, Intel's country manager in Taiwan believes that it would be difficult for any Western computer maker to compete without a Taiwanese supplier: "I don't think any computer company can survive nowadays without buying from Taiwan. Taiwan has become the arms dealer of the computer wars."[4] Taiwanese companies like Acer, Tatung, Inventec, Datatech, and Compal sell components to Apple, Dell, IBM, and AST, among other companies.

The goal may, in fact, be to build a monopoly in some particular core competence area, or as close to a monopoly as possible. The ability to build an end-product monopoly is limited by legal constraints and the fragmentation of distribution channels, but there are often no such constraints on core-product share, and hence core competence share. For years, following its invention of VHS, Matsushita made a substantial majority of the world's VCR components, bolstering and reinforcing its competence in videotape. Consequently, an industry is often much more concentrated at the level of core products than it is at the level of end products. Thus, whereas a plethora of companies produce laptop computers, only two companies—Sharp and Toshiba—produce, in significant volumes, the flat screen displays that make a laptop truly portable. In 1993, Sharp's market share in flat screens (near 40%)[5] was far higher than the brand share of any of its computer-making customers. Given the very different levels of rivalry in the core-product and end-product markets, one shouldn't be surprised to find that the margins Sharp and Toshiba enjoy on their flat-screen sales are somewhat healthier than those gained by companies like AST and Zenith, who assemble the end product.

The notion of core-product share is applicable in service businesses as well. Marriott sells its core competencies in catering and facilities management to companies seeking to contract out management of conference facilities or company cafeterias, as well as delivering its competencies directly to customers via Marriott-branded hotels. Federal Express has created a business where it sells core products in the form of systems and consulting to any company that needs to manage a complicated logistical problem. In this case FedEx is not selling the end product—package delivery—but an intermediate service.

American Airlines' willingness to share its reservation system with its competitors, and sell information services through its IT subsidiary, AMRIS, enables American to leverage its investments in building data management competencies. More important, it reduces the incentives of rivals to make an investment in building a similar competence. Over time, it becomes increasingly difficult for competitors to match the investment as well as the knowledge base that American has. One could argue that the airline business is increasingly an information management business—if one considers the number of point-to-point fares globally, the need to capture an increasing share of customer travel dollars by moving traffic through hubs, and managing customer loyalty through frequent flyer packages. Designing data structures, choosing hardware and software packages, training thousands of airline reservation clerks and travel agents, and making the system operate on a "real time basis" for selectively pricing seats on any specific flight between two points are complex skills. They certainly represent a competence, and American's sale of this competence to potential competitors, in the form of core data management "platforms," works to continually enhance American's core competence leadership.

More and more companies are understanding the value of selling core products. In recent years IBM has begun to reverse a long-standing company policy and is now willing to sell core products (components and modules) to just about anybody—friend or foe. Between 1990 and 1993, IBM's sales of technology to outsiders zoomed from $300 million to $3 billion.[6] The reasons for such a shift are several. In the years when IBM had absolute distribution dominance (when computers were sold almost exclusively through direct channels and IBM had the biggest and best direct salesforce), there was little incentive for IBM to sell core products to outsiders. IBM's own channels gave the company enough volume and market share to stay ahead in the race to improve semiconductor, software, and computer architecture competencies. With the proliferation of channels and new competitors, IBM executives came to realize that they could not guarantee the company's continued leadership in critical core competence areas unless IBM's "aperture" to the market widened. The market coverage of IBM's direct salesforce represented, each year, a smaller and smaller percentage of the total available market. Likewise, the company came to realize that the IBM brand also represented an unnecessarily restrictive gateway to potential markets. Additionally, some of IBM's core competence competitors (NEC, Sony, and Sharp, for example), were substantially more horizontally diversified. These companies had a broader product scope across which to amortize competence-building efforts. To maintain core competence leadership, IBM thus needed the volume it could derive by selling core products and platforms through other channels.

The decision to sell core products to outsiders to be incorporated into products bearing a competitor's brand name often causes a fair amount of consternation to a company's direct salesforce and senior marketing executives. The question that always comes from the internal sales force is, "How can we maintain our competitive differentiation if we sell our core products, our 'crown jewels,' to rivals?" What the marketing and sales function seldom sees is the alternate question, "How can we maintain absolute leadership in our core competence areas if we limit our volumes, and therefore our revenues and market learning opportunities, to our own sales channels?" In our experience, the greater the angst of sales and marketing managers over the decision to sell core products to outsiders, the more likely it is that the firm's in-house channels are less efficient than alternate distribution channels. When, by purchasing a company's core products, competitors can offer products with similar performance characteristics, the internal sales force will be successful only if they can offer customers some additional value-added over and above that inherent in the product itself. If they cannot, and if they are a more expensive channel than the alternatives, there is no reason they should be given an exclusive right to the firm's core products.

In this sense, selling core products to outsiders is often a very healthy discipline for the sales and marketing function—it puts pressure on managers to ensure that they are not merely living off the competitiveness created "upstream" in the business, but are adding sufficient additional value to justify their overheads. Likewise, selling core products to outsiders is a good barometer of whether the company really is a competence leader. If competitors and others don't line up to buy the company's core products, the firm's core competencies are probably not as terrific as some insiders might claim.

We find very few companies where the distinction between core competence share, core-product share, and brand share are clearly drawn. Typically, the "share" over which senior management is most concerned is brand share. This may be an inappropriate focus, particularly if it leads to decisions to outsource core products that are critical to end-product competitiveness. A company that outsources a large share of core product may find itself, over time, becoming more and more dependent on its suppliers. Until it was snapped out of the clutches of Honda by BMW, Rover, the British car company, was substantially dependent on Honda for key auto components such as the engine and the design of vehicle platforms. Honda's equity stake of 20% significantly underestimated the Japanese company's actual control over its British partner. When a company's brand share is significantly higher than its core product share or core platform share, it runs the risk of losing control over its destiny. Again, this is not an argument for doing everything in-house; it is an argument for being very clear on just what skills one deems critical to competitive differentiation and growth, and ensuring that those skills are not inadvertently surrendered through outsourcing.

In recent years U.S. companies have become much more alert to the dangers of relying on potential competitors for the supply of core products. In industries with rapid product cycles, a supplier's decision to withhold a critical core product from a downstream customer can have devastating consequences on the latter's competitiveness. In more than one case, U.S. companies have brought suit against Japanese suppliers for such an alleged breach of good faith. Of course it is very difficult to prove that the supplier was doing anything more than "working out the bugs" before shipping the core product to outside customers.

Dependency around core products is not always asymmetrical; it may be reciprocal. Ford and Mazda have long exchanged products, core and otherwise, as have Philips and Matsushita. And though U.S. computer companies must rely on Japanese and Taiwanese companies for core products, Asian companies must rely on companies like Microsoft and Intel to provide the computer's basic intelligence. Where core products flow both ways, where all partners understand and work to protect their own unique core competencies, and where all partners are alert to both the competitive and collaborative aspects of their relationships, then outsourcing need not lead to "hollowing out." Again, the argument here is not that a company must make everything it sells, only that in deciding to outsource critical components, a company must consider carefully the long-term competitive implications and the nature of dependency that will result.

So our argument is this: Corporate strategy must be more than an amalgamation of individual unit strategies. Because core competencies are the highest level, longest-lasting units for strategy making, they must be the central subject of corporate strategy. Top management must have a point of view on which new competencies to build. It must know whether current competencies are slowly eroding or are being strengthened. It must be able to distinguish between a business to be divested and the competencies within that business that should be retained. It must also be acutely aware of the competence-building efforts of competitors, and must recognize that the company's "competence competitors" may not be identical to current end-product competitors. How one builds a core competence perspective in a company focused single-mindedly on end products or services is the subject of Chapter 10.

Embedding the Core Competence Perspective

he core competence perspective is not a natural one in most companies. Typically, the most basic sense of corporate identity is built around market-focused entities, often called "strategic business units," rather than around core competencies. Whereas it is entirely appropriate to have a strong end-product focus in an organization, this needs to be supplemented by an equally explicit core competence focus. A company must be viewed not only as a portfolio of products or services, but a portfolio of competencies as well.

THE RISKS OF IGNORING CORE COMPETENCIES

A multitude of dangers await a company that can't conceive of itself and its competitors in core competence terms. First is the risk that opportunities for growth will be needlessly truncated. Why didn't CBS, which owned a television network and a successful music recording business, see the opportunity for music television? Instead this "white space" was captured by Viacom's MTV. Too often an opportunity that falls between the cracks of existing market definitions, and has no natural "home," gets overlooked. Most companies work hard to delineate precisely unit-by-unit ownership of existing competitive space, but shouldn't equal attention be given to assigning responsibility for new competitive space?

Second, even if someone in the organization spots a new opportunity, if the competencies that are needed to respond to that opportunity lie in another business unit, there may be no way to redeploy the people who "carry" those competencies into the new opportunity arena. Unit managers are notoriously protective of "their" people, and in few companies are there any explicit mechanisms for ensuring that the best talent gets aligned behind the most attractive new opportunities. The result is imprisoned and underleveraged competencies.

Third, as a company divisionalizes and fractures into ever-smaller business units (a popular trend recently), competencies may become fragmented and weakened. Business unit boundaries may make cross-application difficult and slow the cumulative learning processes through which competencies are enhanced. Individual business units are willing to support competence-building efforts only to the extent that the competence contributes to the competitiveness of today's end products. Often, an individual business unit can sustain neither the investment nor the patience to build a new core competence.

Fourth, the lack of a core competence perspective can also desensitize a company to its growing dependence on outside suppliers of core products. Managers whose only focus is on maximizing brand share may find it expedient to "rent" a competitor's competencies rather than invest to build one's own. This is, as we've argued, an often dangerous short-cut to competitiveness.

Fifth, a company focused only on end products may fail to invest adequately in new core competencies that can propel growth in the future. Tomorrow's growth depends on today's competence-building. Investment in new core competencies provides the seeds for tomorrow's product harvest.

Sixth, a company that fails to understand the core competence basis for competition in its industry may be surprised by new entrants who rely on competencies developed in other end markets. Witness the entry of GM or AT&T into the credit card business. Having built financial competencies to support their core business, they used those competencies to enter new businesses. This happens regularly within the financial services industry because, whatever their end-product focus, financial services companies vie for leadership in a set of more or less common competence areas (see Figure 10-1). Companies are often surprised when a competitor that has built core competencies to support its participation in one end-product market uses that skill to enter another.

And seventh, companies insensitive to the issue of core competence may unwittingly relinquish valuable skills when they divest an underperforming business. In the 1970s, Motorola sold its television plants to Matsushita and exited the television business. Although the decision to get out of the competitive consumer electronics business was probably foresightful, Motorola today might wish it had preserved some of the competencies buried within its former consumer electronics business. Recently, Motorola has recognized that it must rebuild a competence in video displays. To protect core competencies, a company must be able to distinguish between a bad business and the potentially valuable competencies buried within that business.

THE CORE COMPETENCE PERSPECTIVE

For the core competence perspective to take root in an organization, the entire management team must fully understand and participate in the five key competence management tasks: (1) identifying existing core competencies; (2) establishing a core competence acquisition agenda; (3) building core competencies; (4) deploying core competencies; and (5) protecting and defending core competence leadership.

Identifying Core Competencies

A firm can't actively "manage" core competencies if managers don't share a view of what those core competencies are. Thus, the clarity of a firm's definition of its core competencies and the degree of consensus that attaches to that definition are the most rudimentary tests of a company's capacity to manage its core competencies. Whereas most managers will have some sense of "what we do well around here," they may be quite unable to draw any kind of specific

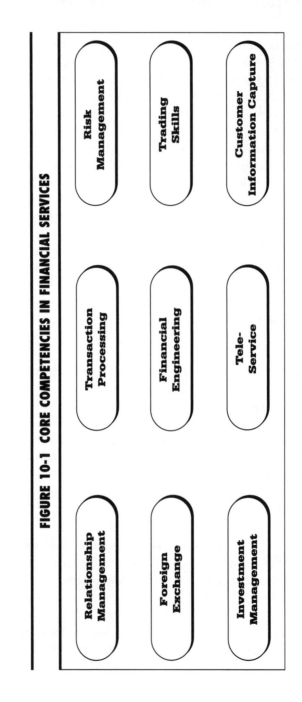

FIGURE 10-1 CORE COMPETENCIES IN FINANCIAL SERVICES

Relationship Management

Foreign Exchange

Investment Management

Transaction Processing

Financial Engineering

Tele-Service

Risk Management

Trading Skills

Customer Information Capture

link between particular skill sets and the competitiveness of end products and services. The first task in managing core competencies is therefore to produce an "inventory" of core competencies.

When we have observed companies attempting to define their core competencies, the process tends to be haphazard and political. The first attempt typically produces a lengthy "laundry list" of skills, technologies, and capabilities—some core, but most not. Every participant in the process wants to ensure that the activities he or she manages are regarded as "core." A substantial amount of effort is required to fully disentangle competencies from the products and services in which they're embedded, to distinguish core from noncore, to cluster and aggregate the skills and technologies in some meaningful way, and to arrive at "labels" that are truly descriptive and promote shared understanding. The time it takes to arrive at an insightful, creative, and shared definition of core competencies is, in a large company, more likely to be measured in months than weeks.

We find that companies typically fall into one of several traps when attempting to identify core competencies. One of the most frequent is delegating the task to the technical community. There is a clear danger in taking such an approach. Core competencies are the soul of the company and as such they must be an integral part of the process of general management. When only the technical community feels ownership, the usefulness of the concept in building new businesses is jeopardized considerably. Too often the concept of core competencies is highjacked by the technical community in a bid for stature and resources.

Other traps include mistaking assets and infrastructure for core competencies and an inability to escape an orthodox product-centered view of a firm's capabilities. Additionally, if executives are too rushed to "get the job done," they may fail to generate a deep and common understanding of what the chosen core competence "labels" mean. A wide group of people must be capable of describing the competence in reasonably similar terms and share an understanding of just what constituent skills are embodied within the competence. When, at Motorola, someone talks about the Semiconductor Products Sector, everyone across the company has a good idea of what products are encompassed within that divisional designation. What is equally important is that everyone share a reasonably precise definition of what is included under the company's broad "wireless" competence.

There is yet another frequent pitfall. Companies often fail to apply the test of "customer perceived value" to their list of competencies. Understanding the link between competence and benefit is critical in identifying competencies that are genuinely core.

We often recommend that several teams work on defining core competencies. Each team should encompass a broad cross-section of employees—functionally, divisionally, geographically, and hierarchically. Seeking a diversity of views ensures that the best possible definition emerges.

It is important not just to identify and agree on what the core competencies are but to identify the elements that contribute to each core competency. For example, expertise in the science of color, inks, dyes, substrates, coating, paper handling, and a host of such elements or discrete skills adds up to the core competence in chemical imaging at Eastman Kodak. It is important that these discrete skills are identified and an inventory of people who possess those skills developed. One company succeeded in developing a hierarchy that extended from competencies to skills and technologies to individual employees—"competence holders." This hierarchy could be accessed through a computer data base so that if someone in the company needed to access a particular competence, he or she could locate the right person. Such visibility to a firm's core competence resources is vital if they are to be fully exploited and easily redeployed.

Further, companies need to benchmark their core competencies with other firms. However, traditional competitors may not be the ones to worry most about. For example, Kodak should be concerned with Fuji, Agfa, 3M, and other such traditional competitors, but must also worry about Canon, Sony, Hitachi, and Toshiba, all of which may be approaching the imaging opportunities very differently.

Senior managers must be full participants in the process of identifying core competencies. The process will involve many meetings, heated debate, frequent disagreements, unexpected insights, and a sense of excitement about potential new opportunities. The task of discovering a firm's core competencies is not one that senior management can delegate, neither can it be squeezed into a two- or three-day "offsite." The goal of the process is to develop a wide and deep understanding of the skills that currently underpin the firm's success, to escape the myopia of the served market, to highlight the "shared property" of the firm, to point the way to new business, to raise sensitivity to the reality of competition for competence, and to provide the basis for actively managing what, after all, are the firm's most valuable resources. The exercise to identify core competencies cannot take a mechanistic, follow-the-checklist approach.

Establishing the Core Competence Acquisition Agenda

Although a company's competence-building agenda is determined by its strategic architecture, a competence-product matrix is often useful in setting specific competence acquisition and deployment goals. The matrix distinguishes between existing and new competencies, and between existing and new product-markets (see Figure 10-2).

Fill in the Blanks   The lower-left quadrant represents the firm's existing portfolio of competencies and products or services. By mapping which competencies support which end-product markets, a company can identify opportunities to strengthen its position in a particular product market by importing competencies that may reside elsewhere in the corporation. We term this "filling in the blanks." Table 10-1 demonstrates how widely Canon has deployed its core competencies across its product line. In like manner, GE has successfully transferred competencies between its power generator business and its jet engine business, both of which rely on advanced materials and engineering skills to produce large turbines. Every company should ask itself where the opportunities are to broaden the deployment of existing competencies to strengthen position in existing markets.

FIGURE 10-2 ESTABLISHING THE CORE COMPETENCE AGENDA

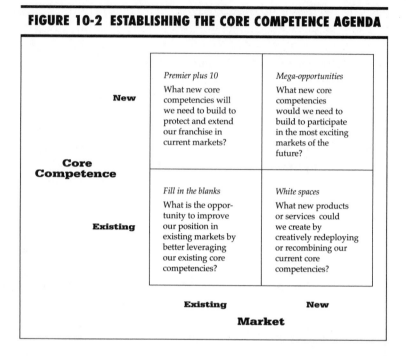

Core Competence (vertical axis, with **New** and **Existing**)

Market (horizontal axis, with **Existing** and **New**)

Premier plus 10

What new core competencies will we need to build to protect and extend our franchise in current markets?

Mega-opportunities

What new core competencies would we need to build to participate in the most exciting markets of the future?

Fill in the blanks

What is the opportunity to improve our position in existing markets by better leveraging our existing core competencies?

White spaces

What new products or services could we create by creatively redeploying or recombining our current core competencies?

Premier Plus 10 The upper-left quadrant suggests another important question: What new core competencies must we be building today to ensure that we are regarded as the premier provider by our customers in five or ten years' time? The goal here is to understand what new competencies must be built to support and extend a company's franchise in its existing markets. For example, IBM has been working hard to improve its business consulting skills because it knows that its customers don't just want to buy computers and software, they want to buy solutions to real business problems. If IBM failed to build such a competence, its franchise as an information technology supplier would be further eroded by competitors such as Andersen Consulting, which possesses strong consulting skills. Whether rightly or wrongly, Sony believed that if it was to protect and extend its franchise in consumer electronics it would, over the long term, need to control more of the "content"

TABLE 10-1 DEPLOYMENT OF CANON'S CORE COMPETENCIES

Product	Precision Mechanics	Fine Optics	Microelectronics	Electronic Imaging
Basic camera	X	X		
Compact fashion camera	X	X		
Electronic camera	X	X		
EOS autofocus camera	X	X	X	
Video still camera	X	X	X	X
Laser beam printer	X	X	X	X
Color video printer	X		X	X
Bubble jet printer	X		X	X
Basic fax	X		X	X
Laser fax	X		X	X
Calculator			X	
Plain paper copier	X	X	X	X
Battery PPC	X	X	X	X
Color copier	X	X	X	X
Laser copier	X	X	X	X
Color laser copier	X	X	X	X
Still video system	X	X	X	X
Laser imager	X	X	X	X
Cell analyzer	X	X	X	X
Mask aligners	X		X	X
Stepper aligners	X		X	X
Excimer laser aligners	X	X	X	X

side of the business. This led Sony to purchase both Columbia Pictures and the recorded music business of CBS.

Obsolete Competencies Another question is suggested by the upper-left quadrant: What new competencies might replace, or make obsolete, the competencies that are currently used to satisfy the needs of existing customers? Canon knows that over time electronic digital imaging may partially replace chemical imaging as a way of recording photographic images. The advantages of digital photography are obvious: an ability to edit at will, reusable "film," low processing costs, and the ability to transfer images easily between different media—PCs, televisions, paper printers. Today Canon is a world leader in the production of 35mm cameras. Not surprisingly, Canon has also been experimenting with electronic photography. Canon's early products have not met with enormous success, but Canon understands that if it is to preserve its franchise in the photography business, it must, over time, develop a competence in digital imaging. Kodak has also recognized the potential threat, and has joined forces with Apple to produce a digital camera. With a similar logic, auto companies have been investing in understanding the potential for electrically powered cars. A company's competence-building agenda should include gaining an understanding of those new competencies that may one day supplant its traditional skill base.

White Spaces The focus here is on the lower-right quadrant. We used the term *white spaces* to refer to opportunities that don't fall within the product-market purview of existing business units. Here the goal is to imagine opportunities to extend existing core competencies into new product markets. Sony's Walkman was a white-space opportunity relying, as it did, on competencies that resided in its tape recorder and headphones businesses. Another example of such a white-space opportunity is the extension of Philips's optical storage competence from audio applications into data storage applications.

Often, the narrowly construed "charters" of market-focused business units blind them to white-space opportunities. In too many companies no one has responsibility for white-space opportunities, nor any incentive to find them. To identify white-space opportunities a company must start with a core competence rather than a product-market perspective and then consider the potential opportunities for applying the particular customer benefit represented by a particular competence.

The need to escape the myopia of the currently served markets should not be a license to ill-conceived diversification. There was little justification for Xerox's purchase of the insurance company, Crum & Forster, nor for Kodak's acquisition of Sterling Drug, nor Ford's dive into the murky waters of the savings and loan industry. We are arguing for a strong core competency logic for diversification. Diversification may appear to be unrelated in product-market terms (as in the case of Cargill, 3M, and Honda) but may be closely related in terms of core competencies.

Mega-Opportunities Opportunities represented in the upper-right quadrant do not overlap the company's current market position nor its current competence endowment. Nevertheless, a company may choose to pursue such opportunities if they are seen to be especially significant or attractive. Here the approach to strategy might be a series of small, targeted acquisitions or partnerships through which the company could gain access to, and understanding of, the required competencies and begin to learn about their potential application.

On a national level, Japan seems to regard aerospace as an irresistible mega-opportunity. Through alliances with a variety of U.S. and European aerospace companies and substantial investment, Japanese companies have slowly built up their own airframe, satellite, and rocket competencies. Whether Japanese companies ever manage to build a commercially successful airliner remains to be seen, but they certainly have not given up on that goal. Opportunities in this quadrant should be approached with great caution, as the firm has little or no experience base to inform its decisions. In the case of Japan's aerospace industry, taxpayers may end up paying a lot to boost the pride of Japanese policy-makers who refuse to accept the dominance of U.S. and European companies in the sector.

Building New Core Competencies

Given that it may take five, ten, or more years to build world leadership in a core competence area, consistency of effort is key. Consistency depends first of all on a deep consensus about which competencies to build and support, and second, on the stability of the management teams charged with competence development. Such consistency is unlikely unless senior managers agree on what new competencies should be built. Without such a consensus, a company may well fragment its competence-building efforts, as various business units pursue their independent competence-building agenda, or the firm may simply fail to build new competencies.

Stability to senior management teams and, correspondingly, strategic agendas is also key. RCA's abortive attempts to produce a video recorder highlights the problems of a lack of stability in the membership of senior teams. While, over two decades, RCA spent more than almost any other company in exploring new video recording and playback technologies, it never brought a successful product to market. The rapid turnover in project leaders and divisional management in RCA and the consequent on-again, off-again support for video research projects undermined the slow, persistent, cumulative learning that is at the heart of competence acquisition.[1] Throwing money at a project, scrapping it when it doesn't yield short-term results, starting it up again when competitors appear to be moving ahead, and deemphasizing the project when a new CEO comes on board is a recipe for inefficient and ineffective competence development.

Deploying Core Competencies

To leverage a core competence across multiple businesses and into new markets often requires redeploying that competence internally—from one division or SBU to another. Some companies are better at this than others, and hence get greater effective use out of their competencies. We sometimes define a company's core competencies in the same way a country defines its money supply: stock (the number of bills printed, or the number of people who "carry" a particular skill) multiplied by velocity (how fast the bills change hands, or how quickly and easily competence carriers can be redeployed into new opportunity areas). Many companies have a sizable stock of core competencies—many people with truly world-class skills—but almost zero competence velocity—the ability to redeploy those individuals behind new market opportunities.

In every diversified firm with which we're familiar, business unit managers accept that cash is a corporate resource and business unit profits go back to the corporation at the end of each year. It is also accepted, however reluctantly, that corporate managers have the right to reallocate cash across businesses. The business unit that produced cash in the current planning period may or may not get all it wants in the next planning period. This allocational right is jealously guarded by top management. Wise capital allocation choices are seen as one of the ways in which corporate officers add value, and hence justify their overheads. We find it paradoxical and disturbing that there is, in many companies, no similar allocation process for the talent that comprises the firm's core competencies.

For more and more companies today, the ratio of market value to asset value is 2:1, 4:1, even 10:1 (see Table 10-2). The difference between asset value and book value is not goodwill, it is core competence—people-embodied skills.[2] The numerator in the ratio reflects investors' beliefs about the uniqueness of the firm's competencies and the potential value that can be generated by the exploitation of those competencies in the marketplace. The allocation and management of the assets that appear on the balance sheet is an elaborate, time-consuming ritual, infused with analytical rigor and attempts at numerical precision. But what about the other three-fourths or nine-tenths of corporate value? Through what mechanism are core competencies allocated? How explicit are the choices about where to put talent? How much pressure is put on divisional managers to justify why they should have preferential access to some particular competence pool? Although human resource executives will proudly proclaim that "people are our most important asset," there is seldom any mechanism for allocating human capital

TABLE 10-2 MARKET AND ASSET VALUES OF SELECTED COMPANIES (END OF 1993)

Company	Market Value ($ billions)	Asset Value ($ billions)	Ratio of Market to Book
Merck	40,596	19,927	2.0
Microsoft	23,348	4,048	5.7
Home Depot	18,651	4,610	4.0
Oracle Systems	9,571	1,229	7.8
Cisco Systems	9,413	802	11.7
Novell	7,880	1,439	5.4
Genentech	5,612	1,469	3.8
Rubbermaid	4,851	1,513	3.2

Source: "The *Business Week* 1000," *Business Week*, 28 March 1994, pp. 72–142.

that approaches, in its sophistication and thoroughness, the procedures for capital allocation. In most Western companies the chief financial officer has more organizational status and raw power than does the head of personnel. In many Japanese companies the situation is precisely reversed—as it should be if a company truly believes that competition for competence is the highest order of competitive rivalry, and if it understands that access to competencies, rather than access to cash, is the most critical driver of growth.

At Sharp, white space opportunities are addressed by "urgent project teams," of which there have been more than 150. These cross-corporate initiatives are known as "the chairman's projects" and attract the best competence resources from across the company. Sharp rightly views competencies, rather than cash, as the scarcest resource in creating new markets. It has an allocational mechanism for ensuring that the best competence resources get assigned to the most promising new growth areas. The spirit of Sharp's urgent project teams, Sony's "gold badge" teams, and variants observed in several other Japanese companies is that the corporation is a reservoir of potential core competencies. In this view, business unit managers are stewards, rather than owners, of the firm's core competence resources in the same way that they are stewards, rather than owners, of the firm's financial resources.

An exercise we sometimes carry out with a company's divisional managers illustrates a critical precondition to the capacity to redeploy competence assets. We provide each divisional or SBU manager with a product-geography matrix, and then ask each executive to rank, 1 through 10, their company's near-term growth opportunities. Not surprisingly, when we compile the completed matrices, there is usually little correspondence between one manager's rankings of growth priorities and any other manager's rankings. Yet in the absence of a corporatewide consensus on new business opportunities—that is, agreement on what projects truly are "urgent" or deserve to be labeled "gold"—there can be no logical basis for the internal reallocation of core competence resources.

One Japanese company regularly publishes a list of the company's top market and product development priorities. Obviously, there is great status attached to working on a high-profile, critical program. If an individual somewhere in the organization believes that he or she can contribute to one of the high priority projects, that individual can "self-promote" himself or herself onto the team. The team leader may not choose to take the applicant, but if the skills offered are critical to the project's success, the team leader can ask that the individual be transferred. At this point, the employee's boss has to justify why that individual's talents are of more value to the corporation in the current job than in the new job. As one might expect, the existence of such a system helps ensure that unit managers do their best to keep key people occupied with truly challenging projects. It also ensures that the best people end up working on the biggest potential opportunities.

The mobility of competencies is also aided when the employees who comprise a particular competence meet frequently to exchange ideas and experience. Seminars and conferences are important for instilling a sense of community among people working in the same competence. The cross-fertilization that results accelerates competence-building. The goal is a group of people who see themselves as corporate resources, and whose first loyalty is to the corporation and the integrity of the company's core competencies, rather than to any single business unit. Geographic proximity can also aid competence mobility. Where a competence is spread across facilities in a dozen countries or more, collective learning and the reallocation of individuals to new projects are difficult. A company should avoid unnecessary geographical fragmentation of its core competencies.

Protecting and Defending Core Competencies

Core competence leadership may be lost in many ways. Competencies may wither through lack of funding; become fragmented through divisionalization, particularly where no single executive feels fully responsible for competence stewardship; be inadvertently surrendered to alliance partners; or be lost when an underperforming business is divested.

Protecting core competencies from erosion takes continued vigilance on the part of top management. Although most senior managers can easily dredge up competitive measures of sales performance, market share, and profitability, few are able to offer a quick and convincing judgment on whether their company is staying ahead of competitors in core competence development. There is no way to protect a firm's core competencies from erosion if the health of those competencies is not visible to top management. Divisional managers should be assigned cross-corporate stewardship roles for particular competencies, and should be held responsible for the health of those competencies. Regular "competence review" meetings should focus on levels of investment, plans for strengthening constituent skills and technologies, internal patterns of deployment, the impact of alliances, and outsourcing.

We are not arguing that the core competence perspective should supplant a product-market perspective; rather, it should complement it. Given how deeply engrained the SBU perspective is in most companies, it will take substantial effort from senior management to build the complementary core competence view. The goal is not to "hardwire" the core competence into the organization through structural changes, but to "soft-wire" the perspective into the heads of every manager and employee. This means (1) establishing a deeply involving process for identifying core competencies; (2) involving strategic business units in a cross-corporate process for developing a strategic architecture and setting competence acquisition goals; (3) defining a clear set of corporate growth and new business development priorities; (4) establishing explicit "stewardship" roles for core competencies; (5) setting up an explicit mechanism for allocating critical core competence resources; (6) benchmarking competence-building efforts against rivals; (7) regularly reviewing the status of existing and nascent core competencies; and (8) building a community of people within the organization who view themselves as the "carriers" of corporate core competencies.

Having safeguarded the firm's existing competencies, escaped the myopia of existing served markets, and built a forward-looking competence agenda, a company can move on to the final tasks in managing the migration path to the future: expeditionary marketing and global preemption.

Securing the Future

. . . .

I n an earlier chapter we argued that a key goal of competing for the future was to maximize the ratio of learning over investment. What is most important, as the future begins to come into view, is to learn faster than competitors about just where the heart of future demand actually lies. An old-timer would call it prospecting, we call it *expeditionary marketing.* When several companies are tracking the same broad opportunity and striving to build roughly similar competencies, the issue is how to maximize one's share of worldwide revenues when the market finally takes off. To do this, a company must have created a preexisting "share of mind" among global customers, a strong distribution presence, and a capacity to quickly rollout the new product or service. These are the keys to *global preemption,* the final milestone on the road to the future.

EXPEDITIONARY MARKETING

When the goal is to create new competitive space, it is usually impossible to know in advance just what configuration of product or service features, offered at what price point and through what channels, will be required to unlock the potential market. Of course every management team hopes for many new product home runs. A product or service scores a "run" when it combines just the right blend of price and performance to penetrate its target market rapidly and deeply. Most companies have a plethora of policies aimed at increasing their hit rate or batting average: thorough market research, careful analysis of current buying behaviors, competitor analysis, and industry structure analysis. But market research carried out around a new product or service concept is notoriously inaccurate. Market research is great for refining existing product concepts, but is of little use in helping a company better target its development efforts around emerging markets.

Every batter would love to hit .400 (or if cricket's the game, get a century), but while policies aimed exclusively at improving the hit rate may produce fewer new business failures, they are likely to so delay a firm's entry into new markets that it loses the advantages of being an industry pioneer. What is obvious, but in practice often forgotten, is that the number of runs a batter actually scores is a product of hit rate (batting average) multiplied by the number of times at bat. A player that bats 1.000, but who only goes to the plate a half dozen times a season (when there's a weak pitcher on the mound and a 30-knot tailwind blowing out to left field) will be much less valuable to a team than a player who bats a modest .250, but gets to the plate three or four hundred times in a season. Similarly, a company may be able to boast about its high batting average in new product introductions, but if that average is the product of a cautious, go-slow approach to creating new markets, the company may well capture less of the future than scrappier rivals with inferior batting averages but more times at bat.

Getting to the future first, and being first up on the scoreboard, requires that a company learn faster than its rivals about the precise dimensions of customer demand and required product performance. To learn faster, a company must maximize its times at bat, rather than sit on the sidelines waiting for the perfect conditions for a home run attempt. If the goal is to accumulate market understanding as rapidly as possible, a series of low-cost, fast-paced market incursions, what we call expeditionary marketing, is imperative.

Think of an archer shooting at a target shrouded by a veil of fog. Intent on hitting the bull's eye, the archer has two choices: Wait until all the fog has cleared (i.e., until a rival has proved beyond a reasonable doubt that the new market is for real) or shoot a series of arrows in the general direction of the target, each time adjusting one's aim as one receives feedback about where the arrow landed. As each arrow flies into the distance and a shout comes back "right of the target" or "a bit too high," more arrows are shot and more advice comes back until the cry is "bull's eye." Although waiting for the fog to clear may guarantee that the arrow hits the target, the patient archer is likely to find that a rival's arrows already blanket the target. What counts most in expeditionary marketing is not hitting a bull's eye the first time, but how quickly one can improve one's aim and get another arrow on the way to the target. Little is learned in the laboratory or product development committee meetings. True learning only begins when a product or service—imperfect as it may be—is launched into the market.

Of course expeditionary marketing represents a practical approach to reconnoitering the markets of the future only if the arrows are not gold plated, and if it doesn't take months or years to recalibrate one's aim and shoot again. Thus, the practical problem of expeditionary marketing is how to reduce the time and cost of product iteration. Speed of iteration refers to the time it takes a company to develop and launch a product or service, accumulate insights from the marketplace, and recalibrate and relaunch. Other things being equal, a company with a 12-month iteration cycle will be able to close in on a potential market much faster than one with a 36-month iteration time. Each product iteration unfreezes one or more aspects of the product or service concept, and thus provides an opportunity for a company to apply what it has learned.

In 1991, IBM launched its first laptop computer, by which time the opportunity for laptops had become blindingly obvious, and Toshiba's and Compaq's "arrows" were scattered all across the target. Toshiba's blistering pace of product iteration allowed it to explore every nook and cranny of the emerging market and thereby take an early lead in the laptop computer business (see Table 11-1). Toshiba thus outran early rivals like Grid and Zenith. Not every one of Toshiba's laptop models met with huge success. Indeed, in its first five years in the market, Toshiba withdrew more

TABLE 11-1 TOSHIBA'S LAPTOP COMPUTERS

Year Introduced	Model	Drive**	Micro-Processor	Display	Price
1986	T1100*	720K	80C88	LCD	$1,999
	T1100+*	620K × 2	80C88	LCD	2,099
	T3100*	720K + 10MB	80286	Gas plasma	4,199
1987	T1000	720K	80C88	LCD	999
	T1200F*	720K × 2	80C86	LCD	2,099
	T1200FB*	720K × 2	80C86	Backlit LCD	2,199
	T1200H*	720K + 20MB	80C86	LCD	2,799
	T1200HB*	720K + 20MB	80C86	Backlit LCD	2,499
	T3100/20*	720K + 20MB	80286	Gas plasma	4,699
1988	T1600*	1.44MB + 20/40MB	80C286	Backlit LCD	3,499/3,999
	T3100*	1.44MB + 20MB	80286	Gas plasma	3,999
	T3200*	720K + 40MB	80286	Gas plasma	5,799
	T5100*	1.44MB + 40MB	80386	Gas plasma	6,499
1989	T1000SE	1.44MB	80C86	Backlit LCD	1,499
	T3100SX	1.44MB + 40MB	80386SX	Gas plasma	5,699
	T3100/40	1.44MB + 40MB	80286	Gas plasma	3,699
	T3200	1.44MB + 40MB	80286	Gas plasma	3,999
	T5100/100	1.44MB + 100MB	80386	Gas plasma	6,999

Year Introduced	Model	Drive**	Micro-Processor	Display	Price
1990	T1000XE	20MB	80C86	Backlit LCD	1,899
	T1000LE	1.44MB + 20MB	80C86	Backlit LCD	2,499
	T1000XE	1.44MB + 20MB/40MB	80286	Sidelit LCD	3,199/3,799
	T2000SX	1.44MB + 20MB	80386SX	Sidelit LCD	4,999
	T2000SX	1.44MB + 40MB	80386SX	Sidelit LCD	5,499
	T3100SX	1.44MB + 80MB	80386SX	Gas plasma	5,999
	T3200SX	1.44MB + 40MB	80386SX	Gas plasma	4,999
	T3200SX	1.44MB + 120MB	80386SX	Gas plasma	5,499
	T3200SXC	1.44MB + 120MB	80386SX	LCD active matrix color VGA	8,999
	T5200	1.44MB + 40MB	80386	Gas plasma	7,199
	T5200/100	1.44MB + 100MB	80386	Gas plasma	6,499
	T5200/200	1.44MB + 200MB	80386	Gas plasma	7,299
	T5200C/200	1.44MB + 200MB	80386	LCD color passive matrix	9,499

*Indicates a model that was withdrawn before March 31, 1991.

**The first drive listed is a floppy disk; the second is a hard disk.

Source: Gary Hamel and C.K. Prahalad, "Corporate Imagination and Expeditionary Marketing," *Harvard Business Review* (July–August 1991): 88. Copyright © 1991 by the President and Fellows of Harvard College; all rights reserved. Reprinted by permission.

models than some rivals launched. But few would count Toshiba's experience in the laptop business, up through the early 1990s, as anything but a success.

Expeditionary marketing does not imply launching products that are manifestly unready or inappropriate to the needs of potential customers. Expeditionary marketing honors the quality maxim, "conformance to customer requirement," but recognizes that customer requirements in emerging markets can only be partially understood. There is much that cannot be known about customer needs, the suitability of particular technologies, and viable price-performance combinations in the absence of direct market experimentation. But expeditionary marketing is not a blind leap of faith; each product iteration should embody all that it is currently possible to know about customer needs and desires.

In expeditionary marketing, cost is just as crucial as speed. If every arrow is gold-plated, management will be unwilling to shoot many arrows into the mist. In the past, the exploration of every conceivable lifestyle niche product by Japanese automakers depended on their having dramatically lower product development and plant tooling costs than Western rivals. Think of the dilemma for a manufacturer whose cost per product iteration is two to three times that of competitors. What will management's attitude be toward the exploration of new competitive space? For such a company the risk of market pioneering will be untenably high. It will launch few new products, and, because of its time-cost disadvantage, will be forced to adopt very conservative designs—"plain vanilla" products that appeal to as broad a segment of buyers as possible. As a consequence, customers will come to view the firm as conservative and slow-moving. It may hold onto some of its loyal, aging customers, but will almost certainly lose the excitement sweepstakes among new buyers. Inevitably, the mantle of leadership will fall on the shoulders of companies that are exploring the limits of customers' expectations. This was precisely the fate that befell Ford and GM in the 1970s and 1980s in their fight with Japanese competitors for the hearts and minds of young buyers.

The way in which many large companies define success and punish failure in new product development is one of the biggest impediments to expeditionary marketing. Verdicts of new product failure rarely distinguish between arrows aimed at the wrong target and arrows that simply fell short of the right target. And because failure is personalized—if the new product or service doesn't live up to internal expectations it must be *somebody's* fault—there is more often a search for culprits than for lessons when initial goals are not reached. Even worse, when some salient new fact comes to light as a result of market experience, the manager in charge is deemed guilty of not knowing it in advance. With risk so often personalized, it is not surprising that when failure does occur, there is often a race to get the body to the morgue before anyone can do an autopsy. The result is a missed opportunity to learn.

Not surprisingly, if the personal price of experimentation is high, managers will retreat to the safety of test-it-to-death, follow-the-leader, do-only-what-the-customer-asks-for conservatism. Such conservatism often leads to much grander, though less visible, failures. Managers seeking to avoid the personal risks of expeditionary marketing may let exciting new opportunities slip through their fingers. Failure is typically, and we believe wrongly, measured exclusively in terms of dollars lost rather than dollars foregone. In which traditional U.S. computer company, for example, has a senior officer lost his or her job, corner office, or promotion for surrendering leadership in the laptop computer business to others? Managers seldom get punished for not trying, but they often get punished for trying and coming up short. This is what promotes the obsession with hit rate, rather than the number of hits actually generated.

Failure is as often the child of unrealistic expectations as it is of managerial incompetence. In the 1980s, General Electric faced a dazzling opportunity: to stake out leadership in the market for the "factory of the future." Integrating CAD/CAM, computer-integrated manufacturing, robots, and automated material handling was an awesome challenge, and one GE was willing to confront. But unrealistic expectations about how fast the market would develop, combined with an all-or-nothing approach to market entry, set GE up for a spectacular failure and a sizable write-off. Take another example: IBM's ill-fated first attempt, in late 1983, to enter the home computer market with PC jr. Widely criticized for having a toylike keyboard and for being priced too high, the PC jr. was regarded by both insiders and outsiders as a failure. Yet at the time, it would have been difficult for anyone to predict exactly what product would appeal to home users whose computer experience to date with home computing was likely to be playing videogames on an Atari or Commodore. The real failure was not that IBM's first product missed the mark, but that IBM overhyped its entry and was thus unable to find a quiet refuge from whence it could relaunch a recalibrated product.

Babe Ruth used to point to the bleachers and then wallop a home run. For lesser mortals, such arrogance opens the door wide to humiliation. In IBM's case, the sizable gap between the company's sky-high expectations for PC jr. and its down-to-earth sales performance led IBM to withdraw from the home market. Not until 1990, seven years after the PC jr., did IBM launch another foray into the home market with its PS1 model. The point is not that the ambitions of GE or IBM were too grand, but rather that what constitutes failure depends on management's initial assumptions about how quickly and easily success should come. Expeditionary marketing is about tightly controlled experiments, not wild predictions of triumph and zillion dollar marketing campaigns.

If the opportunity is oversold and risks undermanaged, failure and premature abandonment of the opportunity are preordained. Overhyping damaged Apple's early experiment with handwriting recognition in the form of the Newton Message Pad. While the Newton was a failure in terms of Apple's optimistic predictions, it may not be a failure in the longer-run battle to create a market for personal digital assistants. Think back a decade. Apple's first "user-friendly" computer Lisa, launched in 1983, was also a flop—though a less grandiose one. But in contrast to IBM, Apple followed up a year later with the first Macintosh, which was faster and more appropriately priced than Lisa. Sony has had some relatively dramatic product failures in its history, including Betamax and digital audio tape (DAT) recorders. Yet this is partly the price of being a pioneer. We should not be surprised if Sony strikes out sometimes; in fact, it is a wonder the company doesn't strike out more often given the number of times it goes to bat. In an average year Sony introduces 1,000 new or updated products—four every working day. Typically, about 200 of these products are aimed at creating new markets.[1] Thus, one can't judge success or failure on the basis of a single product launch. In 1990, Sony launched its Data Discman in Japan, a portable unit that allows users to conveniently carry and view thousands of pages of reference material, textbooks, or novels—all stored on CDs. In 1993 Sony was planning to launch a follow-on product, the Bookman. Clearly it would be as useless to judge Sony's chances of ultimately creating a market for personal digital data players by the success of its first tentative product entry as it would be to judge the outcome of a military campaign on the basis of which side suffered the greatest casualties on the first day of battle.

In a similar manner, Fujitsu was the first company to launch a blazingly fast new generation of telephone switches utilizing a switching technology known as asynchronous transfer mode. Although not all competitors were convinced that the technology was yet ready for the market, a researcher at Bellcore, the joint research arm of the U.S. regional Bell telphone companies, thought he understood Fujitsu's motivation: "It seems that they don't care what the perfect solution is; they go ahead to build first. This is a very good strategy because you want to occupy the market first."[2] Fujitsu got out in the market and started learning from customers about what works and what doesn't while competitors were still speculating in labs.

To create new competitive space, a new yardstick for managerial performance is required. Financial theory teaches us to measure financial returns on a risk- and time-adjusted basis. How often do we make similar adjustments when measuring managerial performance in new business creation? Shouldn't a manager who loses $20 million in the pursuit of an exciting, though nascent, opportunity be treated differently from a manager who loses $20 million through mismanagement of a core business where the company has traditionally been a market leader? Early in the pursuit of new competitive space, the most critical resource is not cash but management talent. New opportunities require a degree of management attention disproportionate to their short-term revenue prospects. If a simplistic definition of failure vests new opportunities with a high degree of personal risk for upwardly ambitious managers, or if management talent is allocated on the basis of the current size and importance of the company's businesses, new markets will not be created and the company's best managers will accumulate in businesses that should run on autopilot. In too many companies the best managers shuffle between the safest businesses. The result is status-quo strategies and a dearth of new business development.

Make no mistake, expeditionary marketing is not a license to fail; it is, though, a mandate to learn when inevitable setbacks occur. When a product aimed at a new market goes astray, management must ask several important questions. First, did we manage the risks appropriately or barge in like a bull in a china shop? Second, did we possess reasonable expectations about the rate at which the market will develop? Third, did we learn anything that will improve our chances on the next attempt? Fourth, how quickly can we recalibrate and try again? Fifth, do we believe that the opportunity is still for real and does its size warrant another attempt? And sixth, if we don't try again, have we just taught our competitors a valuable lesson that they will use to get to the future ahead of us? Failure should be declared only if the answer to all these questions is no. Otherwise, a genuine opportunity may get lost in the embarrassment of a missed attempt. When it comes to expeditionary marketing the rules are very simple: learn faster, learn cheaper.

THE LOGIC OF GLOBAL PREEMPTION

Developing new competencies and reconnoitering new competitive space can be, as we've argued, the work of a decade or more. Yet despite the studied pace of competence acquisition and market exploration, the final dash to the finish line can be an all-out, pell-mell sprint. This is particularly likely when several competitors have been working in parallel to develop needed competencies and market insights, and simultaneously come to believe, after a round or two of expeditionary marketing, that the market is finally "ripe." This last, mad scramble for the finish line is a race to preempt competitors in key markets, to capture market leadership in the biggest and fastest-growing national markets, and bank the rewards of pioneering.

Procter & Gamble's experience in the European market for disposable diapers demonstrates the importance of a capacity for global preemption. Launched first in Germany in 1973, Pampers was not introduced in France until 1978. In the interim, Colgate introduced its own disposable diapers in France in 1976, branded *Calline* (French for Pampers), and quickly established market leadership. Late introduction also cost Pampers market leadership in the United Kingdom, where Pampers was finally introduced in 1981. Only after a long and expensive struggle did Pampers regain the ground it initially gave up to fleet-footed rivals. Lenor, a fabric softener launched by P&G in Germany in 1963, provides an even more dramatic example of the risks of a dilatory pace of new product roll-out. While Lenor was an outstanding success in Germany and created a new product category, it debuted in France nineteen years later as the number-three entrant in the fabric softener category.

In a reversal of such misfortunes, P&G managed to preempt its Japanese rival, Kao, in the race to take superabsorbent diapers to world markets. In 1985 Kao surprised P&G by launching a technologically advanced, superabsorbent diaper in Japan. The new diaper quickly overtook Pampers as the market leader. But with little distribution or brand power outside Asia, Kao could do little to capitalize on its innovation in global markets. Thus, P&G was able to launch its own version of a superabsorbent diaper around the world with virtually no opposition from Kao. In the end, it was P&G, more than Kao, that profited from the new diaper technology. While global distribution power alone can't substitute for a lack of competencies in other areas, it is an absolutely critical multiplier of the returns to innovation.

Take another example. In the United States, Chrysler was the first to launch a minivan, in 1983. Ten years later, and despite tough competition from every other U.S. and Japanese competitor,

Chrysler still held around 50% of the minivan market in the United States, worth about $13 billion in sales. Yet because Chrysler had virtually no market presence in Europe, it ceded leadership there to Renault, which introduced a minivan-type vehicle in 1984. Nine years later Renault had sold 360,000 minivans. Chrysler finally got around to launching its minivans in Europe in 1989, but in its first full year of European operations, Chrysler managed to move only 11,800 minivans.

As the cost of innovation rockets skyward in industries like semiconductors, pharmaceuticals, and telecommunications, the imperative of global preemption becomes ever more pronounced. Consider, for example, a German telecommunications company such as Siemens, competing in the market for large telephone switching gear. In the 1960s the development cost for an electromechanical switch was about $200 million, in 1993 dollars. To recoup these costs, a manufacturer would have needed to capture roughly half the German market. By the late 1970s and 1980s, the cost of developing the new generation of digital switches had risen to about $1 billion. To amortize this investment a German company would have needed to capture a 100% share of its home market, plus a good portion of the broader European market. Looking to the end of the 1990s and beyond, the next generation of switches may cost as much as $2 billion to develop. Having made such an investment, a telecommunications manufacturer would need a 20% global market share just to break even. This inescapable economic logic has prompted wave after wave of industry consolidation and has led to fierce competition for every last scrap of world market share in a host of industries. In telecommunications, where competition was once largely regional—Alcatel versus Siemens in Europe, Northern Telecom versus AT&T in the United States, and NEC versus Fujitsu in Japan—it is now global.

Managers have given much attention to the very important task of reducing product development cycle times. Speedy product development is an important component of the capacity to preempt competitors. Yet the time interval that must be minimized is not just "concept to market," but "concept to global market." A product development cycle that is 50% shorter than a competitor's is of little benefit unless it is coupled with a strong worldwide distribution capability. Although being first to market is important, the real returns go to companies that are first to *global* markets.

The imperative of global preemption is no excuse for a hasty global launch of an ill-conceived and undertested product or service. Early market expeditions will be on a small scale, and may be geographically limited as well (though it is often important to accumulate learning from customers in more than one national market given the diversity of customer needs). But once the market looks set to take off, the innovator must be capable, either alone or in partnership, of "blowing" the new product or service around the world as quickly as possible. After spending more than $100 million over ten years developing its revolutionary Sensor razor, and conducting an initial round of customer research, Gillette launched the product in 19 countries simultaneously. Followers, like Warner-Lambert's Schick division, were quickly buried under Gillette's worldwide promotional avalanche. Gillette left its competitors little room for a second strike.

While the race to globally preempt competitors is competition for market share and position, preparation for a global blitz must start long before the product reaches the market. Just as a company must begin investing in a new core competence area before all the specific product opportunities are clearly defined, so a company must begin to develop global brand and distribution positions in anticipation of the stream of new products and services that will ultimately flow through the firm's global channels. If a company has not developed its global presence in advance of the introduction of its hot new product or service, it will hand much of the market to competitors. This does not mean that huge investments are made merely in the hope that something exciting may be coming down the new product pipeline. There are, as we've indicated, low-cost ways of accessing global markets and preempting competitors, principally through the use of distribution partnerships. This was the strategy Glaxo used in the United States to race ahead of SmithKline in the market for antiulcer drugs. Having a relatively meager distribution capability in the United States at the time of Zantac's launch, Glaxo partnered with Hoffman-LaRoche and immediately gained access to a 1,100-strong salesforce. Many Asian companies have used downstream partners as a low-cost route to global market access. Canon made copiers to be sold under the Kodak name; Samsung made microwave ovens to be sold by GE; and Toshiba first entered the U.S. television market by selling to Sears on a private-label basis.

Everyone remembers the four Ps of marketing: product, price, promotion, and position. We'd like to suggest the 4 Ps of global preemption. The first P is, of course, preemption. We've argued that to capture the maximum returns to innovation, a company must have a capacity for global preemption. The other three Ps are the prerequisites for preemption: proximity, predisposition, and propagation.

Proximity

Competition here is for access to critical national markets and distribution channels. Markets may be "critical" for a number of reasons. A market may offer access to a group of "reference" customers (Japanese teenagers for consumer electronics or hip Californian car buyers). Only when a company has proven itself capable of serving and satisfying the world's most sophisticated customers can it be confident that it is well-prepared for a global roll-out. Second, a market may be strategic because of its size and the opportunity it affords for amortizing development costs. For just such a reason, the U.S. market is absolutely critical to any European company that hopes to be globally competitive. One of the reasons that many of Europe's computer makers have teetered so long on the brink of financial disaster is that none has ever built a strong presence in the United States and thereby gained the global scale economies that are so critical in that industry.

Third, a market may be strategic and therefore important in the battle to preempt because of its rate of growth or because it offers the prospect of future growth. Given the super-heated growth rates in much of Southeast Asia, any company that doesn't today derive at least 20% of its revenues from Southeast Asia (not including Japan) is, by definition, losing world market share. European and U.S. producers of automobiles, consumer electronics, and many industrial products must work hard to ensure that fast-growing Asian markets are not ceded to Japanese rivals. General Electric is one U.S. company intent on depriving its Japanese competitors of hegemony in Asian markets. By the early 1990s GE had become a leading supplier of jet engines to China's growing population of airlines, and businesses like Power Systems and Medical Systems were anticipating that 50% of their future growth would come from Asia. Said one senior GE official, "We really want to have the same market shares in Asia that we do in the U.S."[3]

Given the time it takes to learn the political ropes, find local partners, develop a strong team of indigenous managers, establish whatever local manufacturing may be necessary, gain the required insights into unique customer needs, and establish appropriate distribution channels, any company that is not already working feverishly to build an infrastructure in Asia is likely to be relegated to slower-growing markets.

Fourth, a market may also be strategic because it offers access to a competitor's domestic "profit sanctuary." Having a position in a competitor's home market can allow a company to siphon off some of the profits a competitor might otherwise use to launch head-to-head attacks outside its home market. IBM's early entry into Japan and its strength there as a competitor certainly reduced the ability of Japan's leading computer makers to "cross-subsidize" their international growth from the Japanese home market.

A capacity to preempt competitors, or slow their global advance, is not simply a matter of having built a physical presence in key "strategic" markets. Also important is access to the most effective distribution channels in each key national market. Although the barriers to accessing Japan's distribution system have been widely discussed and have even become the target of "structural" trade initiatives, we believe that a potentially more serious impediment to many companies' capacity to preempt are internal policies and politics that make it difficult to exploit the full panoply of potential distribution channels. Most companies implicitly favor some channels (direct sales, mail order, exclusive dealers, or mass merchandisers) over others. Such favoritism may rest on sound business logic, but is just as likely to rest on an out-of-date business logic that is difficult to change because a powerful internal constituency has a large stake in the continued dominance of one particular channel. For example, for several years Apple's reliance on exclusive dealers slowed the penetration of the Macintosh into corporate accounts, where a direct salesforce would have been more effective. Channel myopia can be a significant impediment to a company's capacity to preempt rivals in the race to the future. Much can be lost if a fire hose–sized new product or service is pushed through a garden hose–sized distribution channel.

Predisposition

To preempt competitors, customers around the world have to be genuinely eager to buy and try a company's new products. Think about what happened when, in 1982, the Coca-Cola Company launched Diet Coke in the United States. Within two years Diet Coke became the number-three U.S. soft drink. Leveraging the powerful Coke brand name, Diet Coke repeated this success in many markets around the world. While in no way disparaging the quality or uniqueness of Diet Coke, one could hardly credit the brand's supersonic take-off to product attributes alone. What existed in people's minds was a deep emotional bond with Coca-Cola, assiduously cultivated by some of the cleverest and least escapable advertising anywhere. In the absence of a preexisting brand franchise, Diet Coke would have faced the same slow, treacherous crawl onto retailers' shelves that faces Coke's wannabe competitors. If the goal is to preempt competitors, it helps to have built a preexisting "share of mind" with customers around the world.

Take another example. In years past, parents stopping off at the freezer section of the local supermarket in search of ice cream bars for the kids would have found only regional or national category-specific brands. On the other hand, a perusal of the candy counter would have revealed several chocolate bars carrying global brand names—Mars, Nestlé, and Cadbury's. In this anomaly, Mars found an opportunity. Why not take its well-known, well-regarded Mars brand and extend it to ice cream novelties? The result was the most successful new product launch in the history of the industry, and the creation of a new product category. Following up this success,

Mars lent its brand to a line of chocolate-milk–based drinks. The experience of Coke and Mars point to an important lesson: A strong, preexisting share of mind can often grease the skids of product acceptance.

Like the Concorde's after-burners, a powerful global brand, fueled with esteem and customer affection, can dramatically accelerate a new product's take-off; what that brand can't do is get a fundamentally un-aerodynamic product off the ground. If the thing can't fly, all that brand fuel simply makes the resulting crash that much more spectacular. No matter how credible a brand is with consumers an Edsel is still an Edsel, and New Coke still ain't Coke Classic. A lousy product can damage the credibility of the brand warrant. Each new product introduction either reinforces or undermines the integrity of the banner brand.

Yet the world's customers are predisposed to pay attention when Coca-Cola, Apple, Sony, Honda, or other company with a similarly strong global franchise launches a new product. Any company with such an enviable brand position has a head start in the race to the future. Marketing experts have opined that it takes on the order of a billion dollars of advertising to build a significant share of mind with consumers across North America, Asia, and Europe. Yet what is the marginal cost for Sony, in terms of brand building, when it launches a new product bearing those four famous letters? Sony's new product introductions benefit from instant street credibility. Now one can legitimately ask which came first: great products or the great brand. Of course it was the product. But what Sony and other global brand leaders have done is to consciously build "banner brands" that span multiple products and businesses and which help customers transfer great experiences with today's products into great interest in and enthusiasm for tomorrow's products.

A trusted brand is a "warrant" to customers that the new product or service will perform to a high standard. Such a warrant may be particularly important when the goal is to establish new competitive space by creating an entirely new product category. The more innovative the product, the more customers are likely to require the security of a brand that has proven itself trustworthy in the past. In large part, IBM's initial success in the then-nascent personal computer business was due to the brand warrant it offered wary and confused customers. Osborne, Kaypro, and even Apple couldn't match IBM's brand warrant. The brand warrant may be a more important guarantor of product quality and performance than the actual product warranty. Making a warranty claim is a hassle. What convinces customers to buy a product from Sony, Canon, or Toyota is less the length of the warranty period than the strength of the quality warrant implicit in the brand.

The goal of a banner brand is simple: to help customers transfer the goodwill that has been built up through positive experience with one of the company's products to other products it offers or intends to offer. Besides having a Canon copier at home, one of us also possesses two Canon 35mm cameras, a Canon 8mm camcorder, a small Canon electronic typewriter, and a Canon fax machine. There was never a decision to be a Canon home, it just worked out that way. Whenever confronted with Canon as a choice in a purchasing decision, one instinctively reflected back on the reliability, performance, and value of other Canon products. Imputed with those virtues, each additional Canon product looked not only like a "safe" buy, but a "smart" buy. As the pace of life has continued to accelerate, and as the complexity of what people buy has increased exponentially, banner brands like Canon and Sony have become mnemonics, standing for quality and value, in the minds of harried, confused customers.

Many companies have fragmented their brands to compete for "share of segment." This was the logic behind GM's multiple brands. From the humble Chevrolet at one end to the luxurious Cadillac at the other, each marque was meant to correspond to buyers with a certain level of income and lifestyle aspirations. With a similar logic, a Philips executive once justified the company's competing and overlapping brands in Britain by arguing that its Pye brand was an entry level brand, its Philips brand a mid- to upper-market brand, and its Grunding brand a high-end, premium brand. The banner brands of Japanese companies have been built on quite a different logic: We promise you the best price-performance tradeoff (i.e., the best value) at whatever price point you buy. So whether one buys a Toyota Corolla for $11,900 (at 1993 prices) or a Toyota Supra for more than $40,000, one expects to buy the best vehicle in its class. Whether one buys a Sony mini-television for $200 or a wide screen behemoth for $6,000, one expects an innovative, aesthetically pleasing product. What Toyota, Honda, and Sony are competing for is less share of segment than share of pocket. The use of a consistent banner brand across a range of products helps make the company a "runner" in every purchase decision.

In our view, the core competencies that support product leadership are the foundation of the corporation, and its banner brand(s) the roof. In between are the various businesses, each resting on a shared foundation, and each supporting a common roof (see Figure 11-1). Of course, many companies have eschewed banner brands. Any U.S. home is likely to have a dozen or more P&G products sitting on shelves in the kitchen, bathroom, and laundry room, none of which shares a common brand with another. Thus, however favorable one's experience with any particular P&G product—be

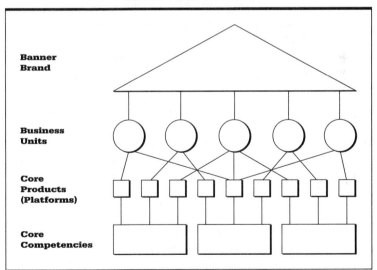

FIGURE 11-1 AN ALTERNATE CONCEPTION OF THE DIVERSIFIED FIRM

Banner Brand

Business Units

Core Products (Platforms)

Core Competencies

it Tide, Pampers, Ivory Soap, Crisco, or Folger's—one is in no way predisposed to buy another P&G product. While few of the world's customers could tell you that P&G is a leader in hair care, most customers would associate the name L'Oreal with hair care, as L'Oreal has plastered its corporate brand across a broad range of hair care products. We are not suggesting that meaningless corporate brands should be substituted for well-loved and long-lived product brands. Nobody wants to buy a jar of Procter & Gamble peanut butter or Unilever face cream! Nevertheless, we believe that any company that fails to take advantage of the logic of global banner branding will find itself, long-term, at a competitive disadvantage.

A banner brand doesn't have to cover a company's entire line of products. Although GM pays a heavy price in terms of customer confusion and missed economies of scope by supporting its vast array of brands around the world (including Opel, Vauxhall, Saturn, Geo, Chevrolet, Buick, Oldsmobile, Cadillac, and GMC), Toyota recognized, in its launch of Lexus, that the Toyota brand couldn't be easily stretched to cover luxury cars aimed at Benz buyers. Interestingly, in launching Lexus, Toyota got the best of both worlds. While Lexus has carved out for itself a unique up-market, "smart money" identity, no Lexus customer can help but know that the product is manufactured by Toyota to Toyota's world-class quality standards. Honda has achieved much the same effect with its up-scale Acura brand. So while Toyota hasn't opted for a single brand, it still has a much more compact and rational brand portfolio than GM or, indeed, Chrysler (Jeep, Eagle, Dodge, Plymouth, and Chrysler).

The banner brand doesn't necessarily have to be the corporate brand. Whether to use the corporate brand as a banner brand is a tactical decision. Very few Americans have ever heard of Matsushita, and fewer still can pronounce it correctly. Yet almost every potential customer is acquainted with the company's banner brands, of which Panasonic and JVC are the best known. Each of these brands spans multiple product categories.

So the banner brand need not be the corporate brand, and there may be good reasons for having more than one banner brand.

Additionally, banner brands and product-specific brands need not be mutually exclusive. Sony puts its brand on everything it makes. Sony is the company's top-level banner brand, but beneath this there are several subsidiary banner brands. Following the enormous success of Walkman, a brand that has become a generic designation for portable tape players, Sony broadened the use of the "man" suffix to denote portability in a broad range of products, including Discman and Watchman. The "Sports" label is another subsidiary banner brand for Sony. Here the message to consumers is about product toughness—the thing can be taken to the beach or the mountains with little fear that a splash of water or a bump will prove fatal. Each Sports product shares a common visual identity, bedecked in yellow and black colors. At Sony, brands are layered, with each layer covering more than one product category, and each layer communicating a distinct message to customers about product attributes.

In the United States, most of Procter & Gamble's customers grew up with Tide, Pampers, Ivory, Crisco, Camay, and many other classic P&G brands. With decades-old product brands in nearly every category, each new generation of P&G customers was as likely to be introduced to the company's brands by mom and dad as by Cincinnati's marketing geniuses. In the United States, with many of P&G's major brand-building investments long since amortized, the company is able to cope with the diseconomies of scale that come from fragmented brand advertising. P&G faced a very different situation when it decided, in the early 1970s, to tackle the huge and ultra-competitive Japanese market. Here P&G had to start from scratch—consumers were entirely unacquainted with P&G's mighty U.S. brands. So the company faced a choice: to fragment its brand-building efforts across a range of product-specific brands, as it had done in the United States, or to add a "maker's mark" to each product brand to more quickly build the brand awareness and brand integrity that is so important to wary Japanese buyers. In a clear break with U.S. policy, P&G chose the latter route, a route favored by its Japanese competitors who often give equal weight to the promotion of corporate and product brands. P&G's logic was simple: If the goal is to build brand awareness and customer credibility in the minimum possible time and with the greatest possible efficiency, it makes no sense to totally fragment brand-building efforts across a range of product-specific brands. So P&G went the Sony route: Use product brands to communicate specific product attributes and overlay this with a corporate brand to communicate integrity and quality.

For years Nestlé has made substantial use of its corporate banner brand; whether on condensed milk, chocolate, Nescafe coffees or, more recently, breakfast cereals. Nestlé's chairman, Helmut Maucher, summarizes the logic of the global banner brand:

> The Nestlé name is now being introduced across all our brands, Maggi, Findus, everywhere. All have the Nestlé [birds'] nest on the back panel. Local products reflect local differences, but the advantage of a worldwide company comes from a common identity like Volvo or Coca-Cola.[4]

Global economies of scale have long been recognized as important to global competition. In industries like telecommunications equipment, jet aircraft, and semiconductors, there is no way to recoup R&D and capital investments without access to global markets. In competing for global share of mind, it is economies of scope, rather than economies of scale, that are critical. Yamaha, which makes and markets a broad range of musical instruments under a single brand (including guitars, pianos, trumpets, organs, and violins), is inherently better positioned to build a significant share of mind than single-segment competitors like Selmer or King, who make only brass and woodwinds, and therefore can't amortize their brand investments across multiple product categories. Similarly, the economies of scope Honda exploited when it put its name on lawn mowers could not be easily matched by more narrowly focused competitors like Snapper and the engine maker Briggs & Stratton Corp.

Because there is an "S-curve effect" in building brand awareness (a customer has to be repeatedly exposed to a brand before that brand begins to stick in the customer's mind), spreading advertising funds across ten distinct brands, for example, yields less than one-tenth the brand awareness that could be achieved by focusing the funds on a single brand. In a systematic study, OC&C, a London-based consulting company, found that the advertising and promotion costs needed to convince customers to try out a new product were, on average, 36% less for a "stretched" brand than for a new product brand. Likewise, looking at the products launched by one particular multinational, OC&C found that six years after launch only 30% of newly branded products were still on the shelf, versus 50% of products that had leveraged a preexisting brand.[5]

Just as it makes no sense to unnecessarily fragment brand-building efforts across individual products, it makes no sense to fragment brand-building efforts across individual business units. Individual businesses may have neither the resources nor the inclination to build a global brand franchise. But once built, such a franchise dramatically reduces the costs of local market entry for all of the company's businesses. Any company intent on preempting competitors around the world must take a coordinated approach to building global banner brands. Building global share of mind, like building core competence leadership, is not a task to be left solely to individual businesses.

Walk through an international airport or look out the window of a towering hotel anywhere in the world. What are the brands you see advertised on billboards or in neon lights? Forget for a moment cigarettes, soft drinks, and alcohol. What are the *corporate* brands you see—whether in Asia, Europe, or Latin America? Most likely they will be Japanese or Korean: Hitachi, NEC, Komatsu, Sony, Fujitsu, Toshiba, Samsung, Hyundai, Mitsubishi. Occasionally you will see ABB, Siemens or Philips, and IBM, but where is Westinghouse, General Electric, United Technologies, or Britain's GEC? A typical Hitachi ad, emblazoned on a LaGuardia airport billboard, reminds customers that the company offers "More than 20,000 electronics products for the home, the office, the factory, the future."

Companies like NEC, Canon, and Honda have often tried to communicate to customers the range of products they offer. Not only is the banner emblazoned on every product, but ads, even if focused on one product, make reference to the firm's entire range of products. In one catchy ad, Honda asked, "How do you fit five Hondas into a two-car garage?" The answer, one has two Honda automobiles, a Honda lawn mower, a Honda portable generator, and a Honda motorboat engine or some other Honda product. Honda has been as intent on creating a global brand franchise as it has been on building core competence excellence in automotive engineering. Of course, to build global share of mind under a banner brand, a company must be committed to global markets. Unlike bricks and mortar, a brand has very little residual value if a company decides to pull out of a market or if its new product pipeline suddenly runs dry.

Obviously, some brands engender a greater predisposition to buy than do others. The attributes of a banner brand that determine its impact on buyer predisposition include (1) *recognition*—the level of brand awareness; (2) *reputation*—the confidence one has that a product bearing a particular brand will live up to the producer's claims; (3) *affinity*—the extent to which the brand is an integral part of the customer's sense of self; and (4) *domain*—the breadth of the brand's potential catchment area in terms of plausible product scope. Multiplied together, recognition, reputation, affinity, and domain determine a brand's share of mind (see Figure 11-2).

Recognition (brand recall) and reputation (brand esteem) are well-known parameters of brand power, but affinity and domain need more explanation. Brand affinity refers to the strength of the emotional tie that connects the consumer with the brand: Is the brand an integral part of one's lifestyle? Does it somehow encapsulate one's aspirations? Is it intertwined with happy memories? The higher the affinity between brand and buyer, the greater the predisposition to consider new product offerings bearing the banner brand.

Affinity is distinct from recognition and reputation. Xerox, Boeing, and Rolls Royce jet engines score high on both recognition and reputation, but low on affinity. Harley-Davidson scores high on recognition and affinity. The affinity Harley-Davidson owners have for "Hog" products drew some 75,000 bikers to Harley's seventy-fifth anniversary and paved the way for Harley's launch of a successful line of clothing and a tony Manhattan eatery. The

FIGURE 11-2 DETERMINANTS OF SHARE OF MIND

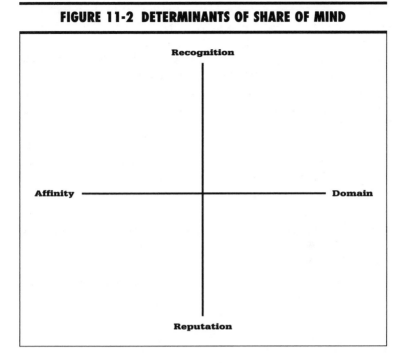

affinity consumers feel for Harley-Davidson goes far beyond bike owners. Disney, another high-affinity brand, found a new way of drawing water from the company's deep well of customer goodwill when it opened Disney retail shops in major malls and city centers around the world. Victorinox, the company that makes and markets Swiss Army Knives, found a novel way to take advantage of its high-affinity brand. While every schoolboy and girl dreams of owning a Swiss Army knife, few adults find it necessary or convenient to carry around a pocket knife on a day-to-day basis. So how to exploit all that underleveraged affinity? Simple—introduce a line of tough, no-nonsense Swiss Army watches. Presto, another hit. Both Harley-Davidson and Swiss Army Knives meet the ultimate test of customer affinity: They have spawned independent and self-perpetuating user clubs.

The contribution a brand makes to predisposing customers to consider new products is also very much related to the brand's domain. Whereas brands like Sony and 3M encompass a broad array of products, others, like Levi, Hershey, Campbell's, or Coca-Cola are limited to a narrow product category. While Campbell's rates high on recognition, reputation, and affinity, it's hard to imagine it adorning anything other than cans of soup or closely related products. Campbell's has, over the years, become hostage to a single product category. Colgate-Palmolive's Colgate brand may have a somewhat broader catchment area, covering toothbrushes, toothpaste, and antiplaque mouthwash, but one could hardly imagine the brand being extended to cover foodstuffs or household cleaning products. The simple principle here is that the longer a brand has been a prisoner of a single product category, the more difficult it is to extend the brand's reach into other product categories.

The wider the potential domain, the greater a brand's value in creating a predisposition to buy. There is, though, a limit to the breadth of any brand's domain. Stretch the brand too far, and it no longer conveys any coherent meaning to customers. Some years ago, Levi Strauss advertised its new line of "David Hunter" slacks and blazers as "classically tailored clothes, from Levi's." Customers thought the tag line an oxymoron, and Levi's quietly withdrew the line. An overextended banner brand may be inappropriate, or simply inconsequential. In advertisements for Sheraton hotels, the moniker "ITT Sheraton" is often used. But who really cares if Sheraton hotels are owned by ITT? The letters "ITT" convey no coherent message to customers given (1) that Sheraton is probably a more familiar brand to most people than ITT and (2) the incoherence of ITT's corporate portfolio, which encompasses businesses as diverse as automobile parts and insurance. On the other hand, when Marriott attaches its brand to its Courtyard group of hotels, customers have a good idea of what to expect.

What ultimately limits a brand's elasticity is the coherence of the brand message. To some extent, it is inevitable that, as the domain of a brand becomes wider, the specificity of the proposition put forward by the brand diminishes, though the proposition may still carry substantial weight with consumers. Banner brands with the broadest domain are those that communicate universal messages about product integrity and quality.

A strong banner brand franchise can become shorthand for a specific skill franchise. "Sony" suggests a cluster of competencies around portable entertainment, digital sound, and video displays. It also conveys quality and innovation. When the company boasts, "Sony, the one and only," few customers argue the point; nor do they take exception with Sharp's contention that it offers "Sharp products from Sharp minds." Before Honda, it would have been difficult to imagine a brand stretching across lawn mowers (where Honda competed with Sears and others), marine engines (Mercury), motorcycles (Yamaha), and automobiles (Toyota). Yet the extension of the Honda brand to cover these product categories makes sense to consumers because they recognize, either explicitly or implicitly, Honda's skill franchise in gasoline engines and its importance to the products Honda makes. Indeed, whatever the product, the engine has always received prominence in Honda advertising.

There is a great deal of subtlety in managing a brand's domain. Unilever thought that it was onto a winner when it extended its leading U.K. margarine brand, Flora, to a new line of salad dressings. After all, the company reasoned, both product lines draw on our experience in fats and oils. Unfortunately for Unilever, customers didn't see the connection. For them, salad dressings are not a logical extension of fats and oils but are closely related to condiments. So while Flora salad dressings were rejected, British customers went right on buying Heinz's Salad Cream.

Although anticipating just how far a brand can be stretched is not always easy, the question to be asked is just how product-specific is the skill franchise embodied in the brand. The Hershey's franchise, "We make great chocolate," is a lot more specific than the Nestlé franchise, "We make first-class food products." Interestingly, one of the broadest fast-moving consumer goods (FMCG) brands in the world is that of the innovative British grocery retailer, Sainsbury's. Unlike the situation in the U.S. grocery business where store brands are often considered second rate and the products they adorn are sold at a discount, Sainsbury's has built a store brand that encompasses everything from grocery staples to luxury chocolates and champagne, and that carries little, if any, discount against leading brands. The preemptive power of the Sainsbury brand is reflected in the fact that when it introduced a house-brand detergent in 1993, the brand quickly captured 30% of the home market, jumping ahead of Unilever's Persil brand and placing just behind P&G's market-leading Ariel.[6] Like Nordstrom's or The Gap, Sainsbury's has built a retailer franchise not around price but value. Because of its enormous buying power and its ability to amortize its brand-building efforts across hundreds of products, Sainsbury's is able to promise customers superior value at any given price point. Such a universal proposition is amenable to a broad range of products. Sainsbury's highly successful banner branding is a direct challenge to the expensive, and sometimes "valueless," product branding of P&G, Unilever, and others.

Propagation

The capacity for preemption rests not only on a physical ability to move the product quickly into channels around the world, but also on an organizational ability to rapidly communicate the advantages of the new product to country managers around the world, to ensure that adequate sales and marketing resources are devoted to the new product in each country, and to quickly spot where the new innovation is not taking root and take corrective action.

In many multinational companies, country managers have been historically quite free to choose which of the company's businesses or products would be included in the local product line-up. Traditionally, local executives were free to adopt or ignore new products created in other countries or at the head office. Aware that customer tastes and preferences varied significantly from market to market, as did the competitive environment, headquarters staff were reluctant to second-guess national managers. Particularly in the early years of international expansion, home office executives, realizing that they had little international experience, granted substantial product-line autonomy to local executives. Indeed, there was little incentive to try and coordinate, much less mandate, worldwide product rollouts. In a world of national markets fragmented by tariffs, regulatory differences, and unique customer preferences, there were few opportunities to capture global-scale economies. With no international media there was little incentive to build a common global brand identity or seek an internationally consistent product positioning. Confronting competitors with similarly national or multinational perspectives, there was little reason to worry about global preemption. In such an environment, local autonomy was the best way to maximize global earnings. But no more.

With increasing economic integration particularly in Europe, the dismantling of tariff and nontariff barriers, the growth of international media and an ever-expanding cadre of internationally mobile customers with a heightened global consciousness, the ever-escalating costs of new product development, and competitors increasingly capable of developing products for a global market and eager to obtain a global return on their investment, the rapid propagation of new business concepts and new products across national subsidiaries has become an imperative for every multinational.

Of course this imperative has often run straight into the traditional strategic prerogatives of country managers. Often lacking an international perspective, local executives have often been prone to overestimate that uniqueness. It was difficult for head-office executives to know whether a country manager's reluctance to take on a new product was based on bona fide market differences, a reluctance to fight an uphill battle to establish the firm in a new product category, or sheer bloody mindedness. But one thing was clear to Philips, Procter & Gamble, Ford, Unilever, Citibank, IBM, and many other multinationals: Organizational boundaries often frustrated the worldwide propagation of new business and product concepts.

To entice country managers to think more globally, many multinational companies are giving country managers worldwide or regional responsibilities for a particular line of business; country managers and their deputies are invited onto transnational business teams where the goal is to optimize a product's market penetration around the world; and high potential executives get international career assignments that make them less prone to parochialism and better able to spot opportunities to extend the geographical reach of a new product or service. As one U.S. executive remarked to us,

> In the old days it was up to the worldwide business manager
> to make the case that a new product was right for local markets.
> Now it is up to the local manager to demonstrate that it is not
> going to fly locally. Our expectation is that every new prod-
> uct will find a global market.

A senior Nestlé manager put it even more simply: "We are [saying] to our people more and more: find the similarities, then we'll discuss the differences."[7] This is not heavy-handed centralization but a recognition that in a world of increasingly global competitors and converging needs, the risks of preemption run ever higher.

The payoff to these efforts to accelerate propagation have been handsome. As noted earlier, Gillette blasted its innovative Sensor razor into 19 countries almost simultaneously, having test marketed the razor in only a fraction of these countries. P&G got one of its recent diaper innovations, Pampers Phases, on the shelf in 90 countries in fewer than 12 months, compared to the 27 months it took to roll out the last Pampers innovation.[8] Pert, a combination shampoo and conditioner introduced in the United States in 1986, was soon on retailers' shelves in 30 countries. P&G's rapid propagation reflected Chairman Ed Artzt's view that, "If we don't do it early on globally, someone else will."[9]

Global brands can be a spur to rapid propagation. A common brand may help create a feeling among far-flung national managers that perhaps local markets are not much different after all, and that success with a particular product concept in one market is transferable to others. In this sense, global brands may serve as a "pivot," helping new product concepts swing from one market to another. The rationale given by Michael Jordon, former chairman of Pepsico International Food and Beverage and now chief executive at Westinghouse, for Pepsico's global food brands (Pepsi, Taco Bell, Pizza Hut) seems to reflect such a logic:

Global brands are emerging because the companies that make and market them are becoming global organizations. . . . The brand is a by-product of organizational experience and business systems (which is what we truly leverage rather than some catchy name). . . . So why do organizations, including my own, continue to strive for worldwide brands? I believe they are really rallying points or symbols for the organization itself, for the experience and knowledge it brings to the marketing of soft drinks, cigarettes, or beer.[10]

Of course, the ultimate goal of preemption is not to leverage a global brand. Whether a global brand is appropriate in any given case is a secondary issue. The primary goal is to drive a new product or marketing concept around the world as fast as possible. Believing that it had a globally competitive product and a universally appealing marketing theme, Unilever worked hard to make its Snuggles brand fabric softener a hit around the world. And even though the English product name got translated and adapted into many local variants, the basic selling proposition—gentleness and cuddliness—and the product mascot—a teddy bear—remained the same around the world.

So the race to the future finally comes down to a mad dash for the finish line. Those companies that have built banner brands that predispose customers to try their new products, that have secured access to critical channels around the globe, and have developed an internal capacity to quickly propagate new product innovations will, other things being equal, capture the competitive high ground.

12

Thinking Differently

. . . .

I f the goal is industry leadership, restructuring and reengineering are not enough. To build leadership, a company must be capable of reinventing its industry; to rebuild leadership, a company must be capable of regenerating its core strategies. In this sense, it is not enough to get smaller and better; a company must also have the capacity to become different. But to ultimately "be" different, a company must first "think" differently. That's why this book has been as much about "how to think" as it has been about "what to do." To have a share in the future, a company must learn to think differently about three things: the meaning of competitiveness, the meaning of strategy, and the meaning of organizations.

THINKING DIFFERENTLY ABOUT COMPETITIVENESS

"Competitiveness" is a growth industry. Presidents and prime ministers vow to improve it, legislators debate it, economists measure it, and editors feature it. In this context, the notion of competitiveness is typically couched in terms of one nation or trading bloc versus another, and the animating question is whether country X is losing or "surrendering" its competitiveness to country Y. When the unit of analysis is a firm rather than a country, the issue of competitiveness revolves around relative competitive position and competitive advantage. In this view, competitiveness comes from a "defensible" market position and "sustainable" competitive advantages. We believe the country versus country formulation of the competitiveness challenge is substantially inaccurate, and the "position and advantage" formulation is incomplete.

Putting National Competition in Perspective

Politicians, professors, and pundits have found votes, book royalties, and headlines in the claim that the United States has become competitively enfeebled. We believe such claims to be invariably exaggerated and misdirected. There is little, if any, "head-to-head" competition between nation states. If Europe's prosperity goes up, America's doesn't go down—it also rises. If Japan's economy grows, the U.S. GNP doesn't decline by a proportionate amount. Competitive battles are fought between firms. Chrysler does indeed "steal" market share from General Motors. The growth of Southwest Airlines does come largely out of the hide of American, United, and Delta. Executives who believe that corporate success turns on trade and industrial policy—as managers in Europe's electronics industry, the U.S. car industry, and Japan's aerospace industry often seem prone to—must be disabused of this dangerous notion.

The competitiveness challenge is not Japan versus the United States versus Europe. It is not about trading blocs. The global economy is so intertwined today that in many cases it hardly makes sense to talk of a "U.S." company, a "European" company, or a "Japanese" company. From Dow Chemical to CPC to Colgate-Palmolive, many leading U.S. companies earn more than 50% of their revenues outside the United States—quite a feat considering the size of the home market "anchor." And if Americans are worried by the fact that U.S. companies don't make as many televisions, camcorders, or CD players as Japanese rivals, they should remember that U.S. entertainment companies, microprocessor makers, and investment banks dominate global markets. Likewise, Unilever, Shell, Ericsson, Glaxo, Nokia, and BMW view Europe not as home but as simply one more market. Although Japanese companies have sometimes been slower to escape the shackles of an ethnocentric view of the world, a new generation of managers is intent on making Japanese enterprise "local" wherever in the world it operates. Neither can one claim that competitive success achieved by one area within the triad must come at the expense of another. The rapid economic development of Asia offers unprecedented opportunity for U.S. and European companies. European companies have an enormous stake in U.S. prosperity, as U.S. companies do in Japanese prosperity, and so on.

Yet no single economy, whether U.S., European, or Asian, is immune from the wrenching changes brought about by technological revolution, deregulation, and corporate entropy. But if the unit of analysis is a nation, America's competitive problems are certainly no worse than those of Europe and Japan. At the time of writing, Europe's unemployment rate is almost double that of the United States. Between the mid-1960s and the end of the 1980s, Europe managed to create just one-fifth of the jobs that were created in the United States. Japan's agricultural, banking, distribution, retailing, computing, and telecommunication sectors continue to lag far behind their U.S. equivalents. When confronted, as we occasionally are, by the "strategic traders," industrial policy wonks, and other self-appointed guardians of U.S. competitiveness, we typically ask, "With whom would you like the United States to trade competitive problems? Do you want to trade with Europe—with its lack of job growth and increasing continental myopia? Do you want to trade with Japan—which has yet to face up to its giant-sized restructuring problem?" End of argument.

What seems to worry the trade pundits is not that U.S. competitiveness is declining in any absolute sense—Americans are today substantially more materially blessed than their parents were—but that U.S. economic hegemony is dwindling in a comparative sense. Simply, other countries are catching up. This is to be expected in a world where capital, technology, and managerial talent are internationally mobile. The unfettered capitalism of the Chinese Diaspora in Taiwan, Hong Kong, and southern China has produced an economic miracle every bit the equal of Japan's. What protectionist-minded politicians and their academic spear carriers see as a competitive "problem," the rest of the world sees as economic development. It is paradoxical that those left of the political center who are most supportive of redistributive fiscal policies at home are the same ones who seem most troubled by the fact that the rest of the world is closing the consumption gap with the United States.

Creating a level playing field in terms of market access, intellectual property rights, and open capital markets is a worthy goal but is, ultimately, a sideshow. U.S. prosperity will be aided hardly a whit by a more "enlightened" or "better-coordinated" trade policy, or by a repentant, free-trading Japan. It will, however, take a substantial leap forward if U.S. workers and companies find a way of aiding and abetting the economic development of those regions and countries striving so desperately to create for themselves the American way of life. Companies like Boeing, General Electric, Procter & Gamble, Coca-Cola, and Merrill Lynch, all of whom are charging into Asia's bubbling cauldron of economic growth, will do far more for U.S. prosperity than any Beltway-born trade policy. Because the vast majority of trade today is intracorporate, taking place, most often, between the parent company and its far-flung national subsidiaries, the growth of U.S. corporate investment abroad acts as a strong stimulus to U.S. jobs creation.

None of this is to argue that the competitiveness of U.S. companies should be taken for granted. But competitiveness is far more an issue of corporate policy than of industrial policy. Hundreds of millions of ECUs and the brightest bureaucrats in Brussels couldn't save Europe's ill-conceived attempts to create a "European" standard in high-definition television. Billions of dollars and rampant protectionism didn't prevent Japan's computer industry from persisting far too long with a mainframe-driven view of the world. And it was the fear of getting pulverized, rather than the extra margins created by protectionism, that pushed U.S. automakers into taking quality seriously.

Those U.S. companies that have been fighting, sometimes successfully, sometimes unsuccessfully, to regain their competitiveness, are not fighting against an unenlightened and unhelpful set of U.S. trade policies, much less against the brilliantly conceived conquest strategies of foreign policy-makers. They are fighting against the demons of inertia, complacency, and myopia. Their competitive enemies are not the corporate warriors of Japan or

Asia, but the unconventional tactics of home-grown rivals. IBM's problems weren't caused by Fujitsu, they were caused by Hewlett-Packard, EDS, and Compaq. Sears wasn't bested by Mitsukoshi, but by Wal-Mart and Nordstrom. Westinghouse didn't fall victim to Mitsubishi, but to General Electric. CBS didn't surrender leadership to NHK, but to Viacom and Turner Broadcasting.

The real competitiveness problem is not that America's too-clever trading partners have tilted the playing field to their advantage. The real problem is that too many large U.S. (and European and Japanese) companies failed to anticipate, much less invent, the new rules of competition in their industries. In this sense, the issue is not foreign competition but nontraditional competition. In the battle for the future, lethargy, convention, myopia, and elitism are much more real and much more substantial enemies than the "unfair" practices of mercantilist trading partners. For anyone who's passionate about competitiveness, the real challenge is not to open the Japanese distribution system or remove the national bias from Europe's public procurement practices. The real challenge is to help IBM develop better industry foresight, to remake the culture at General Motors, to revitalize Philips, to help Intel avoid the pitfalls of success, to help universities reinvent the way they deliver education, to reconceive the delivery of health care, and yes, to help business schools understand how they can substantially improve their contribution to keeping industry competitive.

In our discussion of competitiveness we start with a pro-bigness bias. We believe that large companies are essential to the wealth creation process for a number of reasons.

First, having a capacity to match the resources and global distribution of large competitors brings advantages. It is worth remembering that the global leadership of Intel and Microsoft came on the back of IBM's worldwide distribution presence. The two start-ups rode into world markets on IBM's broad shoulders. A whole raft of small subcontractors, engineering companies, and software makers ride Boeing's coattails into global markets. It is the same in Japan, where Toshiba, Sony, and Canon leverage the ideas and innovations of smaller companies into the global market. There is a symbiotic relationship between big and small. The innovations of small start-up companies create wealth only when they are combined with complementary skills and exploited globally. A Silicon Valley without AT&T, IBM, Eastman Kodak, and Motorola would create little wealth.

Second, large companies also tend to devote a disproportionate share of their resources to training and education. This investment in people is enormously valuable to society. Many entrepreneurs perfected their skills inside large companies. IBM nurtured and trained dozens of entrepreneurs, from Gene Amdahl to Ross Perot, who went on to create their own companies. Large companies contribute to the entrepreneurial process through spinoffs, investment in start-ups, global distribution links, and the training and education of future entrepreneurs. The role of large companies in launching new companies is as vital as the role of venture capitalists.

Third, opening the door to many of tomorrow's mega-opportunities will require significant resources. It is difficult to imagine a small- or medium-sized company building the infrastructure that will be required for interactive television, taking on the task of building the next generation of super-jumbo aircraft, or creating a global, 24-hour-a-day financial trading network. Steve Jobs may have launched the personal computing revolution from his garage, but entrepreneurial fervor is not always enough to crack open a new opportunity. Of course, size is an advantage only when there's a stretching aspiration that engenders great creativity in the use of the firm's resource endowment.

There is a fourth reason why one must be concerned with the fortunes of large companies—they are significant employers. By the time IBM restabilizes it may have shed as many as 200,000 jobs. To put this in context, the venture capital system would have to produce around 15 Microsofts to compensate for IBM's job losses. IBM may be the most dramatic example, but it is almost impossible to pick up a financial newspaper without seeing an announcement of another 10,000 or 20,000 redundancies. Of course, bloated companies must slim down, and the productivity benefits of information technology and process reengineering must be diligently sought. On the other hand, most of the job losses that we have witnessed in large companies are the result not of "global" competition or dramatic increases in productivity. Most of the casualties come when a company crashes into the future, with top management asleep at the switch. This was the case at Philips, at DEC, at Westinghouse, and at many other companies. Top management must not seek to escape its culpability for the carnage caused when it fails to anticipate and shape the future of its industry. Likewise, no one with a social conscience can be unmoved by the plight of those who've paid the enormous personal costs for a company's lack of industry foresight.

We are not arguing for a set of public policy measures that in any way discriminate in favor of large companies. The goal is not to keep dinosaurs alive at all costs. However, society pays a heavy price when, through managerial malfeasance, a company richly endowed with resources and talent self-destructs. The goal is not to embalm dinosaurs through subsidies, protectionism, and preferential procurement policies—as European governments have too often done—but to ensure that large companies don't become dinosaurs in the first place.

The perspective we have provided in this book is of equal value to large and small companies. As keen as we are for the regeneration of large companies, we are equally keen that small companies grow into big companies. Again, the point is not to get big for bigness' sake. Growth creates employment and wealth, which in turn creates the opportunity for personal and societal advancement. There is no honor in being small. Just as bigness without stretch and leverage is obesity, smallness without stretch and leverage is impotence. Thus, anyone running a small company should be enormously encouraged by the fact that there are so many examples of companies that overcame seemingly insuperable resource handicaps and built positions of global leadership.

Searching for the Causes of Competitiveness
Business school professors, consultants, and managers have long sought the causes of competitiveness. Strategy researchers have asked, why do some firms grow and others stagnate? Why are some companies immensely profitable while others lose billions?

Why do some gain market share and others surrender it? From this quest have come a multitude of insights—into the relationship between accumulated volume and costs, into the correlation between market share and profitability, into the things that constitute barriers to entry in an industry, into the dynamics of competitive interaction, and so on. The search for the causes of competitiveness has often been scientifically rigorous, but equally it has often been narrow and shallow.

First, the charge of narrowness. The search for the causes of competitiveness has been narrow in terms of (1) the time frame considered—months and years, instead of decades; (2) the unit of analysis employed—the product or business unit rather than the entire firm or a coalition of firms; and (3) the competitive arena encompassed—market versus nonmarket. Whether it's the time frame of the average B-school strategic marketing case, the length of tenure of a typical SBU head, or the increasingly frantic cycle time for product development, managers or academics seldom consider aspects of competitive strategy that span more than three or four years. Yet there is much that lies outside this restrictive time frame: a 20-year strategic intent, a 15-year crusade to build a core competence, or a 10-year effort to shape an emerging market. A truncated view of the dynamics of competition obscures important strategy issues around notions such as consistency, continuity, resource conservation, and competence accumulation.

We have argued that competition occurs not just between individual product or service offerings, but between firms and coalitions of firms. Top management teams compete in the acquisition of foresight about a broad new opportunity arena such as genetically engineered drugs. Companies compete in building core competencies that transcend the resources of individual business units. Coalitions compete to create new competitive space. Economists, strategy researchers, and managers have too often assumed that competition is limited to the market for goods and services. Yet competition for foresight, competition to build competencies, and competition to shape industry evolution through a coalition are all examples of extramarket, or nonmarket, competition. The fact that this competition takes place outside a "market" doesn't make it any less real. An insensitivity to this broader scope of competition can prevent a company from adequately preparing for the future.

The search for the causes of competitiveness has also not penetrated as deeply as it might. We observe that some firms grow while others contract; some companies are immensely profitable while others hemorrhage cash; some gain market share and some lose it. Observing competitive outcomes is a bit like a physician taking a patient's blood pressure, pulse, or temperature: One can say little more than whether the patient appears to be well or ill. To move from observation to diagnosis a physician must dig significantly deeper. What are the specific symptoms? In what combination do they appear? How persistent have they been and how severe?

A first-level diagnosis of competitive problems typically draws on the tools of industry structure analysis. Understanding a business's competitive position (i.e., the inherent "attractiveness" of the market segments in which it operates) gives some crude indication of the relative *potential* for profits.[1] The theory is that different industries and industry segments have different average profitability levels, and that these differences persist over time. Depending on the array of competitive forces at work, a particular industry segment may be, on average, inherently more or less profitable than another. To wit, it has generally been more profitable, on average, to make ethical pharmaceuticals than over-the-counter pharmaceuticals, to produce large cars rather than small cars, and, if you're an airline, to capture the business flyer rather than the tourist on a budget. Within the broad profitability constraints of its industry or segment a firm's *actual* profitability is determined by its relative cost and differentiation (price) advantages. The fact that one finds successful firms in supposedly "unattractive" industries merely demonstrates that relative advantage may ultimately matter more than industry affiliation.

These, then, are the primary lessons of competitive strategy: Find an attractive industry segment, buy low, and sell high. Easier said than done. Attractive industries—that is, those with above-average profitability—are attractive because they are surrounded by sizable entry barriers (e.g., scale and scope economies, government regulation, research intensity) that keep new entrants out. Likewise, any firm making above-average profits within the industry can be assumed to possess competitive advantages that are not easily imitated. The only avenues open to a firm confronting insurmountable barriers to entry are to redraw industry boundaries so that what is now attractive lies outside the former barriers. This is done by radically shifting the basis for competitive advantage in the industry (as CNN did in news broadcasting) or creating entirely new industry space ideally suited to one's own strengths (as Sharp did with pocket electronic organizers). In either case, whether the company can prosper from its ingenuity will depend on whether it can construct unique and nonimitable competitive advantages. Unfortunately, industry structure analysis provides almost no insight into the two critical tasks of *re*structuring industries and building new, nonconventional advantages.

Industry structure analysis is well-suited to describing the *what* of competitiveness (i.e., *what* is it that makes one firm or one industry more profitable than another). As new *whats* have been uncovered, companies have been exhorted to "compete on time," become "customer-led," strive for "six sigma" quality, adopt "simultaneous engineering," and pursue a host of other desirable advantages. Yet with all the attention given to understanding the particulars of cost, quality, customer service, and time-to-market advantages, the question of *why* seems to have gone largely unanswered: *Why* do some companies seem able to continually create new forms of competitive advantage while others seem able only to observe and follow? *Why* are some firms net advantage creators and others net advantage imitators? There is a need not only to keep score of existing advantages—what they are and who has them—but to discover the "engine" that propels the process of advantage creation. The tools of industry and competitor analysis are much better suited to the first task than to the second. Relying only on these tools, business educators and consultants can be little more than conduits for the transfer of best practice from those firms that are net advantage creators to those firms that are net advantage imitators.

As long as our diagnosis stays focused on the *what* rather than the *why,* there is little chance that companies that have fallen behind in the advantage-building race will ever regain the lead. Laggards will remain laggards. Worse, the strategies of such companies are likely to be transparent to their faster-moving competitors. They can predict which advantages the laggards will have to work on next, and about how long it will take to master the new skills. If the race for global leadership is, in large part, a race to create new competitive space and new forms of competitive advantage ahead of rivals, there is little chance of leadership for a firm whose understanding of the *what* of competitiveness lags by a decade or more the already constructed capabilities of rivals. Understanding the *what* of competitiveness is a prerequisite for catching up. Understanding the *why* of competitiveness is a prerequisite for getting out in front.

The *why* of competitiveness is more than the why of advantage creation; it is also the *why* of industry restructuring and transformation. Just as it is not enough to benchmark the advantages of competitors, it is not enough to understand the existing structure of an industry (i.e., barriers to entry, market segments, and present patterns of rivalry). Typically, the existing industry structure works to the disadvantage of everyone save the industry leader, and most especially to the disadvantage of aspiring entrants. What is needed is a capacity to transform the structure of an industry, as did Wal-Mart in mass merchandising and Canon in copiers. Again, it is not the *what* of industry structure that is of interest, it is the *why* of industry *r*estructuring. *Why* do some firms seem to take industry structure more or less as a given, while others are able to harness the forces of globalization, deregulation, technology, or demographics to transform industry structure to their own advantage?

Industries don't "evolve." Instead, firms eager to overturn the present industry order challenge "accepted practice," redraw segment boundaries, set new price-performance expectations, and reinvent the product or service concept. As Charles Schwab demonstrated in its rivalry with other traders, and as Southwest Airlines showed its larger U.S. rivals, seemingly insurmountable barriers to entry may become, for the incumbent, barriers to retaliation and repositioning when rivals successfully alter industry topography. An *ex post* explanation of how an industry has been transformed—the objective of business school cases and economists' industry studies—is not the same thing as a capacity to reshape an industry *ex ante*. In searching for the wellspring of sustained competitiveness, it is not enough merely to account for competitive outcomes after the fact, to understand in hindsight the evolution of an industry, or to keep score at a particular point in time of relative competitive advantages. *Ex post* explanations and *ex ante* capabilities are two very different things. Understanding industry structure is not the same thing as reshaping it; keeping score of competitive advantage is not the same thing as inventing new advantages. Foresight, stretch, and leverage provide the energy and rationale for proactive advantage building and industry re-engineering.

In recent years process reengineers in leading U.S. consulting companies have superseded industry analysts as the high priests of strategydom. Companies know they're sick, and what they don't want is one more recitation of the symptoms. What they're after is relief. And what they've gotten, more often than not, is relief from the *symptoms* of disease rather than relief from the *causes* of disease. The truth is that most patients are multisymptomatic. This is what makes overweight, out-of-breath corporate patients so attractive to hungry consulting companies—there are just so many problems to fix! A sclerotic product development process, a tumorous corporate bureaucracy, rolls of excess management fat, and a host of anticustomer pathologies all cry out for attention.

Often the approach of process reengineers is more surgery than therapy. Without denying the enormous benefits of simplifying work flows, "working out" unnecessary activities, and collapsing management layers, these activities seldom point to new advantages or opportunities to transform industry structure. At best, they are still in the category of catching up. The deeper questions still remain: Why did this patient get sick in the first place? Why does this patient seem so *prone* to get sick? What could be done to make it more resistant to disease in the future?

If the ultimate goal is to prevent disease rather than merely treat the symptoms, we must dig still deeper. The medical researcher must understand why some individuals seem predisposed to contract certain diseases. Differences in lifestyle are part of the story. The impact of diet, occupation, and exercise on wellness are akin to the impact of institutional factors on competitive outcomes. Institutional factors refer to the environmental milieu in which a firm operates. Although the role of institutional factors in competitive disease is often exaggerated, there is no doubt that monetary and fiscal policy, trade and industrial policy, national levels of educational achievement, the structure of corporate ownership, and the social norms and values that predominate in a particular nation all have an impact on the competitiveness of firms therein domiciled. Yet too often executives have used supposed institutional disadvantages as an escape clause for poor competitive performance.

Take but one example: the *cause célèbre* of Japan's "closed" car market. U.S. auto executives have long blamed import barriers for their poor performance in the Japanese market. (Remember President Bush's ill-fated trip to Japan in 1992 when, accompanied by the chairmen of Detroit's Big Three, he pressed Japanese politicians to open their market to U.S. car makers.) But how do Japanese import barriers explain the abysmal performance of U.S. automakers in the rest of Asia? U.S. car companies run a very poor second to their Japanese rivals across Asia, not just in Japan. Even in Australia, where GM and Ford have operated for decades, Japanese companies have taken far more than their "fair share" of the car market. In 1993 Honda exported more cars from the United States to Japan than did the Big Three. Yet *Business Week* complimented Ford on the fact that it was the first U.S. car company to engineer a right-hand drive model for export to Japan.[2] Whatever the import barriers to selling U.S.-made cars in Japan, one can hardly be sympathetic when it seems to have taken Detroit three or four decades to wake up to the fact that the Japanese drive on the other side of the road!

In blaming institutional factors for competitive ill-health, companies are prone to overlook the institutional disadvantages of their rivals. While the United States may have been a relatively open market, the sheer size of that market and its geographical and cultural distance from Japan made market entry a daunting task for relatively small, resource-poor Japanese companies. One wonders just how much of their enormous resource endowment U.S. car companies would have been willing to trade away to get access to the supposedly "unfair" advantages of Japanese car companies 20 years ago. The point is that U.S. car companies enjoyed substantial institutional advantages: preferential access to a large, continental-scale market, access to customers with the highest disposable incomes in the world, cheap gasoline, and access to the graduates of the best engineering programs in the world. Clearly, the institutional environment does vary from country to country. But it is difficult to argue that a company is systematically disadvantaged by *every* aspect of its institutional environment. Managers are typically quick to point out the institutional advantages enjoyed by a foreign rival, but much slower to recognize their own institutionally derived advantages. Advantages that are typically described as "unfair" are more often simply "different."

Although the impact of lifestyle on health has become a major focus of medical research, the story by no means ends there. How can one explain the jogger who expires mid-stride or the sedentary desk jockey whose more active peers die first? Why do leaders (e.g., Firestone, RCA, General Motors) often end up as laggards in the very industries they pioneered, despite having substantial resource advantages? What possible institutional advantage did IBM lack in its position as the world's leading computer company? How is it that other firms are able to overcome substantial resource disadvantages and successfully challenge industry leaders? What possible institutional advantages did Yamaha have in its quest to become the world's premier musical instrument company? Japan, after all, is not the home of Western classical music.

Beyond lifestyle lies genetics, and it is here that one finally uncovers the hidden causes of competitiveness. The simple fact is that for many—if not most—diseases, the population of individuals who are genetically predisposed to contract a certain disease is not the same population as those who are disease prone as a result of lifestyle. The population distribution of some maladies—sickle cell anemia, muscular dystrophy, Down's syndrome, and male pattern baldness to name a few—are determined almost exclusively by genetics. Diseases like breast cancer, colon cancer, hypertension, and Alzheimer's are now known to have significant genetic "triggers." Disentangling lifestyle and genetic causes of disease is one of medicine's greatest challenges. It is no less a challenge for the student of competitiveness.

Thus, we have argued that the starting point for competitive revitalization is an understanding of a company's "genetic code." In the managerial context, genetics has no biological component but is concerned with the way that managers perceive their industry, their firm, their roles, and the ways in which these perceptions predispose them to behave in particular circumstances. The concern here is over the way that managers are genetically encoded to *think*. Industry structure analysis focuses on the topography of the battlefield and the administrative process perspective on the deployment and organization of forces. Yet if a combatant (GM), or a group of combatants (the major U.S. tire companies, except Goodyear) has been badly mauled in a string of battles, fought over a variety of terrain (low-end, high-end, domestic market, international markets), with varying troop deployments (reorganizations, restructurings), one begins to suspect that the problem lies less on the battlefield than it does in the minds of the generals directing the forces. Do they bring to the battle fundamentally different assumptions, values, and beliefs about strategy, organization, motivation, and the nature of competitive warfare? In short, are they operating from and within fundamentally different managerial frames of reference?

Any process of competitive revitalization that doesn't ultimately address the issue of genetics is likely to produce only symptomatic relief. Our purpose in this book has been to offer a guide to "gene replacement therapy" for senior managers. Making industry and company conventions explicit, understanding how those conventions could imperil the firm's success in the future, delving deeply into industry discontinuities, establishing a process for extending industry foresight, and working collectively to craft strategic architecture are the means for genetic reengineering on a large scale.

THINKING DIFFERENTLY ABOUT STRATEGY

Throughout this book we've argued that a company needs a point of view about the future (industry foresight) and must construct a blueprint for getting there (strategic architecture). Our focus in this book, and especially in this chapter, is the creation of future-oriented corporate strategy. Yet we recognize that "strategy" has a credibility crisis. In many companies the very notion of Strategy—with a capital *S*—has become devalued.

Why, we ask ourselves, in so many companies are strategic planning departments being disbanded or dramatically downsized? Why do senior managers seem relatively unperturbed that they spend so little time thinking about strategy and plotting a course into the future? Why have so many consulting companies largely abandoned the high ground of strategy-making for the day-to-day grind of operational improvement? Is it because most companies already have a clear-eyed and creative view of where they're headed and their problems are only ones of implementation? Unlikely. Is it that "strategy" just never really seems to make much of a difference, never really seems to pay off? More likely, but why?

We believe that the problem isn't with "strategy," but with the particular notion of strategy that predominates in most companies. What is being rejected is not strategy in the sense that we define it, but strategy as a pedantic planning ritual on one hand or a speculative and open-ended investment commitment on the other. In many companies strategy is essentially incremental tactical planning punctuated by heroic, and usually ill-conceived, "strategic" investments. The risk is that the devaluation of strategy will leave many companies rudderless in a world of turbulent seas and force-ten gales. To avoid this, we need a concept of strategy that goes beyond form filling and blank checks.

Strategy as Form Filling

In many companies strategy means turning the crank on the planning process once a year. Yet the fact that a company goes through the motions of an annual planning cycle, and that weighty strategic plans adorn executive bookcases, provides no clue as to whether a company has a truly unique and stretching point of view about the future. Typically, the planning process is more about making the numbers add up—"This is the revenue and profit growth we need this year, now how are we going to produce it?"—than it is about developing industry foresight. The foundation for planning is more often a set of assumptions about what Wall Street expects ("What can we get away with?"), than a point of view about what tomorrow's customers may expect. "Strategic" planning is often functional and tactical planning that barely scratches the surface of deep-down strategy issues. The focus is on marketing "strategy," sales "strategy," and manufacturing "strategy." The units of analysis are the existing businesses, each with its own product-market mandate. "Corporate" strategy is simply an amalgamation of individual business unit plans. The competitors analyzed are those that compete head-on—who play by the same rules. Not surprisingly, planning is almost always incrementalist—a few percentage points of market share gain here, a modest reduction in costs there, and a slightly more profitable niche discovered somewhere else.

In our experience, strategic planning typically fails to provoke deeper debates about who we are as a company or who we want to be in ten years' time. It seldom escapes the boundaries of existing business units. It seldom illuminates new white space opportunities. It seldom uncovers the unarticulated needs of customers. It seldom provides any insight into how to rewrite industry rules. It seldom stretches to encompass the threat from nontraditional competitors. It seldom forces managers to confront their potentially out-of-date conventions. Strategic planning almost always starts with "what is." It seldom starts with "what could be."

Incrementalist planning in a world of profound change is unlikely to add much value. Strategic planning works well when the foundations of planning—assumptions about what is our "industry," what "business" are we in, who are our competitors, who are our customers, and what are their needs—remain unshaken. But in many industries these foundations *are* being shaken. They are being shaken by new competitors who have no stake in the past. They are being shaken by seismic shifts in technology, demographics, and the regulatory environment. Strategic planning is well-suited to the challenge of extending leadership—adding a story or two atop the old foundation. It is not well-suited to the challenge of regenerating leadership—building new foundations. No wonder strategic planning has lost its luster.

To extend industry foresight and develop a supporting strategic architecture, companies need a new perspective on what it means to be "strategic." They need to ask new strategy questions: not just how to maximize share and profits in today's businesses, but who do we want to be as a corporation in ten years' time, how can we reshape this industry to our advantage, what new functionalities do we want to create for customers, and what new core competencies should we be building? They need a new process for strategy-making, one that is more exploratory and less ritualistic. They need to apply new and different resources to the task of strategy-making, relying on the creativity of hundreds of managers and not just on the wisdom of a few planners.

The distinctions between the traditional approach to strategy-making and our approach stand out starkly when we compare elements of the two models:

	Strategic Planning	**Crafting Strategic Architecture**
Planning goal	■ Incremental improvement in market share and position	■ Rewriting industry rules and creating new competitive space

Planning process	■ Formulaic and ritualistic	■ Exploratory and open-ended
	■ Existing industry and market structure as the base line	■ An understanding of discontinuities and competencies as the base line
	■ Industry structure analysis (segmentation analysis, value chain analysis, cost structure analysis, competitor benchmarking, etc.)	■ A search for new functionalities or new ways of delivering traditional functionalities
	■ Tests for fit between resources and plans	■ Enlarging opportunity horizons
	■ Capital budgeting and allocation of resources among competing projects	■ Tests for significance and timeliness of new opportunities
	■ Individual businesses as the unit of analysis	■ Development of plans for competence acquisition and migration
		■ Development of opportunity approach plans
		■ The corporation as the unit of analysis
Planning resources	■ Business unit executives	■ Many managers
	■ Few experts	■ The collective wisdom of the company
	■ Staff driven	■ Line and staff driven

Strategy as Patient Money

Occasionally strategy is more than incremental. Occasionally strategy is truly "corporate" in its orientation. When it is, it is likely to take the form of a major acquisition or divestment, aimed at reconfiguring the company's portfolio in a single go. Think about

Xerox's ill-fated ventures into financial services; GE's purchase, and then disposal, of Utah International; GM's acquisition of Hughes; Grand Met's acquisition of Burger King; Coca-Cola's foray into Hollywood. Occasionally such "strategic" investments build the foundation for a profound and profitable shift in corporate direction; more often they fail to live up to their promise and the expected bonanza never materializes.

Try an experiment. Find a senior finance person in your company. Tell him or her you need funding for a major "strategic" investment. How do finance executives decode the word *strategic* when it comes in front of the word *investment*? We've asked them this question and almost invariably the answer comes back—"The project is going to lose money!" One corporate controller went further, "And if it's a 'global' strategy add three more zeroes on the end!" Next, tell your finance executive that you want support for a "long-term" strategy. How does he or she decode "long-term"? Most probably, as patient money and a payback that is years or even decades away. What does an "ambitious" strategy mean to a fiscally conservative senior executive? A strategy that carries a high degree of risk. Finally, if you argue that the company must be absolutely "committed" to this strategy, how will that be interpreted? What is the measure of commitment in most companies? Being really committed means outspending rivals; it means making big, irrevocable bets. The old saying is to "put your money where your mouth is." Some companies don't know they're committed unless there are nine zeroes after the dollar sign.

In other words, you might just as well say "Las Vegas" as "strategic investment" to most prudent finance officers. Sure, big bets sometimes yield big payouts, but just as often they mean losses. Look at how many "strategic investments" have failed to pay off. Certainly the reason laggards end up as laggards is not because they failed to make "strategic investments." No wonder finance executives are skeptical about strategic investments. In a world of draconian budgetary constraints and hyperefficient operations, no one wants to hear about "strategic" investments. Savvy managers know that for most long-term investments, the long term never materializes. They also know that if they manage to win resources for a "strategic" investment, it's a good idea to move on to another job before the "long term" becomes the near term. As one executive put it to us: "In our company the trick is to change jobs in time to guarantee that the long-term pay-off you promised four years ago in your capital budget proposal becomes someone else's short-term performance target."

Yet we have argued that strategy should be "long term," should be "ambitious," and should provoke extraordinary levels of "commitment." How do you square this circle? Only by building a new managerial frame around the notion of strategy. It is impossible to begin the work of crafting strategic architecture if people are locked inside the traditional strategy frame. Managers throughout the company must understand that "long term" doesn't equal "patient money." Though we won't argue that every project must have positive cash flow from day one, the goal is to get to the future on a pay-as-you-go basis. Long term means a point of view about the evolution of one's industry and how to shape it, not far distant returns.

"Ambitious" doesn't mean taking big risks. Ambition means setting a stretching aspiration, and then using the tools of resource leverage to "derisk" that ambition. We find it interesting that many companies equate innovation and growth with risk-taking. Sure, calculated risks must be taken, but getting to the future first is not simply a matter of having more risk-takers. Getting to the future first is less about making heroic investments than it is about derisking heroic ambitions.

Unless the assumed link between ambition and risk is severed, few managers will have the courage to commit to global leadership. Deeply conservative managers, beleaguered by shareholders, can't be blamed for failing to commit to global leadership when their experience tells them that "being strategic" is little more than financial hari-kari. Yet there need be no 1:1 correlation between stretch and risk. Stretch implies risk only when there is orthodoxy about how and when the aspiration is to be achieved. If managers at Ford simply extrapolate past practices, they might be tempted to believe that developing a car five times as good as the Escort, a potential Lexus-beater, say, would require five times the resources.

As long as a firm is held hostage to the orthodoxies of the past, it is unlikely to gain the courage necessary to commit to undisputed world leadership.

Stretch begets risk when an arbitrarily short time horizon is superimposed on a long-term leadership goal. Impatience brings the risk of rushing into markets not fully understood, ramping up R&D spending faster than it can be successfully managed, acquiring firms that cannot be easily digested, and rushing into alliances with partners whose motives and capabilities are poorly understood. Too often progress toward the future is measured in terms of investment commitments, rather than in terms of accumulated knowledge about technology choices and customer requirements. The job of top management is not so much to boldly "stake out" the future but to help accelerate the acquisition of market and industry knowledge in ways that don't expose the firm to untenable market and competitor risks. Risk recedes as knowledge grows, and as knowledge grows, so does the firm's capacity to move forward.

Similarly being more committed than the next person doesn't mean betting bigger than everyone else; it means being more consistent and more persistent. In our view, commitment is not the financial stake a business unit has in a particular project; it is the intellectual stake the entire company has in a particular point of view about the future. Commitment is evidenced not just by investment levels, but by the application of senior management's attention and interest. Too often top management spreads its time across businesses and opportunities in direct proportion to current revenues or the investment streams. This is a recipe for maintaining the status quo. What is required is a commitment of top management time to a new opportunity arena that is disproportionate to current revenues and investment.

So, the old frame on strategy looked like this:

Long-term   =   Distant return

Ambition   =   Risk-taking

Commitment   =   Big bucks

The new frame we are suggesting here is different:

Long-term   =   A point of view about industry evolution and how to shape it

Ambition   =   A stretching aspiration that is derisked through the tools of resource leverage

Commitment   =   An intellectual and emotional commitment that ensures consistency and constancy

Only when everyone in a company shares this latter perspective will strategy regain its credibility.

THINKING DIFFERENTLY ABOUT THE ORGANIZATION

The need to think differently about strategy cannot be divorced from the need to think differently about organizations. Mobilizing employees at all levels around a strategic intent, leveraging resources across organizational boundaries, finding and exploiting "white space" opportunities, redeploying core competencies, consistently amazing customers, exploring new competitive space through expeditionary marketing, and building banner brands all require new ways of thinking about the organization. Just as the current language and practice of strategy is not up to the challenge of competition for the future, neither is the current language and practice of organizational change.

Over the past few years many companies have been working hard to transform their organizations. Companies have devolved traditional head office functions like planning and human resource management to individual business units; they have sought to enlarge the sphere of operating freedom for employees at all levels; they have divested tangential operations and concentrated on core businesses; they have attempted to encourage personal risk-taking;

they have emphasized individual responsibility; they have inverted the organization chart and put the customer at the top. The watchwords for the would-be engineers of the modern corporation are devolution, empowerment, focus, entrepreneurship, personal accountability, and customer-focus.

These ideas are the antithesis of the highly centralized, overly bureaucratic, control-oriented, "big brain," technology-led organizational archetypes of the 1960s and 1970s. General Electric, 3M, Hewlett-Packard, and a few other similarly devoluted and empowered companies have been the icons of those seeking to build the post-modern organization. Yet there is evidence that, in many cases, the antidote to bureaucracy and needless centralization can be just as toxic as the poison it is seeking to counteract.

We believe that basic organizational choices have too often been posed as either/or, black and white, thesis and antithesis. Managers have been taught to view organizational choices as stark contrasts.

Thesis	Antithesis
Corporate	Business units
Centralized	Decentralized
Bureaucratic	Empowered
Clones	Renegades
Technology-led	Customer-led
Diversified	Core business

This tendency toward black and white is often exacerbated by overreliance on financial reward systems as a tool to shape the actions of individual managers. Financial reward systems typically reward managers for pursuing either "A" or "B" rather than for making subtle and appropriate trade-offs between "A" and "B." To create the future, a company must succeed in creating a *synthesis* of what are too often seen as antithetical organizational choices.

Beyond Corporate versus Unit

In many companies one cannot speak meaningfully of a "corporate strategy" because the corporate strategy is little more than the aggregation of the independent strategies of standalone business units. Where the corporate role has been largely devolved, corporate officers have no particular responsibilities other than investor relations, acquisitions and disposals, and resource allocation across independent business units. In such organizations one has to question just what the value-added of the top team is anyway. Why not have unit managers report directly to Wall Street? Where top management's view of the company is one of a portfolio of unrelated businesses, suboptimization is almost inevitable. "White space" opportunities will go unexploited, existing core competencies will fragment and erode, new core competencies will go unbuilt, and R&D and brand budgets will splinter as divisional executives pursue totally independent strategic agendas.

We are not suggesting that market-focused business units are an inappropriate structural form. Neither are we suggesting that distant, out-of-touch corporate staff should make business unit strategy. What we are suggesting is that rather than seeing the corporation as *either* a single entity or a collection of unrelated businesses, senior managers must seek to identify and exploit the *interlinkages* across units that could potentially add value to the corporate whole.

We believe that there is often substantial "hidden value" buried in the linkages among business units. This value is realized when units identify and jointly explore white space opportunities, when competencies are redeployed from one unit to another or combined in new ways across units, when units cooperate in building strong banner brands serving multiunit customers, and the like. There is a risk that in the pursuit of devolution and decentralization, the substantial value that can be derived from collective action across units is inadvertently lost.

Beyond Centralization versus Decentralization

The potential for extracting value out of the management of inter-linkages only becomes visible when unit executives from across the company participate in a horizontal strategy development process. The identification and management of interlinkages emerge not from a corporate staff exercise but from a process where line managers from across the company come to recognize the potential value-added of collective action. Thus, what we argue for in this book is not absolute decentralization, nor a heavy-handed *corporate* strategy, but what might be described as enlightened *collective* strategy. Because the value of better managing interlinkages is seldom if ever quantified, no vice president is likely to feel responsible for it, nor is anyone pained when the value goes unrealized. Nevertheless, even General Electric, a company where the prerogatives of unit managers have been more jealously defended than perhaps in any other, has come to recognize the potential value in being a "boundaryless" organization. Likewise Hewlett-Packard, a company that has thrived on individual entrepreneurship, has come to recognize that there are some cross-unit opportunities that are just too attractive to sacrifice on the altar of absolute unit autonomy.

Of course, the development of collective strategy requires managers to adopt a more cooperative and less competitive posture vis-à-vis their peers. They must recognize that for every instance of resource sharing, cross-unit support, or sacrifice to the greater good, there may not be an immediate *quid pro quo*. Of course, they must also have good reason to believe that cooperative behavior will be rewarded, and that career advancement depends as much on taking responsibility for collective progress as on making one's own numbers.

Beyond Bureaucracy versus Empowerment

As IBM, GM, Philips, and many other companies have learned, bureaucracy and a rigid sense of hierarchy kill initiative and creativity. In response, companies have been seeking to cut the number of managerial layers. In our experience, managers often forget that reducing the layers of management (reducing levels in the hierarchy) is not the same thing as reducing the dysfunctional consequences of hierarchical behavior. Hierarchical behavior avoids an active multilevel dialogue on critical issues and uses power to settle issues rather than broad debate and high-quality analysis. The conservative, idea-strangling, time-wasting phenomenon of "managing upward" can be observed in many organizations, whether they have three organizational levels or a dozen.

The goal is not simply to reduce organizational levels, or the propensity of corporate staff to second-guess line managers. The goal is to grant individuals the freedom to design their own jobs, fix their own processes, and do whatever it takes to satisfy a customer. Yet are there limits to empowerment? We believe that empowerment without a *shared sense of direction* can lead to anarchy. While bureaucracy can strangle initiative and progress, so too can a large number of empowered but unaligned individuals who are working at cross-purposes. Of course, every employee should be empowered, but empowered to do what? Empowerment implies an obligation and an opportunity to contribute to a specific end. The notion of a shared direction, what we call a "strategic intent," reconciles the needs of individual freedom and concerted, coordinated effort. As tempting as it might be, senior management can't abdicate its direction-setting role. Employees want a sense of direction just as much as they want the freedom of empowerment.

Beyond Clones versus Renegades

In bureaucratic, hierarchical organizations employees are often like sheep. They mill around but have no clear sense of purpose. What companies need, it is so often said, are wild ducks. But any duck that gets too far out of formation and can no longer benefit from the reduced wind resistance that comes from flying in formation will soon get left behind. We prefer a pack of wolves as an analogy. In a wolf pack the leadership role is always clear, but is often challenged and is decided based on capability and strength. The wolves are not all the same and not all are equally capable. They maintain their individuality but they are all members of the same team, and act in unison when on a hunt. The reality of mutual dependency is accepted by all members. Michael Jordan, the famed center of the Chicago Bulls basketball team, was certainly more than a wild duck; he had a keen sense of being part of a team and knew when to sacrifice his own personal glory to the collective goals of the team. He was the leader of a wolf pack. Indeed, all winning organizations are more akin to a pack of wolves than they are to a flock of sheep or wild ducks.

We've argued that a company full of highly socialized, like-minded clones is unlikely to create the future; on the other hand, neither is a company full of self-interested renegades. What is needed are *community activists*, individuals who are not afraid to challenge the status quo, not afraid to speak out, but who also have a deep sense of community and a desire to improve not only their personal lot but that of others as well. The notion of a community of activists brings together the seemingly contradictory ideas of common cause and individual freedom.

Beyond Technology-Led versus Customer-Led

Many companies have recently emphasized the need to become less product- or technology-driven and more customer-driven. Again, there is a danger in posing the choice of whether to be technology-driven or customer-driven as a dichotomy. Clearly, the pursuit of technological leadership, when it is uninformed by customer needs, is a waste of resources. But likewise, no firm is going to find the future first if it waits around to get directions from existing customers.

The goal is not simply to be led by customers' expressed needs; responsiveness is not enough. The objective is to amaze customers by anticipating and fulfilling their unarticulated needs. To do this, a company must gain deep insights into potential classes of customer benefits. Those benefits are not product specific. For example, control over time is a broad customer benefit. This benefit can be delivered in many forms. An airline that has built a core competence in operations might be able to offer better on-time performance; alternately, a company that perfects low-cost video conferencing may allow people to avoid travel time altogether; a videotape recorder gives people more control over their time, as does an answering machine. Companies that create the future are companies that are constantly searching for ways to apply their competencies in novel ways to meet basic customer needs.

This is yet another polarized debate. And again, we think it is fruitless. There is no industry today that is not technology-intensive; the airline or banking industry is no less technologically intensive than the computer or consumer electronics industry. In one case the technology may relate to the management of information, and in another to how many circuits can be jammed on a chip. Lacking a point of view about customers' future needs, there is a danger that a company will invest only in those technologies that correspond to currently expressed customer needs. This is short-sighted. The link between technology and customers is not just currently articulated needs, but also product and service concepts that promise to satisfy unarticulated needs. The goal is to be neither narrowly technology-driven or narrowly customer-driven. The goal is thus to be broadly *benefits driven*—constantly searching for, investing in, and mastering the technology that will bring unanticipated benefits to humankind.

Beyond Diversified versus Core Business

Unrelated diversification was the rage during the 1970s and early 1980s. Companies judged their capacity for growth more by the strength of the balance sheet (could they raise financing) than by the strength of their development efforts. In some companies, acquisitions helped managers cover up anemic growth in the core business. This happened at Kodak, Xerox, Westinghouse, and many other companies. Many of these acquisitions are now being unwound. Dozens of academic studies have shown that acquisitions destroy shareholder wealth more often than they create it. Managers who lack the foresight and imagination to grow their core business are unlikely to have the foresight and imagination to grow acquired businesses. And diversification into areas where a company lacks knowledge and capability invites disaster.

Retrenching around the core business, when "core" is defined in terms of a particular product or market focus, may leave managers with fewer headaches, but may also result in lackluster growth.

Not every market grows forever, and not every product or service category expands endlessly. If Canon had to depend on 35mm cameras for growth, the company would have reached its zenith years ago. If Motorola had to depend on two-way mobile radios of the sort found in taxicabs, its growth would have stalled long ago. Sticking to the core business limits a company's opportunity horizon and its potential for creating new competitive space. The dichotomy between "unrelated diversification" versus "core business," is, like all the other dichotomies here, ultimately sterile.

We have argued for growth and diversification around *core competencies*. Core competencies are the connective tissue that holds together a portfolio of seemingly diverse businesses. Core competencies are the lingua franca that allows managers to translate insights and experience from one business setting into another. Core competence–based diversification reduces risk and investment and increases the opportunities for transferring learning and best practice across business units.

The following summarizes the usual debate around organizational choices and our view of what constitutes a higher-level synthesis of the underlying ideas.

Thesis	Antithesis	Synthesis
Corporate	Business units	Interlinkages
Centralized	Decentralized	Collective
Bureaucratic	Empowered	Directed
Clones	Renegades	Activists
Technology-led	Customer-led	Benefits-led
Diversified	Core business	Core competence

In many companies today, the organizational change agenda can be largely summarized as an attempt to move from "thesis" to "antithesis" in the table. Yet trading one set of problems (bureaucracy, stifled initiative, underperforming "tangential" businesses, and lack of a customer focus) for another set of problems (suboptimization, territorialism, fragmentation, and bounded growth) doesn't constitute progress. As a consequence, much has been written about the need to manage tensions, trade-offs, paradoxes, and contradictions. Unfortunately, much of this misses the point.

The goal is not to find the narrow line between unattractive extremes nor to maintain an uneasy balance between counterposed forces. In short, the goal is not to occupy the middle ground, it is to find the higher ground. Throughout this book we have attempted to avoid elegant and simple-minded dichotomies. Just as we've offered a *rapprochement* between long term and short term, ambition and risk, strategy as a grand vision and strategy as experimentation, we're also offering a *rapprochement* between competing organizational archetypes. We are offering not an alternate perspective, but an enlarged perspective.

FINAL THOUGHTS

We started this book by raising a series of questions. We asked you to rate your organization along a series of dimensions. If you were dissatisfied with the responses, we urged you to read on. Now that we are at the end of the book, we want to pose another set of questions. We want you to rate your organization once again. Not that your organization would have changed fundamentally in the time you have been reading this book, but this rating may give you a sense of where to start and what the unrealized potential may actually be.

Twenty Questions about the Future

Does senior management have a clear and collective point of view about how the future will be or could be different?

Do senior managers see themselves as industry revolutionaries or are they content with the status quo?

Does the company have a clear and collective agenda for building core competencies, deploying new functionalities, and evolving the customer interface?

Is top management allocating as much time and intellectual energy to premarket competition as to market competition?

Is the company exercising an influence over industry evolution that is disproportionately large, given the company's resources?

Do all employees share an aspiration for the enterprise and possess a clear sense of the legacy they are working to build?

Is there a significant amount of stretch in that aspiration—that is, does it exceed current resources by a substantial amount?

Has senior management operationalized that aspiration into a clear set of corporate challenges?

Is it clear to everyone in the company how their individual contribution links into the company's overall aspiration?

Have managers clearly identified current corporate and industry conventions and subjected those conventions to close scrutiny?

Are the conditions under which the firm's existing economic engine might run out of steam clear to all managers?

Do employees at all levels possess a deep sense of urgency about the challenge of sustaining success?

Does the firm's opportunity horizon extend sufficiently far beyond the boundaries of existing product markets?

Is there an explicit process for identifying and exploiting opportunities that lie between or transcend individual business units?

Does the management and allocation of core competencies receive as explicit attention as the management and allocation of more tangible resources?

Are there a sufficient number of ongoing marketplace experiments to ensure that the company learns faster than rivals about the precise location of tomorrow's opportunities?

Does the firm have a capacity for global preemption (either using its own infrastructure or piggy-backing on partners)?

Have all potential opportunities for resource leverage been fully exploited?

Are senior executives confident that they will leave a legacy to future managers and employees that exceeds the legacy they themselves inherited?

Are you having fun?

(The answers to the first 19 questions are irrelevant if you are not enjoying the challenge of competing for the future.)

These questions capture the spirit of our point of view about competition, strategy, organizations, and the value-added of senior management. Our point of view is one that emphasizes building more than downsizing, organic growth more than deal-making, industry redefinition more than process reengineering, long-term possibility more than short-term feasibility, leveraging resources more than allocating resources, and striving more than arriving.

This book has been about making a difference. First, it has been about making a difference to customers by exceeding their wildest expectations, by creating unimagined products and services, and by making the future real and tangible to customers around the globe. Second, it has been about making a difference in the lives of employees by creating high drama and deep meaning in the pursuit of an ambitious aspiration, by providing the hope of a future after restructuring, and by opening every possible avenue for personal contribution. Finally, it has been about making a difference as a manager by inventing new competitive space, by generating new wealth, and by building a legacy that will outlast one's career.

Notes

■■■

CHAPTER 1

[1] "Stocks of Companies Announcing Layoffs Fire Up Investors, but Prices Often Wilt," *The Wall Street Journal*, 10 December 1991, p. C1.

[2] For more information, see Michael Hammer and James Champy, *Reengineering the Corporation* (New York: HarperBusiness, 1993).

[3] "Business School Winner Fails the SEC Test," *Financial Times*, 24 March 1994, p. 12.

[4] J.P. Womack, D.T. Jones, and D. Ross, *The Machine That Changed the World* (New York: Rawson Associates, 1990).

[5] For more information, see George Stalk, Jr., and Thomas M. Hout, *Competing Against Time: How Time-Based Competition Is Reshaping Global Markets* (New York: The Free Press, 1990).

[6] Donald Hambrick, *Reinventing the CEO: 21st Century Report* (Korn Ferry International and the Columbia University Graduate School of Business, 1989).

[7] "Robert Eaton Thinks 'Vision' Is Overrated and He's Not Alone," *The Wall Street Journal*, 4 October 1993, p. 1ff.

CHAPTER 2

[1] "Next Big Thing: Age of Interactive TV May Be Near as IBM and Warner Talk Deal," *The Wall Street Journal Europe*, 21 May 1992, pp. B1 +.

[2] J.M. Laderman and G. Smith, "The Power of Mutual Funds," *Business Week International*, 18 January 1993, pp. 43–40.

[3] However, it should be noted that when governments have lavished protection on a single firm or two, in hopes of producing national or regional champions, the results have typically been less than hoped for. The most successful model seems to be one where government policy-makers and industrialists have a broad consensus about a new opportunity arena, say high-definition television, where government then puts in place a set of modest incentives to encourage development of the technology, brokers to some degree collaboration between several fiercely competing local contenders, and lets the marketplace decide the winner. This was the approach taken by the FCC in the U.S. HDTV standards battle, where several consortia of

two, three, or more firms each raced to get its technology accepted as the standard, and worked with the other coalitions to minimize the risks of getting left out in the cold if their standard was not chosen. This approach is in marked contrast to the less-successful approach of the European HDTV strategy, which was a thinly disguised attempt to prop up Philips, or the Japanese approach in which there was an attempt to force a single, predetermined standard onto the rest of the world.

[4] Brenton R. Schlender, "How Sony Keeps the Magic Going," *Fortune*, 24 February 1992, p. 27.

[5] See, for example, George Stalk, Jr., and Thomas M. Hout, *Competing Against Time: How Time-Based Competition Is Reshaping Global Markets* (New York: The Free Press, 1990).

[6] Louise Kehone, "Rebels Turned Diplomats," *Financial Times*, 8 February 1993, p. 8.

[7] Because of a widespread familiarity with the "digital" opportunity arena we've chosen it for our illustration here. One could, of course, produce a similar map of the genetic opportunity arena, encompassing pharmaceutical, chemical, agricultural, and food products firms, or of the financial services opportunity, or new materials opportunity arena, *ad infinitum*.

CHAPTER 3

[1] Discussion with Gary Hamel.

[2] "Your Digital Future," *Business Week*, 7 September 1992, pp. 48–54.

[3] "Acquisitions Done the Right Way," *Fortune*, 16 November 1992, p. 96.

[4] "Feeling for the Future: A Survey of Television," *The Economist*, 12 February 1994, p. 5.

[5] Ibid., p. 9.

[6] "Reinventing Boeing: Radical Change Amid Crisis," *Business Week*, 7 September 1992, pp. 48–54.

[7] Louise Kehoe, "The Hottest Act in Town," *Financial Times*, 8 March 1993, p. 15.

CHAPTER 4

[1] "Straight Shooter: Robert Eaton Thinks 'Vision' Is Overrated and He's Not Alone," *The Wall Street Journal*, 4 October 1993, pp. 1+.

[2] William Taylor, "Message and Muscle: An Interview with Swatch Titan Nicolas Hayek," *Harvard Business Review* (March–April 1993): 101.

[3] Sally Solo, "From Technology to Market—First," *Fortune*, 23 March 1992, p. 60.

[4] Brenton R. Schlender, "How Sony Keeps the Magic Going," *Fortune International*, 24 February 1992, p. 27.

[5] Steven Levy, "Bill and Andy's Excellent Adventure II," *Wired*, April 1994, p. 102.

[6] Schlender, "How Sony Keeps the Magic Going," p. 23.

[7] John Huey, "Nothing Is Impossible," *Fortune*, 23 September 1991, p. 92.

[8] Robert L. Shook, *Honda: An American Success Story* (Englewood Cliffs, N.J.: Prentice-Hall, 1988).

[9] Karl E. Ludvigsen, *Coming Out of the Car Crisis: Customers to the Rescue* (London: Euromotor Reports Limited, 1993), p. 54.

[10] Levy, "Billy and Andy's Excellent Adventure II," p. 103.

CHAPTER 5

[1] Koji Kobayashi, *Computers and Communications: A Vision of C&C* (Cambridge, Mass.: MIT Press, 1986).

[2] "Hewlett-Packard Digs Deep for a Digital Future," *Business Week*, 18 October 1993, p. 68.

[3] Ibid., p. 67.

[4] The authors would like to acknowledge the help of Greg Trosper, director of Strategic Planning at EDS, and Dr. Jim Scholes for their help in documenting EDS's experience in building a strategic architecture.

[5] "Staid EDS Cuts Loose with Interactive Multimedia Push," *The Wall Street Journal*, 25 March 1994, p. B4.

CHAPTER 6

[1] Of *course* this is an unrepresentative sample! The goal is to understand the process of winning and the process of losing. Yet there is no assumption of "once a winner, always a winner," or vice versa. Winning is only temporary (although losing may be forever). Whatever a firm has done to "win," it will have to do again (at the level of principles, rather than tactics), if it is to win again. Neanderthal man discovered cooking, it is conjectured, when a house burned down and consumed a pig living therein. There is speculation as to how many houses were subsequently set alight in the quest for roast pork before the distinction between tactics and principles was drawn. The firms on the left are not so much losers, as firms that simply stopped winning.

They continue to repeat the rituals of past success (burning down the houses, or "corporate orthodoxies" in business school parlance), but seem unable to distill and reinterpret the principles of earlier successes.

2 " 'Allo, 'Allo Ring of Confidence," *The Times*, 5 February 1993, p. 29.

3 Acts 1, verse 8.

4 Tracy Kidder, *The Soul of a New Machine* (Boston: Atlantic-Little, Brown, 1981).

CHAPTER 7

1 Of course, this conclusion should be regarded as tentative, given the difficulties of finding a proxy for R&D output. Patents are only one measure, and many believe that Japanese companies are quicker to patent small incremental innovations than Western companies.

2 For more historical evidence, see Barbara Tuchman, *The March of Folly* (New York: Alfred A. Knopf, 1984).

3 See, for example: H. Itami with T. Roehl, *Mobilizing Invisible Assets* (Cambridge, Mass.: Harvard University Press, 1989); I. Dierickx and K. Cool, "Asset Stock Accumulation and Sustainability of Competitive Advantage," *Management Science* (December 1989): 1504–1514; J. Barney, "Firm Resources and Sustained Competitive Advantage," unpublished manuscript, Texas A&M University; and C.K. Prahalad and Gary Hamel, "The Core Competence of the Corporation," *Harvard Business Review* (May–June 1990): 79–91.

4 "3M: 60,000 and Counting," *The Economist*, 30 November 1991, pp. 86–89.

5 "A Tighter Focus for R&D," *Business Week International*, 2 December 1991, pp. 80–82.

6 Hermann Simon, *Manager Magazine*, February 1993.

7 For a comprehensive description of the elements of continuous improvement, see M. Imai, *Kaizen: The Key to Japan's Competitive Success* (New York: Random House, 1989); or, more generally, Y. Baba, "The Dynamics of Continuous Innovation in Scale Intensive Industries," *Strategic Management Journal* 10, no. 2 (1989): 89–100.

8 David C. Mowery and David J. Teece, "Japan's Growing Capabilities in Industrial Technology," *California Management Review* (Winter 1992): 9–34.

9 For a detailed treatment of interpartner learning see: G. Hamel, "Competitive Collaboration: Learning, Power and Dependence in International Strategic Alliances" (Ph.D. diss., University of Michigan, 1990).

10 D.J. Teece, "Firm Boundaries, Technological Innovation, and Strategic Management," in *Economics of Strategic Planning*, ed. L.G. Thomas (Lexington, Mass.: Lexington Books, 1986).

[11] The auto industry data in this paragraph comes from "Miles Traveled, More to Go," *Business Week International,* 2 December 1991, pp. 44–47.

CHAPTER 8

[1] "Sega!" *Business Week,* 21 February 1994, pp. 66–74.

[2] Daniel C. Benton and John C. Levinson, "Computer Industry," in *Communacopia: A Digital Communication Bounty* (New York: Goldman Sachs Investment Research, 1992), p. 66.

[3] By early 1994, Sony and Motorola had both announced plans to market personal digital assistants utilizing an operating system developed by General Magic. "Abracadabra," *The Economist,* 5–11 February 1994, pp. 67–68.

[4] Tony Jackson, "How to Stand Out in a Crowd," *Financial Times,* 10 September 1993, UK edition, p. 19.

CHAPTER 9

[1] Sally Solo, "From Technology to Market—First," *Fortune,* 23 March 1992, p. 60.

[2] "U.S. to Challenge Japan on a Screen Near You," *International Herald Tribune,* 18 November 1992, p. 1.

[3] "Samsung's Radical Shake-Up," *Business Week,* 28 February 1994, p. 74.

[4] "Taiwan: 'The Arms Dealer of the Computer Wars,' " *Business Week,* 28 June 1993, p. 36.

[5] "Sharp Gets Set to Ride Hottest Trends in Electronics," *The Wall Street Journal,* 4 October 1993, p. B4.

[6] "Lou Gerstner Unveils His Battle Plan," *Business Week,* 4 April 1994, p. 97.

CHAPTER 10

[1] See Margert B.W. Graham, *RCA and the VideoDisc: The Business of Research* (New York: Cambridge University Press, 1986) and *The Business of Research: RCA and the VideoDisc* (New York: Cambridge University Press, 1989).

[2] A ratio of market to asset value that is substantially more than 1 may also reflect the fact that brand equity seldom appears on the balance sheet. For companies like Gillette (whose ratio of market to asset value was 2.7 at

the end of 1993), Kellogg (2.7), William Wrigley Jr. (6.6), and Snapple Beverage (13.6), a high ratio also reflects the value of the brands the firm owns. Nevertheless, the term *brand equity* is misleading. The value of a brand can decline quickly if it is not well-managed. The premium of market to asset value for the consumer product companies above reflects as much the confidence investors have in the ability of senior management teams to constantly refresh and extend powerful brands, as it reflects the absolute value of a brand asset.

CHAPTER 11

[1] B.R. Schlender, "How Sony Keeps the Magic Going," *Fortune*, 24 February 1992, p. 23.

[2] "Super Phones," *Business Week*, 7 October 1991, p. 61.

[3] T. Smart, P. Engardio, and G. Smith, "GE's Brave New World," *Business Week International*, 8 November 1993, p. 45.

[4] Helmut Maucher, speech given at the World Economic Forum, Davos, Switzerland, 5 February 1991.

[5] "Brand-Stretching Can Be Fun, and Dangerous," *The Economist*, 5 May 1990, pp. 105–110.

[6] "The Erosion of Brand Loyalty," *Business Week International*, 19 July 1993, pp. 32–33.

[7] Z. Schiller and R.A. Melcher, "Marketing Globally, Thinking Locally," *Business Week International*, 13 May 1991, p. 24.

[8] "No More Mr. Nice Guy at P&G, Not by a Long Shot," *Business Week*, 3 February 1992, pp. 46–48.

[9] Schiller and Melcher, p. 21.

[10] Michael Jordon, Chairman, Pepsico International Food and Beverage, "Big Brands in a Borderless World," speech given at the World Economic Forum, Davos, Switzerland, 3 February 1992.

CHAPTER 12

[1] For a comprehensive discussion of the relationship between industry structure and profitability, see Michael Porter, *Competitive Strategy* (New York: The Free Press: 1980).

[2] "Have You Driven a Ford Lately—In Japan?" *Business Week*, 21 February 1994, p. 37.

Bibliography

POINTS OF DEPARTURE

Andrews, Kenneth R. *The Concept of Corporate Strategy.* Homewood, Ill.: Irwin, 1971.

Buzzell, Robert D., and Bradley T. Gale. *The PIMS Principles: Linking Strategy to Performance.* New York: The Free Press, 1987.

Chandler, Alfred. *Strategy and Structure: Chapters in the History of the Industrial Enterprise.* Cambridge: MIT Press, 1962.

Hammer, Michael, and James Champy. *Reengineering the Corporation: A Manifesto for Business Revolution.* New York: HarperBusiness, 1993.

Hofer, Charles W., and Dan Schendel. *Strategy Formulation: Analytical Concepts.* St. Paul: West Publishing, 1978.

Kanter, Rosabeth Moss. *The Change Masters: Innovation for Productivity in the American Corporation.* New York: Simon & Schuster, 1983.

———. *When Giants Learn to Dance: Mastering the Challenge of Strategy, Management, and Careers in the 1990s.* New York: Simon & Schuster, 1989.

Mintzberg, Henry. *The Nature of Managerial Work.* New York: Harper & Row, 1973.

———. *The Structuring of Organizations: A Synthesis of the Research.* Englewood Cliffs: Prentice-Hall, 1979.

———. *Mintzberg on Management: Inside Our Strange World of Organizations.* New York: The Free Press, 1989.

———. *The Rise and Fall of Strategic Planning: Reconceiving Roles for Planning, Plans, Planners.* New York: The Free Press, 1994.

Porter, Michael E. *Competitive Strategy: Techniques for Analyzing Industries and Competitors.* New York: The Free Press, 1980.

———. *Competitive Advantage: Creating and Sustaining Superior Performance.* New York: The Free Press, 1985.

————. *The Competitive Advantage of Nations.* New York: The Free Press, 1990.

Stalk, George, Jr., and Thomas M. Hout. *Competing Against Time: How Time-based Competition Is Reshaping Global Markets.* New York: The Free Press, 1990.

Thurow, Lester C. *Head to Head: The Coming Economic Battle Among Japan, Europe, and America.* New York: Morrow, 1992.

Tichy, Noel M., and Mary Anne Devanna. *The Transformational Leader.* New York: Wiley, 1986.

Tichy, Noel, and Stratford Sherman. *Control Your Destiny or Someone Else Will: How Jack Welch Is Making General Electric the World's Most Competitive Corporation.* New York: Doubleday, 1993.

Womack, James P., Daniel T. Jones, and Daniel Roos. *The Machine That Changed the World: Based on the Massachusetts Institute of Technology 5-Million Dollar 5-Year Study on the Future of the Automobile.* New York: Rawson Associates, 1990.

COMPLEMENTARY PERSPECTIVES

Barney, Jay. "Strategic Factor Markets: Expectations, Luck, and Business Strategy." *Management Science* 32, no. 10 (1986): 1231–1241.

————. "Asset Stocks and Sustained Competitive Advantage: A Comment." *Management Science* 35, no. 12 (1989): 1511–1513.

Clark, Kim B., and Steven C. Wheelwright. *Managing New Product and Process Development: Text and Cases.* New York: The Free Press, 1993.

Cohen, Eliot A., and John Gooch. *The Military Misfortunes: The Anatomy of Failure in War.* New York: The Free Press, 1990.

Davidow, William H., and Michael S. Malone. *The Virtual Corporation: Structuring and Revitalizing the Corporation for the 21st Century.* New York: HarperBusiness, 1992.

Dierickx, Ingemar, and Karel Cool. "Asset Stock Accumulation and Sustainability of Competitive Advantage: Reply." *Management Science* 35, no. 12 (1989): 1514.

Dixon, Norman F. *On the Psychology of Military Incompetence.* New York: Basic Books, 1976.

Drucker, Peter F. *Managing for the Future: The 1990s and Beyond.* New York: Dutton, 1992.

Hamel, Gary, and C.K. Prahalad. "Do You Really Have a Global Strategy?" *Harvard Business Review* 68, no. 4 (1985): 139–148.

———. "Strategic Intent." *Harvard Business Review* 67, no. 3 (1989): 63–76.

———. "Collaborate with Your Competitors—and Win." *Harvard Business Review* 67, no. 1 (1989): 133–139.

———. "Corporate Imagination and Expeditionary Marketing." *Harvard Business Review* 69, no. 4 (1991): 81–92.

———. "Strategy as Stretch and Leverage." *Harvard Business Review* 71, no. 2 (1993): 75–84.

———. "Competing for the Future." *Harvard Business Review* 72, no. 4 (1994): 122–128.

Hariharan, Sahasranam. "Technological Compatibility, Standards, and Global Competition: The Dynamics of Industry Evolution and Competitive Strategies." Ph.D. diss., University of Michigan, 1990.

Itami, Hiroyuki, with Thomas W. Roehl. *Mobilizing Invisible Assets.* Cambridge: Harvard University Press, 1987.

Landis, Gabel, ed. *Product Standardization and Competitive Strategy.* New York: Elsevier Science Publishing Company, 1987.

Nohria, Nitin, and Robert G. Eccles. *Networks and Organizations: Structure, Form, and Action.* Boston: Harvard Business School Press, 1992.

Nonaka, Ikijuro. "The Knowledge-Creating Company." *Harvard Business Review* 69, no. 6 (1991): 96–104.

Nonaka, Ikijuro, and Martin Kenney. "Towards a New Theory of Innovation Management: A Case Study Comparing Canon, Inc. and Apple Computer, Inc." *Journal of Engineering and Technology Management* 8, vol. 1 (1991): 67–83.

Ohmae, Kenichi. *The Mind of the Strategist: The Art of Japanese Business.* New York: McGraw-Hill, 1982.

Prahalad, C.K., and Richard A. Bettis. "Dominant Logic: A New Linkage Between Diversity and Performance." *Strategic Management Journal* 7, no. 6 (1986): 485–502.

Prahalad, C.K., and Gary Hamel. "The Core Competence of the Corporation." *Harvard Business Review* 68, no. 3 (1990): 79–91.

Quinn, James Brian. *Intelligent Enterprise: A Knowledge and Service Based Paradigm for Industry.* New York: The Free Press, 1992.

Senge, Peter M. *The Fifth Discipline: The Art and Practice of the Learning Organization.* New York: Doubleday/Currency, 1990.

Spender, J.C. *Industry Recipes: An Enquiry into the Nature and Sources of Managerial Judgement.* New York: Blackwell, 1989.

Takeuchi, H., and Ikujiro Nonaka. "The New New Product Development Game." *Harvard Business Review* 64, no. 1 (1986): 137–146.

Teece, D.J. "Towards an Economic Theory of the Multiproduct Firm." *Journal of Economic Behavior and Organization* 3 (March 1982): 39–64.

Tuchman, Barbara Wertheim. *The March of Folly: From Troy to Vietnam.* New York: Knopf, 1984.

Ulrich, David, and David Lake. *Organizational Capability: Competing from the Inside Out.* New York: Wiley, 1990.

Wernerfelt, Birger. "A Resource-Based View of the Firm." *Strategic Management Journal* 5, no. 2 (1984): 171–180.

Index

competing on time, concept of, 14
competition, 248–249
  benchmarking, 2
  for competence, 219, *234*,
    233–242, 249, 256
  dynamics of, 300
  as encirclement, 189
  and end products, 219, 245
  foreign, 18
  for future, 34
  global, 7
  for industry foresight, 50, 79
  for intellectual leadership, 50
  intercorporate, 221–223
  interfirm, 34
  for market share, 51
  and migration paths, 50–51
  nontraditional, 6, 18, 57
  premarket, 200
  pricing move of, 4
  rules of, 1, 33, 297
  unstructured arenas for, 40–46
competition for the future
  defined, 24
  differences of, 33
  and profits, 38–40
  three phases of, *52*
competitive advantages, x, 152,
    156, 158, 170, 181, 229, 293,
    301–303
competitive arena, 300
competitive differentiation, 110,
    221
competitive drive, 153
competitive engagement, 190
competitive environment, 60
competitive failure, 157
competitive innovation, 190
competitiveness, 2, 241
  causes of, 299–308
  challenge of, 294
  contributions to, 154
  as growth industry, 293
  meaning of, 293

problems of, 7, 154
quest for, *16*
sustained, 304
competitive parameters, broad
    range of, 155
competitive problems, diagnosis
    of, 301
competitive quests, 119
competitive reality, xii
competitive revitalization, 307
competitive space, xi, 197, 243,
    261, 267, 269, 278, 300
competitive spirit, 153
competitive strategy, 167, 221, 300,
    302
competitive success, 59
competitive vitality, ix
competitors
  benchmarks of, 153
  and differentiation, 226–227
  dismissed by incumbents, 140
  intentions of, 159
  nontraditional, 309
  and resources, 140
complacency, 296
computerized axial tomography,
    185
computers, 172
  applications, *42*
  architectures, 35, 202 ⟩
  and chip designs, 231
  components, 124
  graphics technology, 54
  hand-held, 201
  home, 268
  industry of, 204, 296
  intelligence, 242
  mainframe, 32
  services of, 127
  software, 69
  systems, *42*
computing, 219
  and communication, 83,
    123–124, 133–136

icon-based, 17
paradigm, 87
consistency, 300
consortiums, 80
constancy, 143
consumer electronics, 42, 200, 245
continuity, 300
contrarians, 107–108
control, 5, 142, 143
convergence, 131, 175–176
Cool, Karel, xiv
copiers, 92, 93, 96–97
core businesses, 143, 322, 323
core competencies, 87, 160, 182,
    203, 238, 317, 322
  acquisition agenda of, 249–254
  building of, 4, 222, 254
  complementing, 258
  and customer benefits, 118
  defined, 219, 223–232, 248
  deploying, 254–257
  elements of, 248
  fragmentation of, 258
  and functionality thinking, 96
  and future, 24
  investing in, 273
  leadership in, 238, 258
  at NEC, 124
  versus noncore competencies,
    224–228, 247
  as opportunities, 217
  perspective of, 245–259
  portfolio of, 90
  redeploying, 315
  stock of, 255
core data management, 239
core platforms, 237, 241
core processes, 2
  redesign of, 5
  reengineering of, 3
core products, 237, 239, 240, 241
core strategies, 1
  regeneration of, 3, 5, 16, 17, 19,
    66, 130, 293

corporate brands, 280–281, 283
corporate challenges, 149–158,
    155, 156
corporate clones, 320
corporate confederacies, 43
corporate decline, 73
corporate direction, 143
corporate entropy, 296
corporate genetics
  dangers of, 55–56
  defined, 53
  and diversity, 56–60
  and success, 59
corporate growth, 160
corporate identity, 243
corporate leaders, 100
corporate orthodoxies, 87, 143,
    329n1
corporate regeneration, 85
corporate strategies, 242, 308,
    308–309, 317
corporate success, 294
corporate vitality, 67
corporate vulnerability, 2
cost leadership, 178
cost savings, 233
cost structures, x
country managers, 288–289
CPC, 294
Crandall, Robert, 84
creativity, 145
credit cards, 244
cumulative logic, 207
curiosity, 98–102
customers
  benchmarks of, 153
  benefits for, 79
  care of, 156
  demands of, 262
  driven by, 320
  focus on, 315
  and foresight, 109
  insight, 114
  interfaces with, 79

and long-term investment, 139
and VCR machines, 48–49
R&D budgets, 8, 136, 165, *166*, 317
Reagan, Ronald, 39
realism, 159, 160
recalibration, 270
recovery process, 191
recycling, 186–188
reengineering, 5
  industry, 304
  processes, 12–15, *16*, 108, 197
  programs, 23
  versus restructuring, 13
refocusing. *See* restructuring
regulation, 4, 59, 199, 204, 288–289, 295
remote medical diagnostics, 126
Renault, 272
research productivity, 163
resource
  advantages, 170
  allocation, 174
  conservation, 300
  constraints, 172
  effectiveness, x
  -intensive work, 182
  multipliers, 190
  scarcity, 168
  transformation, 184
resource leverage, 163, 168, 172, 173, 176, 235
  achieving, 175–192
  aspects of, *191*
  capacity for, 168, 173
  and consistency, 176
  co-opting, 188–189
  and future, 25
  starting premises of, 172–174
resources, 174
  abundance of, 168
  accessible, 188
  accumulation of, 180–183
  complementing, 184–186

concentration of, 175–180
conservation of, 186–190
creativity and, 197
dilution of, 176
diversion of, 176
leveraging of, 165
portfolio of, 171
recovering, 190–192
responsibility, personal, 316
restructuring, 5, 9, 125
  goals of, 6–7
  and improvement in business, 10–11
  industries, 302
  programs, 173
  versus reengineering, 13
  social cost of, 10
return on investment, 289
  components of, 9
revenue, 2
  growth, 9–10
  and market structure, *68*
rewards, 195, 197
right-sizing. *See* downsizing; restructuring
RISC architecture, 20, 125, 202, 204
risks, 313
  and future, 197
  management of, 270
  and stretch, 314
risk-sharing, 207
risk-takers, 135, 136, 315
ROCE, 9
Rockwell, xiii
Roddick, Anita, 65, 107
Rodgers, T.J., 65
ROI. *See* return on investment
roller bearings, 228
Rolls Royce, 284
Rolm, 134
RONA, 9
Rover, 196, 241
3-6-3 rule, 67

Professors Gary Hamel and C.K. Prahalad are experts in the dynamics of the global marketplace and the strategies and structures of companies that thrive in today's volatile environment. They have co-authored seven *Harvard Business Review* articles—two of which, "Strategic Intent" and "The Core Competence of the Corporation," have won coveted McKinsey Awards. Both articles are among *HBR*'s bestselling reprints, and "The Core Competence of the Corporation" is the most reprinted article in *HBR*'s history.

Gary Hamel is a professor of strategic and international management at London Business School and chairman of Strategos, a strategy consulting company. As a consultant, Professor Hamel has worked in companies around the globe, including Ford, Motorola, EDS, Nokia, and Dow Chemical. He serves on the board of governors of the Strategic Management Society. He resides in Woodside, California and can be reached at http://www.strategosnet.com or gh@strategosnet.com.

C.K. Prahalad is the Harvey C. Fruehauf Professor of Business Administration and professor of corporate strategy and international business at the Graduate School of Business Administration, University of Michigan. He is co-author, along with Yves Doz, of *The Multinational Mission: Balancing Local Demands and Global Vision*. He has consulted with many multinational firms, among them Eastman Kodak, AT&T, Cargill, Honeywell, Philips, Colgate-Palmolive, Motorola, TRW, Whirlpool, and Ahlstrom.